Programming
Internet
Controls

How to Order:

For information on quantity discounts contact the publisher: Prima Publishing, P.O. Box 1260BK, Rocklin, CA 95677-1260; (916) 632-4400. On your letterhead include information concerning the intended use of the books and the number of books you wish to purchase. For individual orders, turn to the back of this book for more information.

Programming
Internet
Controls

Markus Pope
Jose Mojica
Edward B. Toupin

Prima Publishing

ISBN: 0-7615-0773-6

Library of Congress Catalog Card Number: 96-70103

Printed in the United States of America

96 97 98 99 DD 10 9 8 7 6 5 4 3 2 1

Acquisitions Editor
Deborah F. Abshier

Development Editor
Angelique Brittingham

Project Editor
Kathy Simpson

Indexer
Sherry Massey

Cover Designer
Kari Keating

Publisher Don Roche, Jr.
Associate Publisher Ray Robinson
Senior Acquisitions Editor Alan Harris
Senior Project Editor Tad Ringo
Product Marketing Specialist Julie Barton

To Michael Coley (I hope your mom isn't still mad about the FBI thing)

Acknowledgments

First, I must thank John, because he's always there with an answer when I don't have one. Next, thanks to Debbie, Don, Ian, Julie, Jill, and Kathy at Prima for their wonderful support and hard work on the project. Also, I'd like to thank my contributing authors, Jose Mojica and Ed Toupin. Most of all, thanks to Rayne and Logan, who, as always, are the ones who truly make my books possible. And thanks to you for making me and my family part of your life.

About the Authors

Markus Pope is a member of the research-and-development team at Datastorm Technologies, which has been the leader in the telecommunications industry for more than 10 years. Datastorm Technologies is responsible for bringing you Procomm Plus, Procomm Plus for DOS, and the ever-popular shareware hit Procomm. Recently, Markus shifted his focus from the intricate inner workings of Procomm Plus to writing books about his favorite subjects. (Don't worry— he still works on Procomm Plus in his spare time.) If you're lucky, and if the digital wind is just right, you may be able to catch him floating through cyberspace at markus@socketis.net.

Jose Mojica graduated from the University of Michigan, Ann Arbor, in 1992 with a concentration in computer science and mathematics. Immediately afterward, he worked for two years at Systematic Computer Products, a small company based in Miami, Florida. His duties included creating custom controls in the form of VBXs using Visual C++ 1.5 and creating applications using Visual Basic 1.0 and, later, 2.0. After Systematic Computer Products, Jose worked with Maintenance Automation Corporation, where his duties also included the creation of custom controls and the development of applications with Visual Basic 3.0. After a year, he was made supervisor of all core product development. He left Maintenance Automation to form his own corporation.

Jose is now the owner and president of ABRISOFT, Inc., a company that develops custom controls in the form of OCXs. He is the author of several custom controls written in Visual C++ 4.2 that are being sold worldwide. He is also a consultant for PSDI, one of the top 100 software companies in the world. At PSDI, he aids in the creation of Visual Basic applications and the construction of custom controls.

Late in the summer of 1996, he and his wife, Laurel, became the parents of a son, Alejandro. When Jose is not busy programming or running his company, he enjoys watching movies and playing computer games with his wife.

Edward B. Toupin and his lovely wife, Rena, live in the mountains of Colorado all year round. Rena is a nationally known relocation specialist for one of Denver's largest corporate-owned brokering firms and a full-time law student in real estate litigation, nearing her bars.

Degreed in mathematics, computer science, and electronics technology, Edward is a technical analyst/software engineer for a Denver-based engineering firm. He designs and develops applications under various platforms for industrial control, expert system applications, database management, GIS, integration solutions, network management and communications, mobile satellite, and Internet/intranet communications. Edward also writes books and articles for various publishers, manages the TTC Internet Web site and his employer's intranet Web site, and develops custom Internet/intranet connectivity solutions. One of his endeavors was to implement the first set of 32-bit Internet custom controls as part of the Connectivity Custom Controls.

Edward can be reached at etoupin@toupin.com, CompuServe 75051,1160, or URL http://www.toupin.com/~etoupin/.

Contents at a Glance

Contents

Chapter 11   Plug-in Mail   267

Appendix A Adding Licensing to Your Online Controls 409

Appendix B Diagnosing Problems with Your Online Applications 417

Appendix C Installing the CD-ROM   423

INTRODUCTION

by Markus Pope

One aspect of computer-programming books that's quite annoying is their tendency to try to teach you a programming language along with the concept that the book is about. That tendency cuts the amount of space that the writer devotes to the topic that's listed on the cover. We want to pack as much information into this book as possible, so we assume that you're at least an amateur C++ programmer. Don't worry—even though we expect you to know C++, we don't expect you to be familiar with OLE and COM. (After all, C++ makes building controls so easy that you won't have to be an expert on OLE and COM.) We're not going to get into the bowels of the OLE architecture, but we cover it in detail within the context of building online controls.

Programming Internet Controls is devoted to building ActiveX controls by using Microsoft's Visual C++ 4, hereafter known as Visual C++. (Microsoft refers to the new Visual C++ development environment as the *Developer Studio*.) The step-by-step examples included in this book describe how to use the MFC AppWizard in Visual C++ to create online controls, but you're not out of luck if you don't like using Microsoft's development tools. You can apply the principles that you learn in this book even if you're not using Visual C++. The book has a good balance of control programming vs. modem and Internet technology, so don't be scared off by the title.

Conventions Used in This Book

The book contains quite a few code snippets, which are used to explain the basics of building controls. The book uses two types of code segments. Some of these segments are full listings, showing the code for a complete function, class, or structure. Other segments are fragments of code that contain ellipses to indicate code that has already been covered or code that's not important. Here's what a code fragment looks like:

```
.

.

if( ! strcmp( lpszText, "This book is cool!" ) )
{

    .

    .
```

The book also includes notes and tips, which present special points that may or may not pertain directly to the text that you're reading. Here are samples of those elements:

> **NOTE:** Notes typically refer to the same subject as the text around them, but they make points that are a bit out of context. A note may refer you to text on another, similar subject.

> **TIP:** Tips are suggestions that can make your coding easier, faster, and of higher quality ("Don't run with scissors," for example).

When introducing new words or concepts, we accentuate them by *italicizing* the words or concepts. Text that you type, such as short commands, is **boldfaced**.

How This Book Is Organized

Programming Internet Controls is broken into four parts:

- ◆ Part I: ActiveX Controls
- ◆ Part II: Modem Applications

- Part III: Internet Applications
- Part IV: Appendices

You start in Chapter 2 by learning how to build an ordinary ActiveX control. It's best to start with something simple and then work into the details, so you'll start with a simple edit control. In later chapters, we talk less about ActiveX controls themselves and more about using the technology to enhance your communications applications.

Chapters 3, 4, and 5 cover modem technology. Modem technology has been out of the spotlight for a while (while the media have concentrated on promoting the Internet), but it's still a spicy topic. After all, most PCs sold today come with a modem, and those of us who don't have direct access to the Internet use a modem to connect.

Chapters 6 through 13 cover Internet topics. You learn how to build the full range of Internet clients in these chapters. Even though the chapters concentrate on building controls out of these clients, they are excellent references for any type of Internet programming.

Overview of the Chapters

The following list serves two purposes. First, the list gives you an idea of what's in the book. Second, you can use this section to skip ahead, in case one of the chapters covers something that you already know.

- Chapter 1, "Introducing Online Controls"

    In this chapter, you get the skinny on communications, object-oriented programming, OLE, and ActiveX controls.

- Chapter 2, "Creating Your First Control"

    This chapter introduces the Visual C++ IDE (Integrated Development Environment) in the context of writing ActiveX controls. In this chapter, you create a formatted edit control. This control allows you to specify how data is input by specifying a template. NNN-NNN-NNNN, for example, is a template that you might use to input a telephone number.

- Chapter 3, "Talking to Your Modem"

    This chapter explains how programs interface with modems. The chapter introduces some of the basic concepts of data communications. You learn how to open the COM port, how to send data, and how to receive data. The chapter also touches on modem standards and common modem applications. Finally, the chapter is a good place to find out what you can and can't do with a modem.

◆ Chapter 4, "Plug-in Modem Dialer"

In this chapter, you build your first online control. The modem dialer has a keypadlike interface that allows you to dial numbers the way that you do on a cellular phone—you press the digits of the number that you want to dial and then click the Send button. You write the code that opens the COM port, sets the port settings, initializes the modem, and places the call. This chapter puts the stuff that you learned in Chapter 3 to practical use.

◆ Chapter 5, "Plug-in Terminal Emulator"

This chapter teaches you how to build a basic terminal emulator. A *terminal emulator* is a software version of the firmware that's located in terminals. *Terminals* are used to display the data from host systems. When we were kids, most emulators were used to talk to mainframes; today, terminal emulators are formidable weapons in any cyberpunk's arsenal. You also learn some important concepts that are used in all communications applications.

◆ Chapter 6, "Talking to the Internet"

This chapter explains how Windows applications get access to Internet services and teaches you some of the concepts behind Internet programming. The chapter covers the basics of getting connected, sending data, and receiving data; then it talks about a few of the most common Internet applications. This chapter is the prelude to the cool stuff that you'll do in the rest of the book.

◆ Chapter 7, "Plug-in Ping"

This chapter walks you through the process of creating your first Internet online control. The chapter allows you to do a little warming up before you dive into the more complicated controls, such as FTP and Gopher. Ping is a simple application that allows you to take a pulse over the Internet; it's used to make sure that a particular server is responding to incoming connection requests.

◆ Chapter 8, "Plug-in Finger"

This chapter explains how the finger protocol works and walks you through the process of building a finger control. Finger is a useful tool for finding information on users, servers, and domains, and even for getting the status of certain silly devices that are connected to the Internet. (Engineering students in several learning institutions, for example, have connected Coke and Pepsi machines to the Internet; you learn about that subject at the end of the chapter.)

◆ Chapter 9, "Plug-in WHOIS"

WHOIS is an application that's very much like finger, the subject of Chapter 8. WHOIS is different, though, in that it's commonly used with a specific set of servers known as *NIC servers*. Chapter 9 tells you how to build a WHOIS control and expands somewhat on the principles that you learn in earlier chapters.

◆ Chapter 10, "Plug-in News"

This chapter is where you really start having fun with Internet programming. In this chapter, you build an Internet news control. News is a collection of open forums that users of the Net fill with messages on just about any topic. Those forums are referred to as *newsgroups*. Chapter 10 gives you your first real glimpse of an Internet protocol: NNTP.

◆ Chapter 11, "Plug-in Mail"

This chapter describes SMTP and POP3—the two protocols that are used to send and receive mail on the Internet. Previous chapters of the book are more oriented toward how to handle the socket and the protocol. Chapter 11 focuses more on building interfaces for Internet online controls. This chapter is where you start to "pretty" things up.

◆ Chapter 12, "Plug-in FTP"

This chapter teaches you how to turn an FTP client into an Internet online control. In addition to teaching you the ins and outs of the FTP protocol, Chapter 12 complicates your life by throwing in multiple socket support. FTP uses a command socket to issue commands to the server; then data is sent and received by means of a separate socket.

◆ Chapter 13, "Plug-in Gopher"

Gopher, a protocol that permits document search and retrieval over the Internet, is considered to be the predecessor of the great World Wide Web. Chapter 13 teaches you how to build a Gopher application in the form of an ActiveX control. You write code to download document lists, parse them, and retrieve and display documents. Gopher, in my opinion, lends itself to a prettier interface than many of the other Internet protocols do (except for HTTP and HTML, which are the stuff that Web browsers are made of).

◆ Appendix A, "Adding Licensing to Your Online Controls"

ActiveX control technology allows you to build stand-alone objects that can plug into other applications. A control object can be a simple set of member functions without an interface, or it can be a full-blown application. Companies can create applications as controls and allow other companies to seamlessly integrate those controls into their own software programs. Microsoft includes some tools that you can use to create both design-time and run-time licensing for your ActiveX controls. Appendix A describes how to use Microsoft's licensing technology.

◆ Appendix B, "Diagnosing Problems with Your Online Applications"

Appendix B covers troubleshooting your online controls. In this appendix, you write for the CSocket object a monitor window that intercepts and displays the data that is being sent and received on the socket it represents. In addition, you get the lowdown on using the Microsoft test container to test your controls. (This is useful for any controls that you write, not just for those that talk to your modem or the Internet.)

◆ Appendix C, "Installing the CD-ROM"

Appendix C tells you what's on the CD-ROM that accompanies this book and describes how to install the software.

The chapters described in the preceding list introduce new ideas and reinforce ideas that are presented in earlier chapters. But if you want to, you can skip ahead to Chapter 10 and work on a news client. (If that's what you're interested in, go ahead and skip.) Even though chapters are written to work together, they work just fine on their own.

Reading the Programming Examples

Throughout the book, we use fragments of code to explain how stuff works. For the most part, we teach you how to write the controls step by step. In some cases, though, you won't get a usable program or control simply by concatenating the fragments. Complete source code for each chapter is included on the CD-ROM that comes with the book.

Although we're going to show you how to build usable controls throughout the course of this book, these controls are meant to be examples. Don't use the example controls in a production environment without cleaning them up first. Although we'll do our best to make the examples as defect-free as possible, we can't warrant that there won't be a bug or two lurking about. In some cases, for the sake of space and time, we leave out critical aspects of bug-free programming (error-checking, for example).

PART I

ActiveX Controls

Chapter | 1

Introducing Online Controls

by Markus Pope

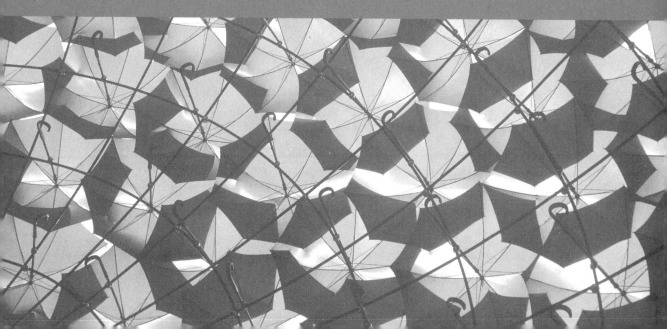

Somewhere barely within the confines of space and time exists a place where you can go to be free—free from the realities that chain people to various locations around the world. In this new world, unlike the old, you can travel to the farthest reaches of the Earth simply by clicking a mouse button or pressing the Enter key. This morning, for example, my daughter and I visited the Louvre; this evening, my wife plans to get some snapshots of Mount Fuji.

I'm talking about an exciting new world that fuels the imagination, embraces the mind, and breaks down the barriers engineered by miscommunication. Here, news is reported within minutes—and sometimes within seconds—of an event. You can talk to the people who are on the front lines of life—people who are on the brink of war, in the mouth of a natural disaster, or otherwise touched by the hand of fate.

I'm talking about the world known as cyberspace, which is made up of countless machines connected by millions of miles of copper and fiber-optic wires, by radios and satellites, with terabits of information fluttering here and fluttering there. Oh, how it fills my heart and soul with happiness.

People project themselves into this brave new world by using devices called clients. *Clients* are software programs that collect and disseminate information in human-digestible form. The notion of clients has been around for quite some time. Not much has changed in the way that clients work—just in their appearance.

What is a book like this one going to offer about client-side Internet programming that other books don't? Throughout the book, you're going to learn about how Internet clients work. I'm going to show you how to build the most common Internet application. But I'm going to take a more object-oriented approach.

The Move Toward Objects

One of the reasons why I love computers so much is that the computer world evolves so insanely fast. There's always something new to talk about and something new to do. Think about what has happened in just the past 15 years. Computers have gone from being mysterious machines found only in the back rooms of large corporations to essential tools in our everyday lives—tools that you and I can't seem to live without.

Since programming was invented, developers have struggled with ways to represent real-world problems in the virtual world created by computer programs. In addition, a tremendous amount of time has been wasted in reinventing the software wheel, so to speak. The move toward objects solves both of these problems—and very effectively, I must say.

Earth As an Object

After years of trying to model the complex workings of the world with a set of straight lines, someone decided that it might be a good idea to represent the real world in the same way that the real world exists in nature: as an object or a set of objects (or as sets of objects).

The American Heritage Dictionary defines an object as something that is intelligible and perceptible by the mind. I'm sure that this definition is true, but I see an object as being a little bit different. When I look around, what I see is a bunch of things that encapsulate all the functionality required to make themselves exist. The glass on my desk, for example, holds water (and does a darned good job of it, too). A glass, as an object, contains everything that it needs to hold water.

But wait—what if there's a hole in the glass? Well, the glass is still a glass and an object; it just so happens that the object is broken. To apply this model to the world of computers, consider an example. A traffic-light simulation is the classic example used in references on object-oriented programming (in addition to a very complex implementation of "hello world").

A traffic light is a complex object that's not represented very well by traditional, linear programming language. Simulating a traffic light with a linear set of instructions takes a great deal of thought, time, and coding. But what if you take a less traditional approach to writing a traffic-light simulation?

Consider what makes up a traffic light in real life:

- ◆ A controller turns the lights red in one direction and green in another.
- ◆ A timer control keeps traffic flowing smoothly by changing the lights at calculated intervals. Often, traffic flowing in one direction is allotted more time than traffic flowing in another direction.
- ◆ Lights shine green, yellow, or red, depending on what the controller does.
- ◆ Finally, some sensors in the road work in conjunction with the timer to prevent unnecessary changing of the light.

In an object-oriented programming language, a traffic light can be represented just as it exists in real life: as an object made up of objects, which are made up of even more objects. Instead of writing a slew of "if this...go there" instructions, you can use an object-oriented programming language to create the components of the traffic light as separate objects. Each object stores its own data and has a set of functions that operate on that data.

Reusing Your Code

How does object-oriented programming save you time and prevent you from reinventing the software wheel? Because you're writing individual objects now, you can borrow components from one system to fulfill the needs of another. You could borrow the timer, controller, and lights from the traffic-light object discussed in the preceding section and create some flashing lights to go around a virtual Christmas-tree object. If you have already written the components that do the flashing, why rewrite them? In the same light (no pun intended), you can use traffic-light objects to create an even bigger traffic-flow simulation.

Another feature of object-oriented programming that saves you coding time is the ability to derive from an object and change it to fulfill slightly different purposes. Suppose that you want to create a flower-bed simulation. You could write the daisies, carnations, and roses from scratch, but doesn't it make more sense to write a flower object, inherit it, and change it slightly to make it a daisy, carnation, or rose? This method certainly would save you a great deal of time and effort.

Windows Objects (OLE and COM)

Microsoft invented *OLE* to solve a fundamental problem with document-based applications: how to store different types of data within the same document and also be able to manipulate that data in the context in which the data was created. Modifying a text editor so that a user can embed a graphic in a document isn't a really tough job. To complicate the situation, however, suppose that someone sends you a document that contains an embedded graphic, and you want to modify the graphic slightly.

Before OLE was discovered, you had to save the graphic by itself, make the modifications, and import the graphic again (kind of a pain, if you ask me). OLE, on the other hand, allows you to modify the graphic right there inside the document that contains it. You don't need to load up a complete other application just to make a few modifications in a document. Instead, the paint program that created the graphic takes over the user interface of the word processing program. But OLE is much more than that, as you'll see in a few minutes.

> **NOTE:** That's referred to as *in-place activation*. Users see the toolbar and the menus of the paint program while they're editing the graphic; they get the toolbar and menus of the word processor when they're modifying the rest of the document.

What's with the reference to *COM* in the title of this section? You'll see references to *COM* in two contexts in this book. First, I'll use the term when I refer to the communications port on your PC or to communications in general. In such a case, I'll try to distinguish the reference in some way. Second, as used here, *COM* stands for *Component Object Model*.

COM is a programming model that defines how objects communicate with one another. In COM, an object exposes something called an *interface*. If a module wants to use that object, it must first obtain a pointer to an interface. Through the interface, the module can call functions provided by the object. Objects written using the Component Object Model are usually referred to as *Windows objects*.

OLE, on the other hand, is a collection of technologies that are based on COM. OLE encompasses not only the in-place activation described earlier in this section, but also drag-and-drop, compound files, embedding, and OLE controls. Drag-and-drop enables the user to pick up a Windows object (such as a file or a link in Windows 95 and Windows NT 4) and drop it on a target. Compound files enable applications to save the data of objects that don't belong to them—a situation called *embedding*. OLE controls are (typically) modular user interface components that perform specific tasks; they can be dropped into applications that are OLE-aware.

> **NOTE:** Microsoft recently renamed OLE controls ActiveX controls. To remain consistent with Microsoft, the book uses *ActiveX controls* instead of *OLE controls*. Please don't confuse ActiveX controls with controls that you would write to enhance your Web site, even though everything that you learn about ActiveX controls here also applies to controls that are used on Web sites.

ActiveX Controls and Containers

Soon after creating the OLE and COM technologies that allow in-place activation, wherein a Windows object can play in the window of another application, Microsoft realized a need to create objects that are capable of two-way communication. Two-way communication implies that a Windows object is capable of calling interfaces exposed in the parent application, just as the parent calls interfaces exposed in the Windows object. That's where the term *ActiveX control* comes from.

What the Heck's a Control?

An *ActiveX control*, simply put, is a Windows object that's capable of two-way communication. In addition to the common set of interfaces that allows the application to talk to the control, a common set of interfaces allows the control to talk back to the application. Suppose that you're building a Web-browser control. You created an application that activates and displays the control, and now you want to make the control look as though it's truly part of the application.

To do so, you create an event notification so that the control tells the application when the user (that's you) right-clicks a graphic. Because the containing application is notified about the mouse click, you can write a routine that displays a right-mouse-button menu. In the right-mouse-button menu, you can do things such as copy the graphic to the Clipboard, copy the graphic to a file, or print the graphic. (Of course, you must write those interfaces as well.) Even though the app and the control are two separate programs, to the user, they look and feel as though they are one.

> **NOTE:** The act of loading an object (be it a control or C++ object) so that you can call its member functions and access its data is called *instantiation*. In such a case, you are creating an instance of an object.

What the Heck's a Container?

Notice in the preceding section that I call the application that instantiates the Web-browser control the *containing application*. Applications that provide housing for ActiveX controls (or for any OLE object, for that matter) are often referred to as *containers*. The container is responsible for getting a pointer to the control's interfaces, using those interfaces to call member functions, and responding to notifications from the control.

That, my friend, is what *Programming Internet Controls* is all about. This book combines the truly fascinating world of writing modem and Internet programs with the awesome power of ActiveX control programming. As a result, you learn to build powerful applets that can plug into just about any application. (Imagine building a fully integrated Internet program, with news, mail, and FTP, or taking those components and selling them as separate applications.)

Now that you know the what, when, and where, you can get on with the joy of modular programming.

Chapter | 2

Creating Your First Control

by Markus Pope

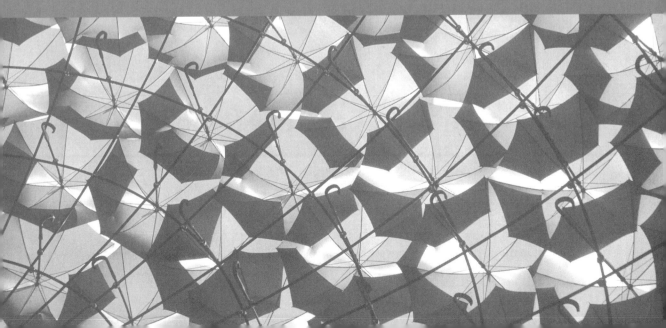

Microsoft is intent on increasing productivity in the computer software industry. This intention is, if you think about it, quite odd, considering that Microsoft is poised to carry the lion's share of all software markets—not just operating systems, word processing programs, and spreadsheet programs. I'm sure that Microsoft has masterminded a plan that entails getting everyone in the world to depend on Microsoft stuff and then threatening to pull the plug if we don't all pay taxes. Problem is (bite my tongue) that Microsoft is darned good at producing high-quality software. (I'm addicted!)

Plan or no plan, Microsoft has done us a big favor, and we're sure as heck going to take advantage of it. Microsoft not only came up with the concepts of Object Linking and Embedding (OLE) and ActiveX controls, but also did most of the work for us. The Microsoft Foundation Class (MFC) library and the application framework, included in Visual C++, take the grunt work out of programming OLE. By taking care of the basics that all ActiveX controls have in common, Microsoft allows us to concentrate on more important things: writing the meat of our applications, playing Diplomacy over the Net, or whatever. (Diplomacy is a very popular strategy game.)

In this chapter, you learn to use the tools that Microsoft provides to create the basic framework for a control. The chapter walks you through the process of writing and testing a control to get you acquainted with the way that a control works and with Microsoft Developer Studio. (*Microsoft Developer Studio* is the new name for Visual C++.) The chapter covers the following topics:

- Creating an MFC control framework
- Implementing the control
- Plugging in the control

Creating an MFC Control Framework

A *framework*, simply put, is a skeleton of an application. You have to write a significant amount of code each time you create a Windows program, and controls are no different. You can create a skeleton that is a fully functioning application and just copy and modify the skeleton when you need to do something new.

Microsoft devoted a considerable amount of time to creating these skeletons. With that fact in mind, you start your project by using Visual C++ to create a skeleton control.

Introducing ControlWizard

Visual C++ provides several wizards that you can use to create your skeleton applications. For purposes of this book, you're particularly interested in the OLE ControlWizard. To start the OLE ControlWizard, choose **File**, **New** in Visual C++ to open the New dialog box. This dialog box allows you to create new source files, resources, and projects. Select Project Workspace and then click the OK button. The New Project Workspace dialog box appears, as shown in Figure 2-1.

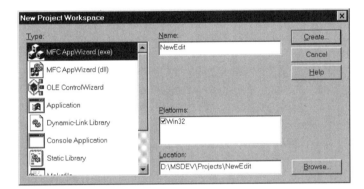

FIGURE 2-1

This dialog box appears when you choose the Project Workspace option in the New dialog box in Visual C++.

From the Type list, you can select a variety of projects, ranging from applications to wrappers for makefiles. Click OLE ControlWizard to highlight it. Next, you need to give your project a name. Call it NewEdit, because you're going to inherit the functionality of the Windows edit control and then modify it a bit to allow formatting. Enter **NewEdit** in the **Name** box and then click the **Create** button. Visual C++ displays the OLE ControlWizard dialog box, shown in Figure 2-2.

> **NOTE:** Notice the Platforms list box and the Location edit box in the New Project Workspace dialog box. *Platforms* refers to the environments that you want your application compiled for, such as OS/2 or MIPS. *Location* refers to the directory where you want your source files saved. You don't need to modify these two fields; the defaults are fine.

This dialog box is where you start specifying how you want to construct the framework. The first question asks how many controls you want in the project. In this case, you want the OCX file to contain only one control. Leave the number of controls at the default setting (1), or use the spin controls to adjust this value appropriately.

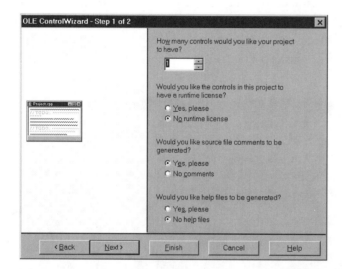

FIGURE 2-2

This dialog box is the first in a series of dialog boxes that help you build the initial framework for your first ActiveX control.

NOTE: You'll hear *OCX* used as a synonym for *ActiveX control*. This is actually a misnomer. OCX is a file extension that's commonly used to name dynamic-link libraries (DLLs) that contain controls. Because most OCX files contain only one control, programmers started using OCX as a nickname for ActiveX controls.

Next, Visual C++ asks whether you want the control to have a run-time license. The default is No, which is just as well, because I don't want to get into that stuff right now. You can always add run-time and/or development-time licensing later; in fact, you can refer to Appendix A, "Adding Licensing to Your Online Controls."

After you specify the number of controls and indicate whether you want to add run-time licensing, Visual C++ asks whether you want to have your source files commented. Answer yes, because you'll be much better off in the long run. Commenting your code is fundamental to programming in any language, especially C and C++. Without the comments, you'll have to read cryptic lines of source trying to figure out what the heck's going on. The option is set to generate comments by default, so you don't have to mess with it.

Finally (on the first page of the OLE ControlWizard, anyway), you specify whether you want to generate help files. Leave this option turned off for the scope of this book. You can always add help files to your projects later. Click **N**ext to continue to the last page of the OLE ControlWizard.

> **TIP:** You can accept the default settings on the first page of the OLE ControlWizard. The last page of the wizard is the most important, especially if you're going to superclass one of the standard Windows controls.
>
> *Superclassing* and *subclassing* are buzzwords that refer to extending the basic capabilities of an object. In this chapter, you're going to inherit the properties of the Windows edit control and write some code to change the control's behavior.

The last page of the OLE ControlWizard (see Figure 2-3) allows you to change the class names associated with the control and to enable and disable some of the framework's features. If you want the container application to be able to call a function in a control that displays an About dialog box, choose the Has an About Box option. Visual C++ adds an About dialog box and supporting code to your project automatically.

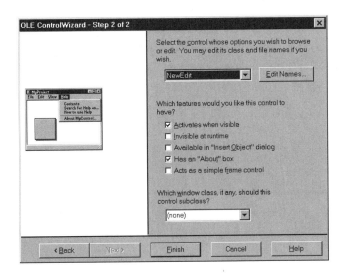

FIGURE 2-3

The last page of the OLE ControlWizard allows you to choose the properties that you want your control to take advantage of.

The default settings on this page are sufficient for what you want to do, with the exception of the last option, which specifies which window class, if any, you want the control to subclass. Your control can inherit the behavior of buttons, status bars, progress bars, edit controls, and even list and tree controls. Select EDIT as the window class to use as the basis for your first control. Then click the **F**inish button to create the framework for the control.

At this point, Visual C++ displays a dialog box, showing all the classes and files that it's going to create for your project. Click the OK button to create the project.

> **TIP:** If you leave out features while using the OLE ControlWizard, and you find later that you need the features you left out, you must add the features to your code manually. So it's a good idea to think about what features you need in your controls before you click the **F**inish button in the OLE ControlWizard!

Navigating the Source

Before you start adding code to the NewEdit control, take a little time to get acquainted with the objects that the OLE ControlWizard created for you. You can view the classes created by the OLE ControlWizard by selecting class view, shown in Figure 2-4. Three classes are displayed: CNewEditApp, CNewEditCtrl, and CNewEditPropPage. Global, although displayed with the project's classes, is not really a class. Global gives you easy access to the global variables in your project.

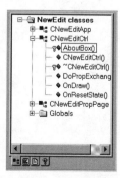

FIGURE 2-4

In Visual C++'s class view, navigating your source code is a snap.

CNewEditApp is derived from COleControlModule, which is derived from CWinApp. CNewEditApp is responsible for initializing the DLL that contains your controls and providing some functions that you can overload to initialize your own data. In fact, the OLE ControlWizard creates definitions for two of those functions—InitInstance and ExitInstance—when you create a control framework. InitInstance, as the name suggests, is where you put code to prepare data members that you stored in the CNewEditApp object. ExitInstance is overloaded so that you have a place to free objects and restore states—clean up after yourself.

CNewEditCtrl, which is where you'll do most of your work, is derived from COleControl, which in turn is derived from CWnd. CNewEditCtrl is the frame window that contains the control (somewhat like the frame window for an MFC executable), with extra code to support events and properties. (I discuss events and properties in "Implementing Events, Methods, and Properties" later in this chapter.)

The OLE ControlWizard automatically creates constructors and destructors for the CNewEditCtrl object. In addition, MFC overloads the DoPropExchange, IsSubclassedControl, OnDraw, OnOcmCommand, OnResetState, and PreCreateWindow member functions. DoPropExchange is called when the control framework is reading from or writing to persistent storage. I'll cover persistent storage in more detail when you start adding properties to your control.

> **NOTE:** *Persistent storage* sounds complicated but is actually simple; it's the medium that stores the data that the control uses. In most cases, this phrase refers to a file in memory or on the hard drive.

IsSubclassedControl, OnOcmCommand, and PreCreateWindow normally are not overloaded, but they are in this case, because you specified that you wanted the control to inherit the functionality of a Windows edit control. IsSubclassedControl is overloaded to return TRUE to tell the framework that you're subclassing a control. OnOcmCommand is used to handle messages (such as WM_COMMAND) that Windows controls normally send to their parent windows (see the sidebar "Subclassed Controls"). PreCreateWindow, which in my opinion is the most significant of these three functions, looks like this:

```
BOOL CNewEditCtrl::PreCreateWindow(CREATESTRUCT& cs)
{
        cs.lpszClass = _T("EDIT");
        return COleControl::PreCreateWindow(cs);
}
```

Subclassed Controls

When you specify that you want to create an OLE control that subclasses a standard Windows control, the framework creates a special window to filter out messages (such as WM_COMMAND and WM_PARENTNOTIFY) that Windows controls usually send to their parent windows. The special filter window catches those messages and sends them to the OLE control by calling OnOcmCommand.

I find the special window useful for handling ownerdraw messages such as WM_DRAWITEM, WM_MEASUREITEM, and WM_DELETEITEM (for painting your own buttons and list boxes, for example).

PreCreateWindow is overloaded so that you can specify which window class you want the OLE control to subclass. A CREATESTRUCT that contains information about the window class used to create the control's window is passed into PreCreateWindow. To change the type of window on which the control is based, set the cs.lpszClass member of the CREAT-ESTRUCT to the name of the desired class. In this case, the member is set to EDIT, which is the class name of the standard Windows edit control.

TIP: Use the _T macro when you specify string constants, because the Visual C++ compiler supports Unicode, Windows' international-character-set support. Character arrays in C and C++, have traditionally been arrays of bytes (8-bit values). Unicode expands these character arrays to arrays of 16-bit integers. _T ensures that the character array is the correct size for the application that you're writing.

The functions that are automatically overloaded also include OnResetState and OnDraw. OnResetState is a good place to put initialization code other than code that initializes your control's properties. The base class implementation calls DoPropExchange, which initializes your control's properties in addition to preparing them for persistent storage.

Now examine OnDraw:

```
void CNewEditCtrl::OnDraw(CDC* pdc, const CRect&
rcBounds, const CRect& rcInvalid)
```

```
{
        DoSuperclassPaint(pdc, rcBounds);
}
```

OnDraw is called when part of the control's window needs to be redrawn. Initially, OnDraw is written to call DoSuperclassPaint. DoSuperclassPaint is called to allow Windows to paint the Windows edit control. Later, you'll hack the OnDraw function so that it executes some formatting code the first time it's painted; for now, don't change it.

In addition to CNewEditApp and CNewEditCtrl, Visual C++ created a CNewEditPropPage class. CNewEditPropPage, which is derived from COlePropertyPage, encapsulates the property pages that appear when the container invokes the control's Properties dialog box. CNewEditPropPage overloads DoDataExchange, which (similar to the DoDataExchange member of a CDialog object) maps member variables in the property pages to properties in the control.

By now, you should have a firm grasp of the classes created by Visual C++ and what they're responsible for. The next section talks about events, methods, and properties.

Implementing Events, Methods, and Properties

The framework is the backbone of the control, whereas events, methods, and properties comprise the implementation. Controls use *events* to notify container applications that something significant has changed in the state of the control. *Methods* are called by containers to invoke behaviors or to set and retrieve properties. *Properties* are member variables that define the behavior of a control. To develop the control, you add your own events, methods, and properties to the control framework.

An FTP (*File Transfer Protocol*) control, for example, may use an event to notify the container when it changes the current directory on the host. The container may then call a method in the control to retrieve the current directory. In addition, the current directory can be implemented as a property. You can add that property to one of the control's property sheets and then change the current directory by invoking the control's Properties dialog box.

Introducing the OLE Tabs in ClassWizard

The ClassWizard (see Figure 2-5) is an extremely useful tool for adding events, methods, and properties to your controls. This section discusses the ClassWizard as it pertains to ActiveX controls; I'll discuss the other options when you need to use them. ClassWizard greatly simplifies your task by adding member variables, functions, and code to your control's source files automatically. To display the ClassWizard, press Ctrl+W.

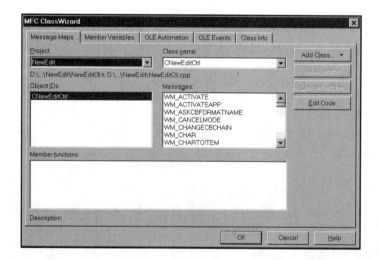

FIGURE 2-5

ClassWizard is the tool to use when you add events, methods, and properties to your controls.

The OLE Automation and OLE Events tabs are of particular interest. In the OLE Automation tab, you can add a method by clicking the Add Method button; to add a property, click Add Property. When you add a method or property to a class, Visual C++ adds it to the External Names list box. Later in this chapter, you add both a method and property to the CNewEditCtrl object.

The OLE Events tab, shown in Figure 2-6, allows you to add stock or custom notifications to your controls. Visual C++'s control framework provides stock events that notify the container of mouse movement and keyboard actions. In addition, you can create custom events that you can fire when properties change or you need to notify the container that something has happened. (In the FTP example earlier, the container was notified when the FTP control changed directories.)

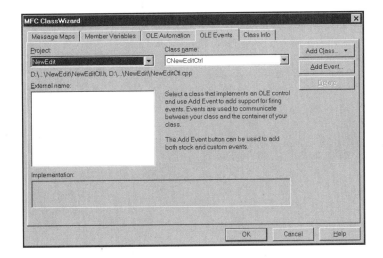

FIGURE 2-6

The OLE Events tab of the ClassWizard allows you to create notifications so that your control can warn the container application about changes in the control's behavior.

Adding Properties

In this section, you're going to create an edit control that allows you to format the data as it's typed into the control. To do so, you need to add a member variable to the CNewEditCtrl class to track the string that specifies the format of the control. Because you're going to have the container specify the format of the edit control, you may as well convert the string that contains the format into a property. Follow these steps:

1. Press Ctrl+W to display the ClassWizard, if necessary.
2. Select CNewEditCtrl in the Class Name list. (The Class Name list is in every tab in the ClassWizard.)
3. Click the OLE Automation tab and then click the Add Property button. Visual C++ displays the Add Property dialog box.
4. Type **FieldFormat** in the External Name box.
5. In the Implementation section, choose Get/Set Methods. Changing the implementation to Get/Set gets rid of the member-variable and notify-function fields and replaces them with two function calls: the Get function and the Set function.

    As you see in Figure 2-7, Visual C++ creates two member functions as you type the name of the property. (In this case, it sets the Get/Set functions to GetFieldFormat and SetFieldFormat.)

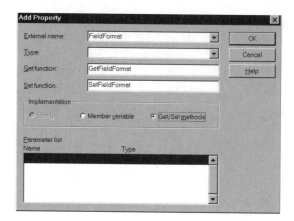

FIGURE 2-7

Type the name of the property in the Add Property dialog box, select the variable type of the property, and choose OK to add the property to your source files. Don't forget to set the implementation appropriately.

6. After you set the name of the property, you need to choose the property type. Because you want the format property to represent a string, select BSTR in the **T**ype list. (BSTR is a character array.)

7. Choose OK to add the property to the source code.

Visual C++ adds the following two member functions to your CNewEditCtrl class:

```
BSTR CNewEditCtrl::GetFieldFormat()
{
        CString strResult;
        // TODO: Add your property handler here
        return strResult.AllocSysString();
}
void CNewEditCtrl::SetFieldFormat(LPCTSTR lpszNewValue)
{
        // TODO: Add your property handler here
        SetModifiedFlag();
}
```

Getting the Property

GetFieldFormat instantiates a CString object and returns a BSTR pointer that points to the CString's contents. But look at the code—it doesn't really do anything, because Visual C++ doesn't automatically tie a Get/Set property to a member variable. (Visual C++ does, however, do that when you set the implementation to member variable instead of Get/Set.)

To fix this problem, you need to add a member variable to CNewEditCtrl and tie it to the FieldFormat property. You can add a member variable to a class declaration manually, but Visual C++ provides a quick way to do it without forcing you to open a header file. In class view, right-click the CNewEditCtrl class and then choose Add Variable from the pop-up menu that appears. Visual C++ displays the dialog box shown in Figure 2-8.

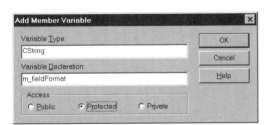

FIGURE 2-8

Use the Add Member Variable dialog box to add member variables to your classes instead of wasting time by modifying header files manually.

Type **CString** in the Variable **T**ype box and **m_fieldFormat** in the Variable **D**eclaration field, set the Access type to Protected, and click the OK button to add the variable to the project. Then expand CNewEditCtrl in class view. m_fieldFormat now appears after the SetFieldFormat function. Double-click GetFieldFormat in class view to edit the code, and replace GetFieldFormat with this new version of the code:

```
BSTR CNewEditCtrl::GetFieldFormat()
{
        return( m_fieldFormat.AllocSysString() );
}
```

This code looks much better. Instead of instantiating a CString object and returning a BSTR pointer to that object, the code returns a BSTR pointer to the m_fieldFormat member variable.

Setting the Property

Now you need to change the SetFieldFormat member function to set the value of m_fieldFormat. Refer to the SetFieldFormat code fragment at the end of the "Adding Properties" section earlier in this chapter. The call to SetModifiedFlag sets the modified flag for the control. You should call this function any time you change the control's persistent data. Along with calling the SetModifiedFlag member variable, you have to change the code so that m_fieldFormat is set equal to the string pointed to by lpszNewValue. That change is simple, because the CString class overloads the equals operator to allow direct assignment of strings.

Examine the SetFieldFormat function in the following example:

```
void CNewEditCtrl::SetFieldFormat(LPCTSTR lpszNewValue)
{
        if( m_fieldFormat != lpszNewValue )
        {
                m_fieldFormat = lpszNewValue;
                SetModifiedFlag();
        }
}
```

The first thing that this code does is determine whether the current contents of m_fieldFormat are the same as the string passed in by the control framework. If not, the code sets m_fieldFormat to the passed-in string and then makes a call to SetModifiedFlag. If the contents of m_fieldFormat have not changed, there's no reason to set the modify flag of the control.

At this point, you have the basic implementation of the FieldFormat property. What do you need to do to make the FieldFormat property affect your control? First, you probably don't want to display the format string, which is rather ugly. So you need to implement a second CString object to contain the string that's actually displayed in the edit control.

Adding Methods

Add another private CString to the CNewEditCtrl class, and call it m_fieldDisplay. You learn about the full implementation of m_fieldDisplay later in this chapter. For now, you need to create a way for the container to get the contents of the edit control. Follow these steps:

1. Press Ctrl+W to display the ClassWizard, if necessary.

2. Click the OLE Automation tab and then click the **Add Method** button. Visual C++ displays the Add Method dialog box.

3. Type **GetDisplayString** in the External Name box.

4. Select BSTR in the Return Type list (see Figure 2-9).

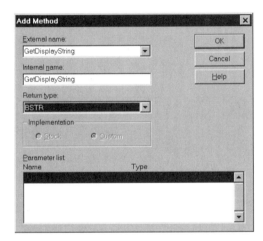

FIGURE 2-9

Use the Add Method dialog box to expose functions in your control to the container.

5. Choose OK to add the `GetDisplayString` function to your control.

6. Double-click `GetDisplayString` in class view to edit the code.

7. Replace the contents of this function with the following:

```
return( m_fieldDisplay.AllocSysString() );
```

You have added both a property and a method to your control, but you have a great deal of work left to do. The next step is to make the control display the contents of `m_fieldDisplay`.

Displaying the Formatted String

To notify the user that he or she is entering a formatted string, you need to display the format string. But you don't want to display `m_fieldFormat`, because it's ugly. Instead, write a function that converts the format string to a display string and then puts the result in `m_fieldDisplay`. Call this function `ConvertFormatForDisplay`.

ConvertFormatForDisplay simply loops through each character in m_fieldFormat. If a character is a format character, the corresponding character in m_fieldDisplay is set to a space. (Format characters indicate whether a digit is alphabetical, numerical, punctuation, and so on.) If a character is part of the background (the constant text), it's copied to m_fieldDisplay. Your ConvertFormatForDisplay function looks like this:

```
void CNewEditCtrl::ConvertFormatForDisplay()
{
        int i, len = m_fieldFormat.GetLength();

        m_fieldDisplay.Empty();
        for( i = 0; i < len; i++ )
                if( m_fieldFormat[i] != '#' &&
m_fieldFormat[i] != '~' )
                        m_fieldDisplay += m_fieldFormat[i];
                else
                        m_fieldDisplay += ' ';
}
```

I chose the pound sign (#) and the tilde (~) as format characters. I'll leave it up to you to change the code so that you can specify numbers or alphabetical characters only. (A suggestion: Use # to specify digits and ~ to specify letters.)

Now that you have the code in place to handle the initial state of m_fieldDisplay, you can modify the SetFieldFormat function to set the contents of the edit control to m_fieldDisplay. To do so, add the following lines of code just below the line that reads m_fieldFormat = lpszNewValue:

```
        ConvertFormatForDisplay();
        SetWindowText( m_fieldDisplay );
```

Getting Input for the Control

Next, you want to put in a handler for the WM_CHAR message, which is sent to the control when the user presses keys on the keyboard. You're going to trap each keystroke and format the data that the user types as he or she types it.

To add the WM_CHAR handler, follow these steps:

1. Double-click OnDraw in class view. This action opens the file that contains the source code for the CNewEditCtrl implementation.

2. At the top, you should see the **M**essages list; select WM_CHAR. Visual C++ displays a dialog box, asking whether you want to add a handler for the WM_CHAR message.

3. Click Yes. Visual C++ adds a function called OnChar to your CNewEditCtrl class declaration.

4. Double-click OnChar to edit the source code.

5. Replace the contents so that your OnChar handler looks like the following example:

```cpp
void CNewEditCtrl::OnChar(UINT nChar, UINT nRepCnt,
UINT nFlags)
{
        int nPos = GetCurrentCaretPos();
        int len = m_fieldFormat.GetLength();

        if( nChar >= ' ' && nChar <= '~' )
        {
                if( nPos < len )
                {
                        if( m_fieldFormat[nPos] != '#' &&
m_fieldFormat[nPos] != '~' )
                        {
                                SetCurrentCaretPos( nPos + 1 );
                                OnChar( nChar, nRepCnt, nFlags );
                        } else
                        {
                                m_fieldDisplay.SetAt( nPos, nChar );
                                SetWindowText( m_fieldDisplay );
                                SetCurrentCaretPos( nPos + 1 );
                        }
                } else
```

```
                        ::MessageBeep( MB_ICONEXCLAMATION );
        } else if( nChar == 0x08 && nPos > 0 )
        {
                nPos-;
                if( m_fieldFormat[nPos] == '#' ||
m_fieldFormat[nPos] == '~' )
                {
                        m_fieldDisplay.SetAt( nPos, ' ' );
                        SetWindowText( m_fieldDisplay );
                }
                SetCurrentCaretPos( nPos );
        }
}
```

OnChar determines whether the character is a displayable character. Displayable characters have character values greater than or equal to space and less than or equal to tilde. When OnChar receives a displayable character, and when the current location in the format string is a format character, the code updates the corresponding character in m_fieldDisplay with the new character and resets the text in the edit control. If there's room, but the current location in the format string is not a format character, the code moves to the next character and calls OnChar recursively. (Not using recursion is more efficient but more complicated.)

When OnChar receives a nondisplayable character, the code looks to see whether the character is a backspace; if so, the caret's position is decremented by 1. Then, if the caret's new position in m_fieldFormat corresponds to a format character, the character in m_fieldDisplay is set to space—appearing to the user as though he pressed Backspace and deleted a character (which is good, because that's what he intended to do).

NOTE: *Caret* is another name for the traditional text cursor. Because the mouse pointer is so often called a cursor, many developers—and Microsoft—refer to the traditional cursor as a caret.

Tracking the Caret

One important aspect of the OnChar function—the element that makes it work—is the location of the caret in the edit control. To track the position of the caret, the OnChar handler uses two functions: GetCurrentCaretPos and SetCurrentCaretPos. Examine the implementation of these two functions:

```
int CNewEditCtrl::GetCurrentCaretPos()
{
        DWORD dwStart, dwEnd;
        SendMessage( EM_GETSEL, (WPARAM)&dwStart,
(LPARAM)&dwEnd );
        return( (int)dwStart );
}
void CNewEditCtrl::SetCurrentCaretPos( int nPos )
{
        SendMessage( EM_SETSEL, (WPARAM)nPos, (LPARAM)nPos );
}
```

GetCurrentCaretPos sends an EM_GETSEL message to the edit control and passes it two DWORD values. EM_GETSEL returns the text that is selected in the edit control. The first DWORD contains the start of the currently selected text. The second DWORD contains the end of the currently selected text. You don't care much about the end in this case, so GetCurrentCaretPos returns the start of the selection, which in most cases is the current caret position.

> **NOTE:** You could expand GetCurrentCaretPos to determine which is greater—the start or the end—and return the appropriate value, but don't worry about doing that for this project.

Contrary to GetCurrentCaretPos, SetCurrentCaretPos sends an EM_SETSEL, which selects text in the edit control. Luckily, passing the same value for start and end has the effect of setting the current caret position.

You're close to completing the implementation of the m_fieldFormat property. All that you have left to do is add a couple of functions that make the format control work a little better and make m_fieldFormat persistent. I'll save the discussion of persistence for

"Serializing Properties" later in the chapter. The remainder of this section shows you how to finish the m_fieldFormat implementation.

Setting the Caret's Initial Position

If you were to build and use the NewEdit control at this point, and then set the format string, you would notice that the initial position of the caret is not the first valid format character. To change that situation, you create two functions: GetFirstFormatSpace and GetNextFormatSpace. GetFirstFormatSpace simply makes a call to GetNextFormatSpace, specifying zero as the starting position. GetNextFormatSpace searches for the next format character in m_fieldFormat, starting with the specified position. The following example shows what those two functions look like:

```
int CNewEditCtrl::GetNextFormatSpace( int nPos )
{
        int i, len = m_fieldFormat.GetLength();
        for( i = nPos; i < len; i++ )
                if( m_fieldFormat[i] == '#' ||
m_fieldFormat[i] == '~' )
                        return( i );
        return( 0 );
}
int CNewEditCtrl::GetFirstFormatSpace()
{
        return( GetNextFormatSpace( 0 ) );
}
```

Both functions are simple. GetNextFormatSpace loops through each character in m_fieldFormat, and upon finding a format character, it returns the position of that character to the calling routine. If GetNextFormatSpace reaches the end of the format string before finding a format character, it returns zero. To implement these two functions, change the SetFieldFormat member function to look like this:

```
void CNewEditCtrl::SetFieldFormat(LPCTSTR lpszNewValue)
{
        int nPos;
        if( m_fieldFormat != lpszNewValue )
```

```
        {
                m_fieldFormat = lpszNewValue;
                ConvertFormatForDisplay();
                SetWindowText( m_fieldDisplay );
                nPos = GetFirstFormatSpace();
                SetCurrentCaretPos( nPos );
                SetModifiedFlag();
        }
}
```

Notice that the preceding code adds an integer variable to store the position returned by GetFirstFormatSpace. Next, the code inserts a call to GetFirstFormatSpace after the call to SetWindowText and then makes a call to SetCurrentCaretPos to set the new position of the caret. This code positions the caret at the first valid format character in m_fieldFormat.

Adding Events

Now that you have completed the implementation of the control, you're ready to add two events: one to notify the container when the user clicks inside the control, and the other to notify the container when m_fieldDisplay changes. The first event is easy. Visual C++ provides stock events for mouse clicks and keyboard actions.

To add the mouse-click stock event, follow these steps:

1. Press Ctrl+W to display the ClassWizard, if necessary.
2. Click the OLE Events tab and then click the **A**dd Event button. Visual C++ displays the Add Event dialog box, shown in Figure 2-10.
3. Select Click from the **E**xternal Name drop-down list. Click is a stock event that notifies the container when the user clicks inside the control window.
4. Choose OK.

To add a custom event, follow these steps:

1. Press Ctrl+W to display the ClassWizard, if necessary.
2. Click the OLE Events tab and then click the **A**dd Event button to display the Add Event dialog box.
3. Type **TextFull** in the **E**xternal Name box.

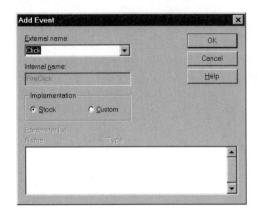

FIGURE 2-10

Use the Add Event dialog box to add notifications to your controls. Notifications tell the container when the behavior of the control changes.

4. Choose OK. Visual C++ adds an inline member function called `FireTextFull` to your `CNewEditCtrl` object. `FireTextFull` calls the `FireEvent` member of `COleControl`, which in turn signals the container with the `TextFull` event.

To implement the event, you need to call your new `FireTextFull` function. Add the following line to your implementation of the `OnChar` function, after the line that contains `::MessageBeep( MB_ICONEXCLAMATION )`:

```
FireTextFull();
```

Now when the caret reaches the end of the edit control, our `NewEdit` control calls `FireTextFull` to notify the container. Then the container can call the `GetDisplayString` function to get the contents of the edit control.

The following section explains how you can make data within your control persistent—that is, save it to some type of storage.

Serializing Properties

Property serialization is a fancy term that Microsoft invented to explain how an object is written to a storage device. (*Storage device* usually refers to the hard drive.) You know what properties are. What is serialization?

Serialization means putting a group of objects in a single-file line so that they can be accessed linearly. In property serialization, an object's data is laid out on the storage device in a specific way, so that you know how to read that data back into the object when the object is restored from the storage device.

In this section, you add serialization for only the FieldFormat property. Start by changing the DoPropExchange function to look like this:

```
void CNewEditCtrl::DoPropExchange(CPropExchange* pPX)
{
        ExchangeVersion(pPX, MAKELONG(_wVerMinor,_wVerMajor));
        COleControl::DoPropExchange(pPX);
        PX_String( pPX, _T( "FieldFormat" ),
m_fieldFormat, _T( "" ) );
}
```

Notice that the preceding code adds a call to the PX_String function. PX_String writes a character array to, or reads a character array from, the storage device specified by pPX. In addition, PX_String can initialize the character array with a default value, in case some kind of error occurs while the code is writing the property. The code passes in the name of the property—FieldFormat—as a constant, as well as the member variable to which the property corresponds. Now you have a persistent property.

But you still have to make some rude hacks to your control to get the serialization to do anything. First, add an integer called m_nOnFirstDraw to your CNewEditCtrl class declaration. Next, replace the DoSuperClassPaint call in your OnDraw function with the following code:

```
        int nPos;
        if( m_nOnFirstDraw )
        {
                m_nOnFirstDraw = 0;
                ConvertFormatForDisplay();
                SetWindowText( m_fieldDisplay );
                nPos = GetFirstFormatSpace();
                SendMessage( EM_SETSEL, (WPARAM)nPos, (LPARAM)nPos );
        } else
                DoSuperclassPaint(pdc, rcBounds);
```

This code determines whether m_nOnFirstDraw is true. If so, the code converts m_fieldFormat for display, sets the contents of the edit control to your display string, and sets the caret to the first format space in the format string.

That's all there is to it. When a container restores the NewEdit control from a storage stream, you retain the format of the NewEdit control that was saved. Now it's up to you to make the display string—m_fieldDisplay—persistent.

Using Property Pages

When Visual C++ creates the framework for a control, it also creates a property page. A *property page* is a tab in a dialog box that's displayed when the container invokes a control's Properties dialog box. Property pages give users an easy way to change the properties of your control. In this section, you top off the control by adding the FieldFormat property to the default property page provided by the framework. Follow these steps:

1. Start by switching from class view to resource view, as shown in Figure 2-11.

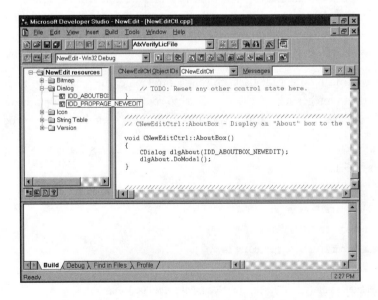

FIGURE 2-11

In Visual C++ resource view, you can edit existing resources or add new ones.

2. Expand `NewEdit` resources to reveal your control's resources.

3. Next, expand the dialog-box folder. Notice that there are two dialog-box definitions. The first one, `IDD_ABOUT_NEWEDIT`, is an About dialog box that's created by the OLE ControlWizard. `IDD_PROPPAGE_NEWEDIT` is the property-page dialog box where you're going to add an edit box to modify the `FieldFormat` property.

4. Double-click `IDD_PROPPAGE_NEWEDIT` in resource view, select the static text control in the Controls dialog box, and add a static text control to your dialog box.

5. Using Figure 2-12 as a reference, change the text of the static control to `&Format String:`.

   You can modify the text of the static control by double-clicking the control and typing new text in the **C**aption box. When you double-click a control, the Control Properties dialog box appears (also shown in Figure 2-12).

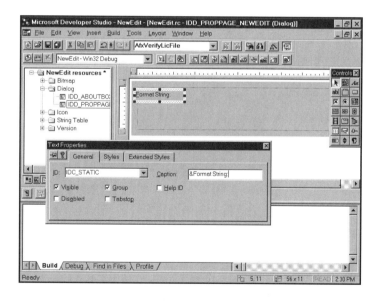

FIGURE 2-12

Use the Controls dialog box and the mouse to add a static text control to the `IDD_PROPPAGE_NEWEDIT` *dialog box. Double-click the static text to change its caption.*

6. When you have the static text that describes the property that you're allowing the user to modify, add an edit control next to the static text.

7. Double-click that control to display the Edit Properties dialog box.

8. Replace the contents of the **ID** box with **IDC_FORMATSTR**. (The ID is what you'll use to tie the edit control to the `m_fieldFormat` member of `CNewEditCtrl`.)

9. Close the Edit Properties dialog box by clicking the close button.

10. Hold down the left Ctrl key and double-click the edit box. Visual C++ displays the Add Member Variable dialog box, shown in Figure 2-13.

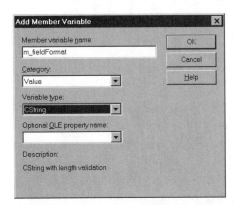

FIGURE 2-13

In the Add Member Variable dialog box, you can tie the edit control to the FieldFormat *property of* CNewEditCtrl.

11. Type **m_fieldFormat** in the Member Variable **N**ame box, change the Variable **T**ype entry to CString, and leave **C**ategory set to Value.

12. In the Optional **OLE** Property Name box, type **FieldFormat** to indicate that you're tying the m_fieldFormat member of CNewEditPropPage to the FieldFormat property of the control.

13. Click the OK button to create the member variable.

After you click OK, Visual C++ adds an m_fieldFormat member to CNewEditPropPage and also adds the following two function calls to the DoDataExchange method:

```
DDP_Text(pDX, IDC_FORMATSTR, m_fieldFormat,
_T("FieldFormat") );

DDX_Text(pDX, IDC_FORMATSTR, m_fieldFormat);
```

DDP_Text associates the m_fieldFormat member of CNewEditPropPage to the FieldFormat property. Then DDX_Text is used to tie the m_fieldFormat member of CNewEditPropPage to the IDC_FORMATSTR edit control in the property page.

Now you're ready to build and use your first control. To build the control, choose **B**uild, **R**ebuild All or press F7. The following section describes how to play with your new control, using the Visual C++ OLE Control test container.

Plugging in the Control

After you build the NewEdit control, you can test it with the OLE Control test container provided by Microsoft. This container is great, because you don't have to build a special container just to test your controls. Run the test container by choosing OLE Control Test Container from the Tools menu in Visual C++. You get a glimpse of the test container application in Figure 2-14.

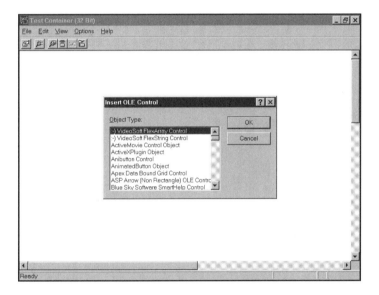

FIGURE 2-14

Use the OLE Control test container application, which is included with Visual C++, to test your controls. This application saves you the work of creating your own container.

Notice the Insert OLE Control dialog box in Figure 2-14. (You can display this dialog box by choosing Edit, Insert OLE Control.) To insert the NewEdit control from this dialog box, select it in the list. Visual C++ inserts the NewEdit control into the client area of the test container.

Activating and Testing Your Control

You're probably already trying to type data into the control, and the silly thing just beeps at you. That's what it's supposed to do. Remember that this is a masked edit control. Initially, the mask is empty, so there's no room to type any characters. In this section, you set the format string. Follow these steps:

1. Choose **E**dit, Properties, NewEdit Control **O**bject in the test container. The NewEdit control displays the IDD_PROPPAGE_NEWEDIT dialog box that you worked on in "Using Property Pages" earlier in this chapter. Figure 2-15 shows the Properties dialog box.

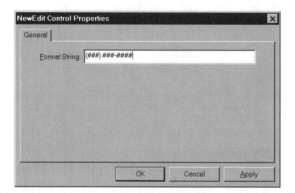

FIGURE 2-15

*Visual C++ created this Properties dialog box for your control framework. The **F**ormat String box makes it easy to change the* FieldFormat *property.*

2. Type **(###) ###-####** in the **F**ormat String box.

3. Choose OK to close the Properties dialog box. Notice that NewEdit removes the # characters and displays the format string in the NewEdit control.

4. Click the edges of the control so that the caret appears after the first parenthesis.

5. Start typing a telephone number. What you type is formatted automatically, based on the FieldFormat property.

6. In the test container, click the button in the toolbar that has the picture of a button and two parentheses (the Invoke Method button). The Invoke Control Method dialog box appears.

7. Make sure that the GetDisplayString function is selected in the **N**ame box, as shown in Figure 2-16.

8. Click the Invoke button. The telephone number that you typed appears at the bottom of the dialog box.

Now look at the events that you created in the final stages of developing your NewEdit control. Close the Invoke Control Method dialog box, and open the Event Log dialog box. To open the Event Log dialog box, click the button in the test container's toolbar that has a picture of waves, or choose **V**iew, Event Log.

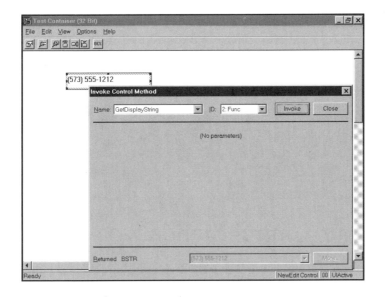

FIGURE 2-16

The test container allows you to call methods that you added to your control's interface. The NewEdit *control, for example, exposes a method called* GetDisplayString, *which returns the contents of the edit box.*

Click the edges of the NewEdit control. Notice that an event called Click() registers in the Event Log, as shown in Figure 2-17.

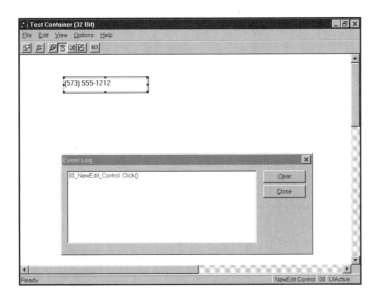

FIGURE 2-17

The Event Log dialog box allows you to view the two events that you created earlier. One event fires when you click the control; the other event fires when you fill up the edit control.

If you haven't filled the format string yet, do so now. Notice how the Event Log dialog box registers a TextFull() event when you try to type past the end of the format string. Pretty cool, huh?

> **NOTE:** Each component of an application that you write can be a stand-alone control. Think of what that does for maintenance of your programs! Because the components of your application are separate but work together as though they are one, you can update each of them independently.

Registering Your Control Manually

You need to register your control in the Windows Registry, so that Windows knows where to find it when an application wants to use it or loads the object's persistent data from a storage device. To register your control manually, choose Tools, Register Control in Visual C++.

> **NOTE:** The intricate details of how Microsoft stores information about your control in the Registry could constitute a large discussion, but describing those details in this book would be a waste of time. If you want to pursue this topic on your own, look in Books Online for articles on the Registry, ActiveX controls, and GUIDs.

Registering Your Control Automatically

You don't have to register your control manually when you use Visual C++ 4.0, because after you compile and link your control, Visual C++ automatically handles registration. (Did you notice the Registering OLE Control message at the bottom of the Visual C++ window?)

Visual C++ registers your control by calling the DllRegisterServer function that Visual C++ creates when you ask for an OLE-control framework. Visual C++ also creates DllUnregisterServer, an exported function that takes care of registering your control so that you don't have to. You can call this function yourself to register your control as part of an application or an install program.

> **NOTE:** You'll find the source code for DllRegisterServer and DllUnregisterServer in the NEWEDIT.CPP file, which is included in your NewEdit control framework.

Chapter Summary

This chapter introduced you to the ActiveX control technology. Along the way, you learned to simplify your development by taking advantage of the features in Visual C++. Using Visual C++ and MFC, you can create modular software systems without forcing yourself to learn about OLE and COM. Although ActiveX controls are based on OLE and COM, MFC conceals the OLE and COM deep within the classes created for the control framework.

As part of this chapter, you used the OLE ControlWizard to create an ActiveX control framework. You know how to add properties, methods, and events to a control. You also know how to test a control by using the OLE test container included with Visual C++.

In Chapter 3, "Talking to Your Modem," we take a break from control technology to talk briefly about modem programming in Windows.

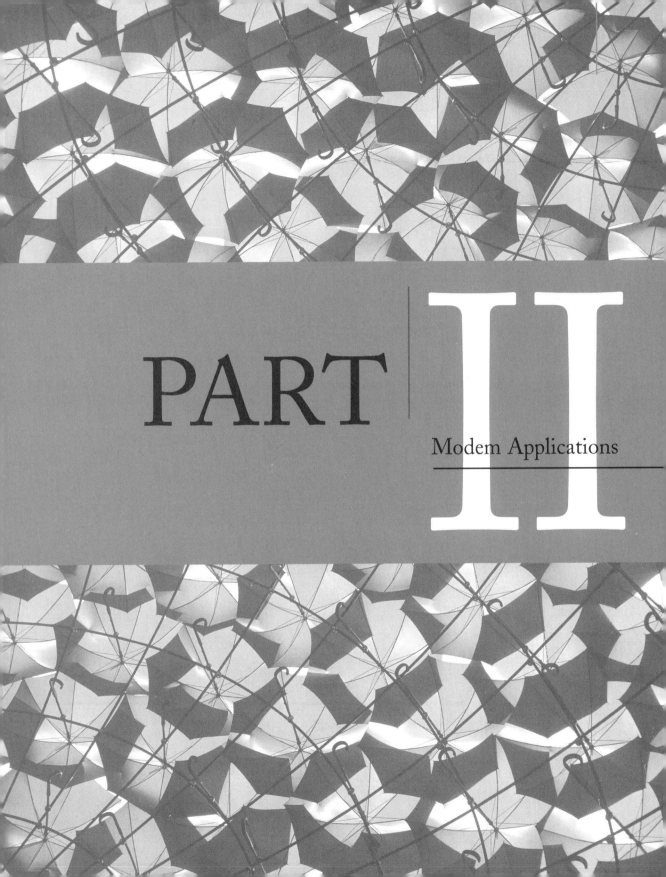

PART II

Modem Applications

Chapter | 3

Talking to Your Modem

by Markus Pope

In Chapter 1, you learned how to write an ActiveX control. In this chapter, you take a short break from coding ActiveX controls so that I can give you some background in modem technology. This chapter lays the foundation for the next two chapters, which show you how to write a simple dialer control and a small terminal emulation. The chapter covers the following topics:

- Modem technology
- Serial ports
- Common modem applications

Modem Technology

Modem technology is, in my opinion, fairly arcane. Did you ever wonder what became of the teletype machines that you see in older movies? Teletypes never went away; they just changed form. Modems, like old-fashioned teletype machines, convert data to audible tones (electrical current) that can be transmitted over telephone lines. When the audible tones are received by another modem, they're converted back to data.

People use modems to relay messages and to transfer important documents from machine to machine. You can transfer programs, documents, and graphics, and also communicate with someone in real time. By contrast, teletypes were often used for unidirectional communication—to broadcast news, for example.

Although some people may argue, modem technology was invented in the early 1800s. It all started when a man named von Soemmering built a machine that converted pulses of electrical current to human-readable output. He built the machine out of an aquarium that generated bubbles when the machine received pulses. After that, everybody (and their dogs, too) was creating machines that could transmit and receive messages.

But communications devices at that time were fraught with error because of poor power and line conditions. The machines relied too heavily on synchronization because there was no way to tell when one chunk of information started and the next began. That's when a man named Emile Baudot hit the scene. At the end of the 19th century, Baudot created an encoding scheme that greatly improved the reliability of communications. (*Encoding* refers to the act of interpreting alphabetic data into electrical current.) Baudot's scheme consisted of characters that were represented by a fixed number of high and low pulses.

Even though Baudot is thought of as being the father of telecommunications as it exists today, he was only a stepping stone in the evolution of the modern modem. Modemlike devices would still be fragile if it were not for a man named Kleinschmidt, who added a frame around encoded characters. The frame consisted of a low voltage to indicate the start of a character and a high voltage to indicate the end of a character. Two communicating devices could synchronize themselves by watching for the start and end of characters.

> **NOTE:** In 1987, Joe Campbell wrote an excellent book that details the history of modem communications. The book, called C *Programmer's Guide to Serial Communications* (ISBN 0-672-22584-0), is a fundamental tool for anyone who is developing modem applications.

As you can see, the technology used in modems is very old. And the technology really hasn't changed in the past 200 years—it's just gotten better.

Three Basic Modem Technologies

Modems support three basic forms of communication:.data, fax, and voice. I find the term *data* to be somewhat confusing when it's used in this context. What does *data* mean? Doesn't a fax machine transmit documents in the form of data? When you hear the term *data* used in conjunction with modems, it refers to terminal communications.

A *terminal* is a window in which a programmer can display data for a user. Unlike a computer monitor, though, a terminal has built-in logic that formats data on a display screen. A terminal is like a small computer, except for that fact that it's designed to perform that single simple function.

Not so long ago, computers were big machines that occupied entire rooms in large corporations. Users used terminals to talk to those massive machines. Since the start of the computer revolution in the late '70s, computers have become tiny machines that we all love and depend on. But the big machines haven't gone away. Now manufacturers can make machines that have a few nonillion times more power and take up a tenth as much space as before. Users still talk to those machines using terminals, but with an added twist.

Because manufacturers can make computers that fit in the palm of your hand, the computer has replaced the terminal as the medium of communication between the user and the *big metal* (the geeky term for *mainframe*). People use the big metal to make complex calculations quickly; then they retrieve and massage the data by using personal computers. A *terminal emulator*—a program that can act as a terminal—is the way that PCs communicate with the big machines.

Now that so many people have home computers, terminal emulators are being used for more tasks than just talking to big metal. Nowadays, we use computers to communicate with one another. We call computer bulletin boards to leave messages and chat with our friends; we send one another documents, graphics, and files.

Fax machines came about because businesses needed a faster way to transfer documents than through couriers. Fax machines translate paper documents into bits and bytes, and then send the data over telephone lines, using special modems that are designed specifically to transmit fax data. When computers replaced typewriters in the office, someone figured out that it's much faster to fax documents right from word processing programs than to print them and then send them via fax machines. The result was the birth of the fax/modem.

Historians attribute the facsimile to Alexander Bain, a philosopher and inventor who lived in Scotland during the 1800s. In 1842, he created a timing mechanism that allowed one clock to set and control the timing of another—thereby allowing for synchronization of all clocks in a system. In 1843, Bain patented a device called the recording telegraph, which could send and receive messages. Of course, his inventions were nothing like the fax machines sitting on our desks today.

The fax machine as we know it wasn't invented until after the turn of the century. In 1902, Arthur Korn created the first photoelectric device capable of scanning and transferring documents from one place to another, over wire or radio. During the 1950s, the National News Service created a network of fax machines to transfer news.

It's not clear to me why people still use fax technology to send documents. Fax protocols are timing-sensitive, they have basically no error correction, and they're extremely slow. The transfer protocols that are used in terminal programs (such as Procomm Plus, by Datastorm Technologies) are much faster and much more reliable than fax protocols. I guess people send documents by fax because the procedure is less complicated and because so many fax machines are still in operation. No one has seen fit to write a faxlike program that uses something like ZMODEM to transfer documents.

I don't think I've ever seen a PC modem that supports only fax transfer, although such modems probably exist. In fact, nowadays almost all new modems support both data and fax. Fax/modems combine both data and fax communications, so you get the best of both worlds. You can fax your documents right from Microsoft Word or connect to a local bulletin-board system by using your terminal program.

Today's modems aren't limited to just data and fax calls. Voice modems can answer incoming phone calls, play greetings that you recorded with your sound card, and record messages left by callers. Suppose that you receive a phone call, the caller leaves a message, and (when the caller hangs up) the computer calls your office and forwards the message to your voice-mail system. That's technology!

Voice software packages let you define scripts that play when the voice modem answers an incoming call. You can set up a greeting that asks the caller to press 1, 2, or 3, based on who the caller wants to leave a message for. If the caller presses 1, for example, he is prompted to leave a message for Mom and Dad. If the caller presses 2, he can leave a message for the kids. And if he presses 3, he can leave a message for the dog and cat.

Voice modems often incorporate all three modem technologies. Instead of having a terminal to connect you with the online world, a fax machine to send faxes, and an answering machine to answer incoming calls, you can use your PC to do all three things. You lose the cost involved in maintaining the three separate systems, and you lose the mess.

Direct Connections

Typically, when you talk about data communications, you're talking about using your modem to talk to other machines. That may not always be the case, so let's expand on this term a bit. Earlier, we talked about the computer replacing the terminal as a way to communicate with the big metal in the back room. In such a case, it's not necessary to have a modem. Installing special telephone lines for each user connected to a mainframe could get ugly.

A PC talks to the modem through a *serial port*—a card that takes parallel data, serializes it, and transmits it to a device. (Refer to the discussion of serialization in Chapter 2. The concept of serialization is the same in this chapter as it is in Chapter 2.) A serial port also takes serial data and makes it parallel, so that the computer can use the data. A special cable—called a *null modem cable*—can connect the serial port on the PC to the serial port on the mainframe. This type of connection is referred to as a *direct connection*.

Direct connections don't have much to do with the applications that you're going to build in this book (except, possibly, the terminal emulator in Chapter 5). While you write your online controls, keep in mind that there's more to communications than just talking to modems. A dialer, for example, uses a modem, but a terminal emulator may use a direct connection.

AT Command Set

Modems speak an ancient language known as the *Hayes AT command set*. During early modem days, Hayes built modems that had a command-driven interface, whereas other modems used menu-driven interfaces (such as the Racal Vadic). Command-driven interfaces turned out to be more flexible and powerful, so the command set that Hayes used was adopted as an industry standard.

A *command interpreter* is a program that accepts input in the form of basic commands, such as those that you would give to a trained animal. Then, interpreting a command that you typed, the interpreter performs the corresponding function.

AT, which stands for *attention*, is the basis of the command set used in Hayes modems. Following is a typical modem-initialization string:

```
AT&C1&D2E1V1Q0{CR}
```

Notice that the command string starts with AT. AT tells the modem that until it receives a carriage return (Enter), the characters that follow AT form commands.

Table 3-1 shows what the commands do.

Table 3-1   AT Commands

AT Command	Function
&C1	Tracks true state of carrier detect
&D2	Hangs up when the PC drops DTR
	(DTR stands for *Data Terminal Ready*. DTR is a line in the serial port that the PC uses to control the modem.)

AT Command	Function
DT	Dials a number, using touch tones
E1	Echoes back what you type
V1	Responds to commands verbally
Q0	Responds to commands

Each of these commands performs specific functions. The {CR} included in the command string earlier in this section represents the carriage return. If you type that command string to your modem, your modem does each of the things listed in Table 3-1.

In Chapter 4, you learn how to use AT commands to make the modem dial a number.

> **TIP:** Before you start writing modem-enabled programs, it's a good idea to become familiar with the various things that you can make the modem do with AT commands. Take some time to glance through your modem manual.

> **CAUTION:** Even though the AT command set has become a standard in the modem industry, don't make the mistake of believing that all modems respond to the same commands. The AT command set doesn't accommodate many of the new standards, such as compression and error correction, so modem manufacturers have implemented their own variants.

Modem Standards

Since 1983, a spectrum of modem standards has emerged, the first of which was error correction. Because error-correcting protocols exist, that technology is used in modem hardware. Finding a modem that doesn't support error correction, in fact, is nearly impossible.

The next new standard was data compression, which shrinks data so that it can be transmitted in less time, thereby increasing the transfer rate artificially. Instead of being limited by how fast the hardware works, transmission speed is limited by the efficiency of the data compression. Figure 3-1 demonstrates data compression.

FIGURE 3-1

Modems that support data compression shrink large chunks of data to increase throughput.

Several error-correction and data-compression standards exist, the most common of which are V42, V42bis, V32, V32bis, VFC, and V34. V42 and V32 introduce error-correction protocols; and V42bis, V32bis, VFC, and V34 introduce compression protocols. (When we were kids, we dreamed of having modems that could transfer 1,200 characters per second; now we're slowed by modems that boast transfer rates of up to 115.2K per second!) Check your modem reference for the commands that enable error correction and data compression—they vary, depending on the modem.

Serial Ports

Now that you have some background on modem technology, consider how you're going to use the modem. Earlier in the chapter, you learned that the software routes data through the serial port. As you can see in Figure 3-2, you must know how to communicate with the serial port to talk to the modem.

Serial ports are simple devices, and Windows makes using them even simpler. In the days of DOS programming, you had to talk directly to the serial port to set its speed, parity, and stop bits, and to send and receive data. Windows, however, provides a layer (a few layers, actually) between the programmer and the hardware. This abstraction lessens the burden of serial-port programming on the programmer. Programmers are no longer forced to communicate directly with the serial port. Instead, programmers now use the Windows stream I/O functions, with help from a few specialized functions.

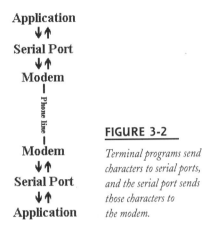

FIGURE 3-2

Terminal programs send characters to serial ports, and the serial port sends those characters to the modem.

Opening a Port

In 32-bit Windows, similar to UNIX, serial-port programming is integrated into the file system. To open a port, for example, you make a call to CreateFile. Some functions still are used specifically to manipulate the serial ports; I'll get into those functions later in the chapter. First, I'll show you how to open a port.

The beauty of exposing the serial ports through the file system is that you can treat them as streams. A *stream* is an input or output channel for data. When a serial port is opened as a stream, you can use functions such as WriteFile and ReadFile to send and receive data. Following is a call to CreateFile to open the serial port associated with COM2 (the name of a standard input and output stream, such as PRN, CON, and AUX):

```
hComm = CreateFile( "COM2", GENERIC_READ |
GENERIC_WRITE, 0, NULL, OPEN_EXISTING,
FILE_ATTRIBUTE_NORMAL, NULL );
if( hComm != INVALID_HANDLE_VALUE )
{


} else
```

```
MessageBox( "Error opening COM2", "Error",
MB_OK | MB_ICONEXCLAMATION );
    .

    .
```

The handle returned by CreateFile is used to make calls to stream I/O functions. The handle returned by CreateFile is checked against INVALID_HANDLE_VALUE to ensure that the stream opened successfully. When you're done with the stream, you can close it, as shown in the following code segment:

```
    .

    .

CloseHandle( hComm );
    .

    .
```

That's not all that you have to do when you open a port, but it's enough to get you started. The following section shows you how to send and receive data when you have the stream open.

Sending and Receiving Data

Sending and receiving on a port opened with CreateFile is simple. All you have to do is make calls to WriteFile and ReadFile, passing the data that you want to send or the buffer that you want to read into. Following is a small piece of code that opens the serial port, sends some data, and then closes the port:

```
void CommObj::WriteSomeData()
{
DWORD dwBytes;
char szOut[256];

        m_fhComm = CreateFile( "COM2", GENERIC_READ |
GENERIC_WRITE, 0, NULL, OPEN_EXISTING,
FILE_ATTRIBUTE_NORMAL, NULL );
        if( m_fhComm != INVALID_HANDLE_VALUE )
```

```
            {
            wsprintf( szOut, "ATDT6571318\r" );
                    WriteFile( m_fhComm, szOut, lstrlen( szOut ),
&dwBytes, NULL );
                    CloseHandle( m_fhComm );
            } else
                    MessageBox( "Arf. Couldn't open port!", "Error",
MB_OK | MB_ICONEXCLAMATION );
}
```

`CommObj` is an imaginary class that contains information about the COM port that's opened with `CreateFile`. If the code successfully opens the COM port, a buffer is set to a modem command and a telephone number. `ATDT` tells the modem to dial (using tone) the number that follows. (Remember that *AT* means *attention*.) Next, the code takes the handle returned by `CreateFile`, which is the `m_fhComm` member variable, and passes it to `WriteFile`, along with the data that you want to send. Finally, the code closes the port by using `CloseHandle`.

What do you suppose happens when this function is called? Nothing, probably, because the code doesn't set the state of the DTR (Data Terminal Ready) signal on the modem. Many modems require the DTR to be high before they dial—a strange situation, but that's the way it works. (*High*, when used in reference to signals, means that the line carries a voltage that's higher than the ground voltage.) The following section shows you how to use `EscapeCommFunction` to set the state of the modem.

Reading data from the COM port isn't much harder than writing data; to do it efficiently, you need to check for incoming data before you call `ReadFile`. To do so, use `WaitCommEvent`, which returns a set of flags that you can check against `EV_RXCHAR`. `EV_RXCHAR` tells you when data is ready to be read from the serial port. If you were to implement a timer that checks for incoming data, your `OnTimer` function probably would look something like this:

```
void CommObj::OnTimer(UINT nIDEvent)
{
            DWORD dwEvents, dwRead;
            char szIncoming[256];
            if( WaitCommEvent( m_fhComm, &dwEvents, NULL ) )
```

```
        {
            if( dwEvents & EV_RXCHAR )
                    ReadFile( m_fhComm, szIncoming, 256,
                            &dwRead, NULL );
        }
        CDialog::OnTimer(nIDEvent);
    }
```

> **CAUTION:** You have to be careful with a routine such as the preceding, because WaitCommEvent is asynchronous only when you're using overlapped I/O. In this example, WaitCommEvent does not return until it receives some type of event, so your application gets stuck in the OnTimer routine until data is received. I'll give you the lowdown on WaitCommEvent in the next chapter, when I show you how to write a routine or two to handle incoming data. You'll get to use overlapped I/O and some threading.

Understanding Port Settings

In the preceding section, CommObj::WriteSomeData probably wouldn't work as expected because the code didn't set the state of the serial port—specifically, DTR. To fix the problem, you must use some specific API calls to modify the port settings. *Port settings* are the many states of a serial port that you can alter, including baud rate, parity, data bits, stop bits, and the states of the control lines (Data Terminal Ready and Request To Send).

You can make the modem dial in the WriteSomeData member function simply by raising DTR with a call to EscapeCommFunction. You need to add to the code a line that looks something like this:

```
EscapeCommFunction( m_fhComm, SETDTR );
```

This line raises the DTR signal so that the modem can dial. Conversely, you need to drop DTR before you close the port with CloseHandle. If you replace SETDTR with CLRDTR in the preceding example, the DTR line is dropped.

Request To Send (RTS) is used in conjunction with the Clear To Send signal (CTS). RTS and CTS are raised and lowered to control the flow of data into and out of the serial port. When RTS is raised (by calling `EscapeCommFunction` with the SETRTS flag), the modem is clear to send data to the PC. When RTS is lowered, the modem refrains from sending data to the PC. CTS works in the opposite direction. If CTS is raised, the PC is clear to send data to the modem; if CTS is lowered, the PC refrains from sending data. The raising and lowering of RTS and CTS to control the flow of data is known as *hardware flow control.*

Baud rate, parity, data bits, and *stop bits* refer to the way that data is transmitted across the telephone line.

Baud rate refers to the speed of the connection. When you set the baud rate, you limit the number of characters that you can send in a given amount of time. Don't confuse this setting with *characters per second* (cps). When you use one of the modems that is on the market now, you set the baud rate high (57600 baud, for example), and the modem uses compression to try to come close to that value in cps. In reality, when your PC-to-modem rate is set very high, you never get the equivalent in cps.

Parity is a primitive form of error detection. (Don't confuse error detection with error correction.) Back in the old days, about 10 years ago, characters were represented with 7 bits, allowing us to use the 8th bit in each byte as a checksum. *Even parity* means that the 8th bit is turned on when the byte has an even number of ON bits. *Odd parity* means that the 8th bit is turned on only when the byte has an odd number of ON bits.

> **NOTE:** Now that you know how parity works, can you see how inefficient it is? Upon examining the chances of detecting an error, you find that you have about a 50–50 chance. Most of the time, you'll just set parity to none (turn it off).

Parity, data bits, and stop bits are related. *Data bits* represent the number of bits that are in each byte that's transmitted and received. This setting usually is 8 bits but can be 7 when it's used with even or odd parity. *Stop bits* (actually, start/stop bits) are delimiters that surround a character. Because data that is transmitted asynchronously can arrive in bits and pieces—no pun intended—the hardware has to know where one character ends and another begins. The stop-bits setting determines the number of bits that separate the bytes in a data stream.

NOTE: Synchronous transmissions do not require data bits and stop bits. Instead, data that's transmitted synchronously is transmitted by means of electrical pulses. All bits in a character are sent between the pulses, which makes synchronous communications fragile (although faster than the asynchronous kind). Asynchronous transmissions aren't subject to latency, because each character is surrounded by a start bit and a stop bit.

To set the other port settings, you need to make a call to `SetCommState` and pass a DCB (device control block) structure. A *DCB structure* simply contains information about the COM port. Typically, you make a call to `GetCommState` first. That way, you can make sure that you have a valid DCB structure. Then, after modifying the baud rate, parity, and so on, you pass the same DCB structure into `SetCommState`. You learn how to do all these things in Chapter 4.

Sending Commands to Your Modem

As you saw in the `CommObj::WriteSomeData` example, sending commands to your modem is trivial stuff. After you open the port and call `EscapeCommFunction` to raise DTR, you're ready to start pumping out those commands. I feel confident that you can handle the job, but I'd like to point out a few things about sending modem commands that aren't obvious:

- Be sure to terminate each command with a carriage return. Although a few modems treat carriage returns and line feeds as though they are the same character, most require the carriage return for command termination.

- Initializing the modem at the same baud rate at which you're going to dial is a good idea. Some modems have problems when you switch baud rates while setting up to dial.

- You may want to send a few carriage returns before you start your initialization or dial. That way, you know that the modem isn't in the middle of collecting a previous command.

Common Modem Applications

At this point, you know quite a bit about modem technology, and you know how to build ActiveX controls from Part I. You're about ready to do some programming. First, examine some common modem applications. The following sections may give you some ideas for applications of your own.

Terminal

A terminal emulator is built into almost every operating system. and one is shipped with every modem. HyperTerminal, by Hilgraeve, is the terminal emulator that's included with Windows 95. HyperTerminal has some good terminal emulations and file-transfer protocols, and it's easy to use.

Figure 3-3 shows you what a typical terminal emulator looks like.

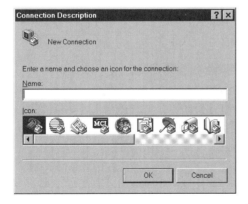

FIGURE 3-3

Hilgraeve's HyperTerminal, which is included in Windows 95, is a typical terminal program.

I'm not suggesting that you write your own fully featured terminal program, because there's no money in it now—the market's already full of terminal programs. But plenty of companies are looking for technology that they can plug into their own applications (specialized applications). If you come up with terminal emulations and protocols that you can plug into any application (maybe an ActiveX control?), you may make a big hit!

Fax

With the introduction of PC fax capability, fax machines are becoming obsolete. Although most companies still have at least one fax machine for receiving faxes, they are turning more and more to personal fax/modems and fax servers in efforts to increase productivity and lower costs.

Think about what it costs you when you get up to use the fax machine. On the way to the fax machine, you're invariably interrupted; that costs time. When you finally make it to the fax machine, it's congested with faxes, so you're forced to come back later; that costs more time. And if you're lucky enough to get a fax into the machine, you have to babysit the silly thing until it reaches the receiver.

With a fax/modem or fax server, you can fax straight from your workstation. You lose no time waiting at the fax machine, being interrupted on the way, or babysitting your faxes. You simply tell your word processing program to print your documents to the fax printer driver. You still have to go to the fax machine, however, if you're faxing documents that are already printed (unless you have a scanner). Figure 3-4 shows the fax status window for Procomm Plus, by Datastorm Technologies.

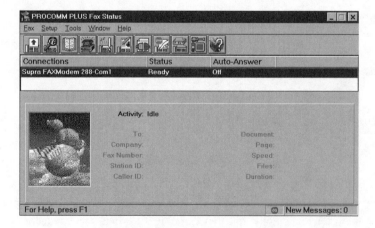

FIGURE 3-4

Procomm Plus is probably the most popular communications program used by the PC community.

Voice

Voice is still new to the online world. Most of the mainstream communications companies haven't touched the voice market, but its time is approaching quickly. Using a single machine to connect to the online world, receive incoming faxes, and answer telephone calls would be very attractive.

Because voice is an infant market, you could make money by building a killer voice application; there aren't many apps of that type right now. But I'm inclined to believe that it's more profitable to write components from which larger companies can leverage. People are more into buying a complete solution now than they are into searching for the best version of each online technology.

Internet Connectivity

With the media frenzy over the Internet, 90 percent of the households in America are sure to have an Internet connection by 2010, if not sooner. Not everyone has direct access to the Internet, however. Most home computer users use modems to dial up Internet Service Providers (ISPs).

Internet Service Providers are companies that have computers connected directly to the Internet. Users pay these providers for temporary access to the Internet. You call into an ISP's computer, using your modem, and you're given a network address that's valid for the length of your call. Thereafter, you can use the Internet just as though you are directly connected. Trumpet, a complete TCP/IP network stack, is the most common application used to connect users to the Internet.

> **NOTE:** Windows 95 and Windows NT feature built-in TCP/IP network stacks. You install a dial-up network adapter and then use the Windows 95 or Windows NT RAS (remote access service) dialer to connect to your service provider. Windows 95 and NT's dial-up TCP/IP network stack is really slick.

Chapter Summary

This chapter touched on the history of modem communications; it also talked about what's in the modem market and about the future. Now you have a short background in Windows communications programming. You also got to look at some of the most popular applications that use modem technology. It's time to get on to the art of programming and put this information to good use.

What's next? Chapter 4, "Plug-in Modem Dialer," teaches you how to use the COM port on your machine. In addition, you learn how to add more complicated interfaces to your ActiveX controls, using dialog boxes (more complicated than the interface you built for the edit control in Chapter 2).

Chapter | 4

Plug-in Modem Dialer

by Markus Pope

Now you're ready to put what you've learned to use. In this chapter, you make a small ActiveX control (slightly more endowed than the one in Chapter 2) that a container can use to make data, fax, or voice calls.

The dialer control serves as a layer between the container and the modem hardware. You start by creating an interface for the dialer. Next, you make it dial. Then you enhance the dialer by making it send and receive data.

This chapter covers the following topics:

♦ What a dialer is made of

♦ Creating a dialer control

♦ What you can do with a modem dialer

About the Dialer

A *dialer* is a small program that uses the modem to dial the phone. The concept of a modem dialer is simple. In this chapter, you're going to add some features to the dialer to make it easy and fun to use. In addition, you'll implement the dialer as a control, so you can plug it into any application that supports OLE automation.

What kind of program would you plug a dialer into? It may seem that this control has few possibilities. But if you build the dialer correctly, its uses are virtually limitless.

Suppose that you have a database of 1,000 telephone numbers, and you want to call each number to market a product. Wouldn't it make sense to plug a dialer directly into your database application? Then, to dial a number from the database, all you do is click a button that causes the database to call a few member functions. (The database app would have to support ActiveX controls, of course.)

You can also make the dialer support data and fax. (This chapter doesn't get into fax capability, but you can add a few methods to send and receive data when you're connected, and with those methods in place, a container should be able to implement fax.) It's difficult to think of an application that wouldn't benefit from the capability to send and receive data.

How a Modem Dials a Phone Number

I provided technical support for a communications package for a long time. The concept that people most commonly misunderstood was how the modem dials a number. The standard answer is that modems dial just like you dial a telephone. Some people couldn't get connected because they had to dial 8 or 9 to get an outside line. Other people couldn't get connected because they weren't including 1 to dial a long-distance number or because they were including an area code in a local call.

A modem is nothing more than a telephone that can send digital data over phone lines. If you have to dial 8 or 9 to get an outside line with a telephone, you have to do so with a modem.

You learned in Chapter 3 that modems dial by using AT commands. Consider the following string:

```
ATDT8,555-1212
```

In this string, AT stands for *attention*; D tells the modem that you want it to dial; and T tells the modem that you want it to use touch tones to dial instead of pulsing. The remainder of the string—8,555-1212—dials 8 to get an outside line and then dials the telephone number. (The comma causes the modem to pause before dialing the numbers following the 8, allowing the phone system time to attach an outgoing line.)

Modems support a few other dialing aids. If you have several extensions on your phone line, you may need to include the X3 command (as in ATX3DT). X3 informs the modem that the dial tone on the phone line is unreliable. Modems can sense for a dial tone before dialing (by means of the X4 command), and most do so by default. If you're using X4 and the modem doesn't sense a dial tone, the modem hangs up and issues a warning.

Breakdown of Dialing Types

You can make your dialer control support several dialing types. *Dialing types* are types of calls you can make with your modem: data, fax, voice, long distance, local, international, and so on. There are countless ways to dial a telephone number, so making your control dial all combinations is an experiment in futility, but a subset of dialing types probably is necessary if you're going to market your control.

Currently, you don't have to dial an area code and long-distance prefix for local calls. Long-distance calls require the area code (or city code, if you're outside the United States) and a long-distance prefix of either 0 or 1. International calls require an international dialing prefix (011, in the United States), the country code, the city code, and the telephone number. Internal calls don't require you to dial 8 or 9 to get an outside line, and calling-card dialing requires you to dial multiple numbers.

> **NOTE:** You can use the ; command in a dialing string to tell the modem to dial the numbers that you've given it so far but to return to command state instead of going online. This command allows you to send multiple dial commands to the modem. Most modems support 40-character command strings; older modems support 20 characters; but calling-card and long-distance dialing may require 60 or even 80 characters.

Differences Between Data, Fax, and Voice Calls

How do each of these dialing types—data, fax, and voice—affect the way that you dial?

Data calls are very simple. The string ATDT8,555-1212, used alone, tells the modem to dial a number and wait for data tones. But if you initialize the modem to fax mode before making the dial, the modem expects to receive fax tones. Other than the fax initialization, dialing a fax number is the same as dialing a data number. Voice calls, on the other hand, are slightly different.

To make a voice call, you dial just as though you're dialing a data or fax number. After the modem finishes dialing, you pick up the handset, and the dialer hangs up the modem. You have to be careful, though—if the phone is hooked to the modem, the call may be cut off when the modem hangs up the line.

Create the Dialer Control

Before you can add code to the dialer, you have to create the ActiveX control framework. Use the OLE ControlWizard to create a framework, and call this one Dialer. You're going to create the interface from scratch, so leave the subclass field set to none. Visual C++ creates three classes: CDialerApp, CDialerCtrl, and CDialerPropPage.

> **NOTE:** Chapter 2 covers the OLE ControlWizard and the ClassWizard, and also explains how to add member variables and methods. The following section assumes that you understand these topics.

CDialerApp is in charge of handling everything necessary to load and instantiate your control. CDialerCtrl handles interaction with the user and the container. CDialerPropPage encapsulates the dialog box that appears when the container asks your control to display its properties to the user. As you did with the edit control in Chapter 2, you'll do all your work in CDialerCtrl and CDialerPropPage. In addition, you'll add a couple of classes to handle the keypad and the modem.

Building the Keypad

Common practice in Windows is to develop from the top down—that is, start with the interface and then implement the features. I recommend this approach because it lets you see the results of your programming faster. Besides, the most important part of a program is the interface.

Switch to resource view, and add a dialog-box resource. (You should remember how to switch to resource view.) To add a dialog-box resource, right-click Dialer Resources in resource view, and choose **I**nsert. Select Dialog, and click the OK button. Visual C++ displays a dialog-box template, as shown in Figure 4-1.

Select the OK and Cancel buttons that are added to your template automatically, and delete them. Display the dialog-box properties by double-clicking the dialog box. Change the **ID** to IDD_KEYPAD, set the Style list box (below the Styles tab) to Child, and set the styles shown in Table 4-1. Check the check boxes in the Styles, More Styles, and Extended Styles tabs of the dialog-box Properties dialog box to set the styles in Table 4-1.

Table 4-1   Style Bits for Keypad

Style	Setting	Location
Titlebar	Off	Styles
Border	None	Styles
Control	On	More Styles

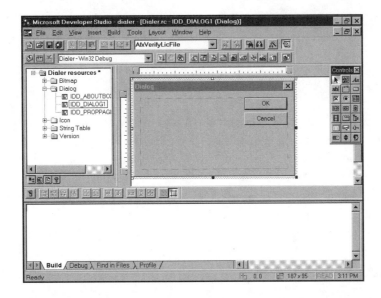

FIGURE 4-1

When you choose to create a dialog box, Visual C++ creates a dialog-box template and adds OK and Cancel buttons.

When Titlebar is turned off, the dialog box that appears is not movable. This is preferred, because you're going to place the dialog box inside the window allocated for the control. You want the keypad's location to be controlled by the control and the control's location to be controlled by the container. You can choose to have a border; the example is leaving it up to the container to display the border. When you turn the control style on, your dialog box acts as though it's truly part of the parent. If you choose to add other dialog boxes to your control, things like tabbing between Windows controls would work between all of the dialog boxes as though they were one. Close the dialog-box properties after you finish setting the style bits.

Now what you need to do is add an edit box to display the telephone number and push-buttons to represent the numbers found on real keypads. Figure 4-2 shows what your keypad should look like. The ID for the edit control is IDC_DISPLAY. Make each of the numbers in the keypad have IDs such as IDC_KEYPADx, where x is the number on the face of the keypad. 1 has an ID of IDC_KEYPAD1, for example, and 9 has an ID of IDC_KEYPAD9. That leaves IDC_KEYPAD_CLR for the Clr button, IDC_KEYPAD_SND for Snd, and IDC_KEYPAD_HANGUP for Hangup.

Save the dialog-box resource, and switch back to class view. Open the ClassWizard so that you can add a dialog-box object to the project. With the ClassWizard open, Add Class and New. Visual C++ displays the dialog box that you see in Figure 4-3. Type **CKeypad** in the **N**ame box, and choose Cdialog for the **B**ase class.

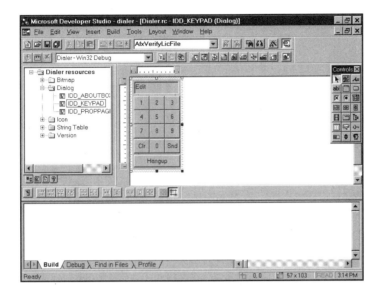

FIGURE 4-2

This is the keypad dialog box for the dialer included with this book. Notice that it resembles a cellular-phone keypad.

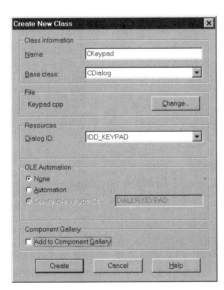

FIGURE 4-3

Use the ClassWizard's Create New Class feature to add a dialog-box class to your project.

Notice under Resources that ClassWizard lets you set the dialog-box resource that's associated with the new class. Choose IDD_KEYPAD (the dialog box that you just created), and click the Create button. Visual C++ creates a header file and source file containing the definition and implementation for the CKeypad object. Before you start plugging in code to make the thing work, make some modifications to CDialerCtrl so that it displays the keypad dialog box.

Add m_keypad as a protected member variable in the CDialerCtrl object. You can do that by double-clicking the CDialerCtrl object in class view and adding the declaration manually, or by using the automated method that you learned in Chapter 2. If you're adding the member variable manually, add the following line to the protected section of CDialerCtrl, in DIALERCTL.H:

```
CKeypad m_keypad;
```

You have a little more work to do before the dialer control uses the keypad dialog box. Save and close DIALERCTL.H. Open DIALERCTL.CPP, and select WM_CREATE in the **M**essages list. Add the OnCreate handler to the project. Edit OnCreate, and make it look like this:

```
int CDialerCtrl::OnCreate(LPCREATESTRUCT
lpCreateStruct)
{
        CRect crcClient;
        if (COleControl::OnCreate(lpCreateStruct) == -1)
                return -1;
        m_keypad.Create( CKeypad::IDD, this );
        m_keypad.GetClientRect( &crcClient );
        SetControlSize( crcClient.right,
crcClient.bottom );
        m_keypad.ShowWindow( SW_SHOW );
        return 0;
}
```

The first thing that you do here is call the Create member of m_keypad, passing it the ID stored in the CKeypad class definition and a pointer to the control window. Create creates the IDD_KEYPAD dialog box as a child of the window attached to CDialerCtrl. (Remember that CDialerCtrl is derived from COleControl, which is derived from CWnd.) Next, you call the GetClientRect member to get the dimensions of the dialog box and use SetControlSize to set the size of the control to the size of the dialog box. Finally, call the ShowWindow member to make the dialog box visible.

What about making the control paint the dialog box? You need to modify the control's `OnDraw` member, which is overloaded by default, so that it displays (paints) the dialog box when the control is invalidated. Don't worry; it's easy. Edit `OnDraw`, and replace its contents with the following:

```
m_keypad.Invalidate();
```

`Invalidate` causes the dialog box (actually in a separate window) to redraw itself.

You aren't ready to try to compile; you forgot to add the KEYPAD.H header file to the DIALERCTL.CPP source file. With the header file, the compiler doesn't know what a `CKeypad` object is. Add the following line just above the line that includes DIALERCTL.H in DIALERCTL.CPP:

```
#include "Keypad.h"
```

Feel free at this point to build the control and plug it into the OLE Control test container, as you did with the edit control in Chapter 2. Aside from a glitch in the initial painting, which can be corrected by sizing or moving the control, the test container displays a keypad that looks a lot like the keypad on your telephone. In "Testing Your Dialer Control" later in this chapter, you build a small container that you can use to test the dialer. Figure 4-4 shows what the dialer control looks like when it's plugged into the program that you build in "Testing Your Dialer Control."

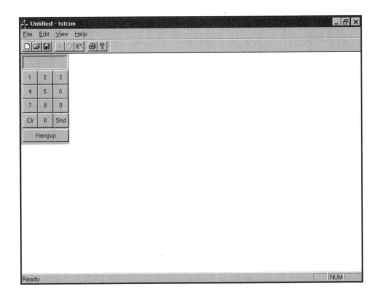

FIGURE 4-4

The dialer control plugs nicely into just about any application. It took about 5 minutes to plug the dialer control into the sample container shown here.

The next step is to implement the numbers on the keypad. When the user clicks a number on the keypad, you need to add that number to a string and then display that string in the IDC_DISPLAY edit box. When I was creating the sample dialer control included with this book, I found it easier to implement the handlers for the buttons manually, so that's what you'll do.

Open KEYPAD.CPP, and mosey on down to the message-handlers section. (Look for the comment CKeypad message handlers.) Add a message handler for each number button, 0 through 9. Your handlers will look something like this:

```
void CKeypad::OnKeypad1()
{
        AddToPhoneNumber( _T("1") );
}
```

This is the handler for the first number button in the keypad. AddToPhoneNumber, a function that you're going to create later, appends the specified number to the end of the telephone number. In addition to the OnKeypadx message handlers, add ones called OnKeypadClr, OnKeypadSnd, and OnKeypadHangup, but leave these functions empty for now.

After you're through adding the message-handling routines, you need to map them to controls, using the keypad dialog box's message map. Find the message map in KEYPAD.CPP, and change it to look like the following routine.

```
BEGIN_MESSAGE_MAP(CKeypad, CDialog)
        //{{AFX_MSG_MAP(CKeypad)
        ON_BN_CLICKED(IDC_KEYPAD1, OnKeypad1)
        ON_BN_CLICKED(IDC_KEYPAD2, OnKeypad2)
        ON_BN_CLICKED(IDC_KEYPAD3, OnKeypad3)
        ON_BN_CLICKED(IDC_KEYPAD4, OnKeypad4)
        ON_BN_CLICKED(IDC_KEYPAD5, OnKeypad5)
        ON_BN_CLICKED(IDC_KEYPAD6, OnKeypad6)
        ON_BN_CLICKED(IDC_KEYPAD7, OnKeypad7)
        ON_BN_CLICKED(IDC_KEYPAD8, OnKeypad8)
        ON_BN_CLICKED(IDC_KEYPAD9, OnKeypad9)
        ON_BN_CLICKED(IDC_KEYPAD0, OnKeypad0)
        ON_BN_CLICKED(IDC_KEYPAD_CLR, OnKeypadClr)
```

```
    ON_BN_CLICKED(IDC_KEYPAD_SND, OnKeypadSnd)
    ON_BN_CLICKED(IDC_KEYPAD_HANGUP, OnKeypadHangup)
    //}}AFX_MSG_MAP
END_MESSAGE_MAP()
```

The message map for CKeypad allows the framework to handle the details of intercepting messages generated by Windows controls. You don't have to deal with the WM_COMMAND message directly; the framework simply calls the member function assigned to the control in the message map.

Open the KEYPAD.H file, and add the following code between the line that reads //{{AFX_MSG(CKeypad) and the one that reads //}}AFX_MSG:

```
    afx_msg void OnKeypad1();
    afx_msg void OnKeypad2();
    afx_msg void OnKeypad3();
    afx_msg void OnKeypad4();
    afx_msg void OnKeypad5();
    afx_msg void OnKeypad6();
    afx_msg void OnKeypad7();
    afx_msg void OnKeypad8();
    afx_msg void OnKeypad9();
    afx_msg void OnKeypad0();
    afx_msg void OnKeypadClr();
    afx_msg void OnKeypadSnd();
    afx_msg void OnKeypadHangup();
```

These are the prototypes for the message-handling functions that you just added to KEYPAD.CPP. You could have used the Visual C++ shortcut, as you did with the WM_CREATE message earlier, but sometimes it's faster to do it by hand. Besides, programming wouldn't be much fun if Microsoft took all the work out of it.

You're almost ready to compile the control and look at your progress. Before you can do that, you need to implement CKeypad::AddToPhoneNumber. Just add a void AddToPhoneNumber(LPCSTR lpNum) declaration to your CKeypad class definition. Then add the following function to the bottom of your KEYPAD.CPP file:

```
void CKeypad::AddToPhoneNumber( LPCSTR lpNum )
{
        m_cszNumber += lpNum;
        SetDlgItemText( IDC_DISPLAY, m_cszNumber );
}
```

After you get that done, add an m_cszNumber member variable to the CKeypad class; give it a type of CString; and make it private. AddToPhoneNumber takes the specified string and appends it to the string stored in m_cszNumber. Then it tells the IDC_DISPLAY edit box to display the string. At this point in the project, you should be able to compile and play with the edit control.

How'd everything turn out? You probably noticed that you can type numbers by clicking 1 through 0, but you have to modify the number in the edit box directly to correct mistakes. You can fix that easily enough. Edit the OnKeypadClr member function. This is where you're going to put the code to back out a number that's been entered. My OnKeypadClr function follows; change your blank implementation so that it looks like mine:

```
void CKeypad::OnKeypadClr()
{
        if( ! m_cszNumber.IsEmpty() )
        {
                m_cszNumber = m_cszNumber.Left(
m_cszNumber.GetLength() - 1 );
                SetDlgItemText( IDC_DISPLAY, m_cszNumber );
        }
}
```

First, make sure that there are numbers in the string to back out. If there are numbers in the string, you use the Left member of CString to extract all but the last character from m_cszNumber and assign the result to itself (no need to declare a temporary variable). After you truncate the string, you tell the IDC_DISPLAY edit box to display it. Now if you compile and test the control, you can click the number buttons to enter numbers and the Clr button to delete them.

> **NOTE:** Set the Read-only style for the IDC_DISPLAY edit-box control in the dialer so that you can use the edit box for display. If you don't set the Read-only style, that's fine, but you should at least consider setting the Number style. Setting the Number or Read-only style ensures that the user doesn't accidentally introduce an unwanted modem command.

Opening the Port and Setting the Port Settings

You can make some quick hacks to OnKeypadSnd to make the modem dial, but you won't get much out of that, and you'll run into problems when you try to use your dialer in a production application. Instead, create a class that encapsulates the port. Encapsulating the port allows you to keep the details of modem communication hidden from your keypad object. The keypad simply tells the port object what port to open, what settings to use, and the data to send. Your port object knows how to open and maintain a port.

Create two new source files, and add them to the project. Do this by choosing **File, New,** Text File. Choose **File,** Save **As** to save one file as COMPORT.CPP and the other as COMPORT.H. Open COMPORT.H, and define a class called CComPort that looks like this:

```
class CComPort
{
protected:
        HANDLE m_hComm;
        DWORD m_dwThreadID;
        HANDLE m_hThread;
public:
        CComPort();
        BOOL OpenPort( LPCSTR lpszPort );
        void ClosePort();
        void SetPortSettings( DWORD dwBaud,
BYTE cbParity, BYTE cbDBits,
BYTE cbSBits );
```

```
        HANDLE CommHandle() { return( m_hComm ); }
};
LRESULT CommEventThread( LPVOID pComObj );
```

m_hComm is where you're going to store the handle for the port, when it's open.
m_dwThreadID and m_hThread are used with a parallel thread that watches for comm events
to occur (events that are related to the communications port you have open). CComPort
initializes the data that you're going to store in your object (it's the constructor for
CComPort objects). OpenPort and ClosePort are the worker functions that call CreateFile to
open the port and CloseHandle to close it. SetPortSettings takes care of changing the settings for the modem (the common ones, anyway). CommHandle simply returns m_hComm so
that it can be used with some of the comm functions. CommEventThread is defined outside
the class because it's the controlling thread for your comm event handler.

> **TIP:** Because you're going to be including the COMPORT.H header file in a few
> modules, make inclusion of the contents of the header file conditional. Do that by
> putting this at the top of the file:
>
> ```
> #ifndef _COMPORT_H
>         #define _COMPORT_H
> ```
>
> Then put this at the bottom of the file:
>
> ```
> #endif // _COMPORT_H
> ```
>
> That way, you can include the header in as many modules as you like, and you won't
> have to worry about duplicate definition errors during compilation. I do this with all
> the header files that I create. It's a good habit to get into.

Open the COMPORT.CPP file that you created, and add the following code:

```
#include "stdafx.h"
#include "ComPort.h"


CComPort::CComPort()
{
        m_hComm = INVALID_HANDLE_VALUE;
}
```

```
BOOL CComPort::OpenPort( LPCSTR lpszPort )
{
}
void CComPort::ClosePort()
{
}
void CComPort::SetPortSettings( DWORD dwBaud,
BYTE cbParity, BYTE cbDBits, BYTE cbSBits )
{
}
LRESULT CommEventThread( LPVOID pComObj )
{
}
```

These are the functions that you declared in the CComPort class definition. Now you're going to fill in the code that makes them work. I've already done this with the CComPort constructor. You need to start with the OpenPort member function.

To implement that OpenPort member, you have to call the file I/O (or stream I/O) function: CreateFile. In 32-bit Windows, CreateFile is used to open a wide variety of files and devices—data pipes, sockets, and serial devices, as well as data files. To open a serial port as a stream, you simply call CreateFile as in this implementation of the OpenPort member:

```
BOOL CComPort::OpenPort( LPCSTR lpszPort )
{
        m_hComm = CreateFile( lpszPort, GENERIC_READ |
GENERIC_WRITE,         0, NULL, OPEN_EXISTING,
FILE_ATTRIBUTE_NORMAL | FILE_FLAG_OVERLAPPED,
NULL );
        if( m_hComm != INVALID_HANDLE_VALUE )
        {
                m_hThread = CreateThread( NULL, 0,
(LPTHREAD_START_ROUTINE)&CommEventThread,
this, 0, &m_dwThreadID );
                if( m_hThread != INVALID_HANDLE_VALUE )
                {
```

```
                    EscapeCommFunction( m_hComm, SETDTR );
                    return( TRUE );
            } else
                    CloseHandle( m_hComm );
        }
        return( FALSE );
}
```

The code opens the port by calling `CreateFile` with the `GENERIC_READ` and `GENERIC_WRITE`, `OPEN_EXISTING`, and `FILE_FLAG_OVERLAPPED` flags. This opens the port for reading and writing, and prepares the stream for overlapped I/O.

Overlapped I/O is important for what you're going to do, because it allows functions such as `WaitCommEvent`, `ReadFile`, and `WriteFile` to return after they're called. Without it, your program would get hung up each time it made a call to `WaitCommEvent`, because `WaitCommEvent` waits for an event to occur on the specified port when overlapped I/O is not used.

The code also sets up a separate thread to handle comm events because it's more convenient and makes the code cleaner. Besides, you want the `CComPort` object handling events independent of the processes that's using the `CComPort object`. The code makes a call to `CreateThread`, passing it the address of the `CommEventThread` function, a pointer to the `CComPort` object, and a variable that will contain the ID of the new thread.

> **NOTE:** In overlapped I/O, I/O functions often return immediately after they're called. After an overlapped I/O process is complete, Windows sets an event that you passed to the function to a signaled state. When you implement `CComPort::SendString` and `CommEventThread`, I'll show you how to use an `OVERLAPPED` structure and `CreateEvent` to create the event used by the I/O functions.

As discussed in Chapter 3, many modems won't perform correctly if you don't raise the state of the DTR signal before attempting to use them. That's what the call to `EscapeCommFunction` is doing. `EscapeCommFunction` lets you set the state of DTR and RTS, send a break, and fool around with the software flow control characters. (Software flow control uses characters Ctrl+S and Ctrl+Q to control the flow of data over a line.) `EscapeCommFunction` is also used in the implementation of the `ClosePort` member function. `CComPort::ClosePort` looks like this:

```
void CComPort::ClosePort()
{
        if( m_hComm != INVALID_HANDLE_VALUE )
        {
                if( m_hThread != INVALID_HANDLE_VALUE )
                        CloseHandle( m_hThread );
                EscapeCommFunction( m_hComm, CLRDTR );
                CloseHandle( m_hComm );
        }
}
```

Be sure that your implementation of ClosePort cleans up the thread that's created in the OpenPort member. Although the operating system makes sure that this kind of stuff isn't left around when the program is closed, you should always clean up after yourself. After you clean up the thread, make a call to EscapeCommFunction to turn off DTR. (You can see how to do that in the preceding example.) Finally, you can call CloseHandle, passing it the handle returned by the CreateFile call in OpenPort to close the port.

Unlike DTR and RTS, for which you use the EscapeCommFunction call to set their states, port settings have to be set with a combination of the GetCommState and SetCommState functions. You can use SetCommState by itself to set the port settings, but the structure that it requires is large. Making a call to GetCommState first, to fill the structure, saves you quite a bit of time. Following is a copy of the SetPortSettings member function:

```
void CComPort::SetPortSettings( DWORD dwBaud,
BYTE cbParity, BYTE cbDBits, BYTE cbSBits )
{
        DCB dcb;
        GetCommState( m_hComm, &dcb );
        dcb.BaudRate = dwBaud;
        dcb.Parity = cbParity;
        dcb.ByteSize = cbDBits;
        dcb.StopBits = cbSBits;
        SetCommState( m_hComm, &dcb );
}
```

You declare a DCB structure (DCB stands for Device Control Block). Call `GetCommState` to fill in the DCB structure with the current COM port settings. Change the appropriate structure members—in this case, the ones that correspond to baud rate, parity, data bits, and stop bits—and call `SetCommState` to set the new state of the COM port.

> **NOTE:** There are enumerated types for baud rate, parity, and stop bits. Look up the definition of DCB in the Visual C++ help file for a complete list of those types and descriptions of all the members of the DCB structure.

Look at the `CommEventThread` function so that you can get to the part where you actually add a `CComPort` object to your control. It's a little bit more complicated than the functions that you've dealt with so far. The main goals of `CommEventThread` are to handle events and to keep the new thread in a loop until it's appropriate to exit. You start with a `while` loop, as shown in the code that follows:

```
LRESULT CommEventThread( LPVOID pComObj )
{
        DWORD dwEvent;
        CComPort *pPort = (CComPort *)pComObj;
        OVERLAPPED ovl;

        memset( &ovl, 0, sizeof( OVERLAPPED ) );
        ovl.hEvent = CreateEvent( 0, TRUE, TRUE, NULL );
        while( pPort->CommHandle() != INVALID_HANDLE_VALUE )
        {
                if( ! WaitCommEvent( pPort->CommHandle(),
&dwEvent, &ovl ) )
                {
                        while( GetLastError() == ERROR_IO_PENDING
&& pPort->CommHandle() !=
INVALID_HANDLE_VALUE )

                                GetOverlappedResult(
pPort->CommHandle(),
&ovl, &dwEvent, FALSE );
                }
```

```
        if( pPort->CommHandle() != INVALID_HANDLE_VALUE )
        {
                switch( dwEvent )
                {
                }
        }
    }

    if( ovl.hEvent != INVALID_HANDLE_VALUE )
            CloseHandle( ovl.hEvent );


    return( 1 );
}
```

The while loop continues until m_hComm points to an invalid handle. m_hComm is going to point to an invalid handle after you close the port. Inside the loop, you make a call to WaitCommEvent to retrieve pending events. Because you're using overlapped I/O, WaitCommEvent returns false immediately. Then you go into another loop, checking the return on GetLastError to see whether it's ERROR_IO_PENDING and making sure that the comm handle is still valid. Inside that loop, you're calling GetOverlappedResult to see whether the WaitCommEvent call has completed.

Normally, WaitCommEvent doesn't return until an event occurs. You don't want that, because then you can't terminate the thread if the port is closed. So you enabled overlapped I/O, and now you have an outer loop that keeps you in the thread while the port is open. The nested loop waits for the WaitCommEvent call to complete but also keeps an eye on the port. If the port is closed while a WaitCommEvent is in progress, you don't care. Your loops are busted, and the thread terminates.

> **NOTE:** Simply calling CloseHandle on the handle to the thread won't work. Windows keeps the thread open until the thread exits or calls ExitThread.

When an event fires, the inner loop is busted, and you evaluate the event that occurs. That's all you're going to do with this function right now. In "Making the Modem Place a Call" later in this chapter, you'll add the EV_RXCHAR event to the event thread so that the

CComPort object handles incoming data. For now, take a break from the CComPort class implementation and work on adding a CComPort object to your control.

First, get the build environment out of the way. To add the new files to the project, choose Insert, Files into Project in Visual C++. Visual C++ displays the dialog box that you see in Figure 4-5. Select COMPORT.CPP, and click the Add button. When you do this, your project no longer compiles. You should get an error message stating that afxRegApartmentThreading is an undefined symbol.

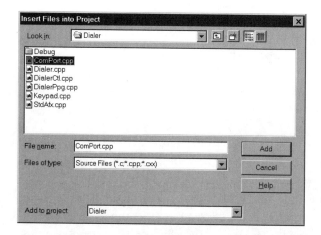

FIGURE 4-5

This dialog box pops up when you choose Insert, Files into Project in Visual C++. It allows you to add files to the project that aren't created automatically by Visual C++.

Open DIALERCTL.CPP, and find the member function that's called UpdateRegistry. After you find it, look at the parameters that UpdateRegistry is passing to AfxOleRegisterControlClass. afxRegApartmentThreading is the sixth parameter in the list. Highlight it, and change this parameter to 0. This informs the control framework that your control doesn't conform to apartment model threading.

When Visual C++ creates a framework, it defines VC_EXTRALEAN. This definition prevents the inclusion of the communications functions (and a few other things) when a framework program is compiled and linked. Because you need access to the communications API, you need to undefine VC_EXTRALEAN. Open STDAFX.H, and comment out the line that defines VC_EXTRALEAN, as follows:

```
// #define VC_EXTRALEAN        // Exclude rarely-used
// stuff from Windows headers
```

That takes care of the compiler errors. Now you need to add the COMPORT.H header file KEYPAD.H and KEYPAD.CPP. Open KEYPAD.H, and include the COMPORT.H header file at the top. Then open KEYPAD.CPP, and include COMPORT.H between the includes for DIALER.H and KEYPAD.H. Now add the following line to the CKeypad class declaration in KEYPAD.H, just after the declaration of m_cszNumber:

```
CComPort m_port;
```

Making the Modem Place a Call

With the CKeypad object instantiating a CComPort object, you can start adding code to make the modem dial a number. Before you add any more code to the CKeypad class members, though, add to the CComPort class a few members that allow you to send data to, and receive data from, the modem. Add the following member function to the CComPort class in COMPORT.CPP (don't forget to add a prototype for the function to the CComPort class declaration in COMPORT.H):

```
DWORD CComPort::SendString( LPCSTR lpStr, int nBytes )
{
        DWORD dwBytesWritten;
        OVERLAPPED ovl;

        memset( &ovl, 0, sizeof( OVERLAPPED ) );
        ovl.hEvent = CreateEvent( 0, TRUE, TRUE, NULL );
        if( ! WriteFile( m_hComm, lpStr, (DWORD)nBytes,
                &dwBytesWritten, &ovl ) )
        {
                if( GetLastError() == ERROR_IO_PENDING )
                        GetOverlappedResult( m_hComm, &ovl,
&dwBytesWritten, TRUE );
                else
                        return( 0 );
        }
```

```
        if( ovl.hEvent != INVALID_HANDLE_VALUE )
                CloseHandle( ovl.hEvent );
        return( dwBytesWritten );
}
```

As you've probably guessed, the SendString function is used to send strings of data to your modem. It takes a pointer to a character buffer and a maximum number of bytes to write as arguments. (It has to know the number of bytes, because it's valid in online communication to send NULLs, or zeros.)

SendString creates an event that can be used for the overlapped WriteFile call. Then it calls WriteFile, passing it the handle to the COM port, the pointer to the buffer, a maximum number of bytes to write, and an OVERLAPPED structure. If the WriteFile fails, you check to see whether the error is ERROR_IO_PENDING. If so, you make a blocking call to GetOverlappedResult. GetOverlappedResult waits until the I/O process is complete and then signals the event associated with the OVERLAPPED structure. SendString returns the number of bytes written to the COM port to the calling routine.

Reading from the COM port is somewhat less straightforward. Implement a ReadString member. But instead of making calls to ReadFile, read the data from a buffer stored in the CComPort class. Then, in your implementation of CommEventThread, you'll check for incoming data and put it in the buffer stored in the CComPort class. CComPort::ReadString looks like this:

```
int CComPort::ReadString( LPSTR lpStr, int nMaxBytes )
{
        int nBytesRead = 0;

        while( nBytesRead < nMaxBytes && m_nHead != m_nTail )
        {
                lpStr[ nBytesRead++ ] = m_cbBuff[ m_nTail++ ];
                if( m_nTail >= BUFFERSIZE )
                        m_nTail = 0;
        }
        return( nBytesRead );
}
```

For this function to work, you have to define two private integer variables in the CComPort class: one called m_nHead, and the other called m_nTail. m_nHead is known (appropriately) as the head pointer, and m_nTail is the tail pointer. Also add a BYTE array called m_cbBuff, which is going to act as a circular buffer. (Make it at least 2,048 bytes.)

Imagine that you're using a roulette wheel to store your incoming data. When a character comes in, you put it in a slot. Another character comes in, you put it in the next slot, and so on. Because there's no end to a roulette wheel, your buffer keeps going, and going, and going. You need some way to keep track of the data, though. So you use a head pointer to indicate the last character put into the buffer and a tail pointer to indicate the last character read from the buffer. The number of characters in the buffer, then, is the distance between the head and the tail pointers. When a head or tail pointer gets to the end of the buffer, it's moved back to the beginning of the buffer.

> **NOTE:** When the head pointer surpasses the tail pointer, an error condition occurs where the data is being put into the buffer faster than it's being read out of the buffer. This is known as a *buffer overrun*. You're not going to do anything to detect buffer overruns in this chapter, but the procedure is worth looking into on your own. (This condition is solved by creating a buffer that allocates extra memory if it's needed—an idea for a new class.)

ReadString is checking to see whether there are any characters in the receive buffer by comparing the head pointer with the tail pointer. If the tail pointer isn't equal to the head pointer, there's data waiting to be read. ReadString copies a character at a time to the buffer that's passed in. It aborts when the head and tail pointers are the same and returns the number of bytes actually copied into the destination buffer.

There's got to be some way of detecting when data is ready to be put into the buffer. This requires some modifications to the CommEventThread function and the addition of one other member function. Edit the CommEventThread function, and add a call to SetCommMask below the line that calls CreateEvent, as follows:

```
        .
        .
ovl.hEvent = CreateEvent( 0, TRUE, TRUE, NULL );
        SetCommMask( pPort->CommHandle(), EV_RXCHAR );
```

```
while( pPort->CommHandle() != INVALID_HANDLE_VALUE )
        .

        .
```

SetCommMask allows you to specify the comm events that you want to be notified about. The results of the WaitCommEvent call indicate which events have fired. Add a switch block after the WaitCommEvent conditional, as follows:

```
            .

            .

            if( ! WaitCommEvent( pPort->CommHandle(),
&dwEvent, &ovl ) )
            {
                while( GetLastError() == ERROR_IO_PENDING
&& pPort->CommHandle() !=
INVALID_HANDLE_VALUE )
                    GetOverlappedResult(
pPort->CommHandle(),
                        &ovl, &dwEvent, FALSE );
            }
            if( pPort->CommHandle() !=
INVALID_HANDLE_VALUE )
            {
                switch( dwEvent )
                {
                    case EV_RXCHAR:
                        pPort->AddToBuffer();
                        break;
                }
            }
            .

            .
```

EV_RXCHAR is the comm event that notifies you when there's data that can be read from the port. In response to the EV_RXCHAR event, you make a call to AddToBuffer. AddToBuffer is responsible for taking characters out of the comm subsystem's internal buffer and putting them in the m_cbBuff member of CComPort. Examine the AddToBuffer member:

```
=BOOL CComPort::AddToBuffer()
{
       BYTE cbBuff[256];
       DWORD dwBytesRead;
       int i;
       OVERLAPPED ovl;

       memset( &ovl, 0, sizeof( OVERLAPPED ) );
       ovl.hEvent = CreateEvent( 0, TRUE, TRUE, NULL );
       if( ! ReadFile( m_hComm, cbBuff, 256,
&dwBytesRead, &ovl ) )
       {
               if( GetLastError() == ERROR_IO_PENDING )
                       GetOverlappedResult( m_hComm, &ovl,
&dwBytesRead, TRUE );
               else
                       return( FALSE );
       }
       for( i = 0; i < (int)dwBytesRead; i++ )
       {
               m_cbBuff[ m_nHead++ ] = cbBuff[i];
               if( m_nHead >= BUFFERSIZE )
                       m_nHead = 0;
       }
       if( ovl.hEvent != INVALID_HANDLE_VALUE )
               CloseHandle( ovl.hEvent );
       return( TRUE );
}
```

The first thing that AddToBuffer does is create an event that you can pass to ReadFile for overlapped I/O. Similar to SendString, it then makes a call to ReadFile and checks to see whether ERROR_IO_PENDING occurs. You're stuck at GetOverlappedResult until the I/O operation is complete. After the operation is complete, the bytes read are moved to m_cbBuff. As each character is added, the head pointer is moved along the circular buffer.

Now go back to the CKeypad implementation and work on making the modem dial. At the start of this chapter, you created the handlers for the buttons in the keypad dialog box. You implemented most of them but didn't touch OnKeypadSnd and OnKeypadHangup. Replace CKeypad::OnKeypadSnd, in KEYPAD.CPP, with the following code:

```
void CKeypad::OnKeypadSnd()
{
        char szCommand[100];


        if( m_port.OpenPort( "COM3" ) )
        {
                m_port.SetPortSettings( 57600, NOPARITY,
8, ONESTOPBIT );
                wsprintf( szCommand, "ATDT%s\r",
(LPCSTR)m_cszNumber );
                m_port.SendString( szCommand,
lstrlen( szCommand ) );
        } else
                MessageBox( "Couldn't open port!", "Error",
MB_OK ¦ MB_ICONEXCLAMATION );
}
```

szCommand is a character buffer that's used to build the dial command that makes the modem dial. After declaring szCommand, OnKeypadSnd calls the OpenPort member of m_port (the CComPort object), passing in the name of the port to open. My modem, for example, is on COM3, so I hard-coded COM3 as the port to open. OpenPort is followed by a call to SetPortSettings, which I hard-coded to 57600, n, 8, 1.

> **TIP:** It's OK to hard-code things that aren't volatile, although some programmers may disagree. Don't, however, hard-code the COM port and port settings in a commercial application. If you do, you're asking for a maintenance nightmare and limited code. (How many people do you know who use COM3?) I've done it here only because this is an example application and it saves some time.

All you have to do before you can dial the modem is open the port and set the port settings. After that's done, OnKeypadSnd constructs a dialing command by concatenating m_cszNumber to ATDT. Finally, it makes a call to the SendString member of m_port to send the dialing command to the modem.

Did you notice how easy it was to add communications capabilities to your dialer control after you created the CComPort object? (You gotta love C++.) Now you have all the code that you need to make a connection.

Hanging up the Call

Most modems are set, by default, to hang up the line when they sense an on-to-off transition in DTR. Add a member function called FlashDTR to the CComPort class. FlashDTR, as you can judge by the name, lowers the DTR line for a few seconds and then raises it again. FlashDTR looks like this:

```
void CComPort::FlashDTR( DWORD nMS )
{
        DWORD nTimeout;
        EscapeCommFunction( m_hComm, CLRDTR );
        nTimeout = GetTickCount() + nMS;
        while( GetTickCount() < nTimeout )
                ;
        EscapeCommFunction( m_hComm, SETDTR );
}
```

FlashDTR calls EscapeCommFunction to lower DTR. Then it uses GetTickCount to get the number of milliseconds since Windows started. It adds the timeout passed in by the calling routine and loops while GetTickCount is less than the sum. After the delay, FlashDTR calls EscapeCommFunction to set the state of DTR high again. To hang up the line, you make a call to FlashDTR and drop DTR for about 2.5 seconds, as follows:

```
void CKeypad::OnKeypadHangup()
{
        m_cszNumber.Empty();
        SetDlgItemText( IDC_DISPLAY, m_cszNumber );
```

```
        m_port.FlashDTR( 2500 );
        m_port.ClosePort();
    }
```

Giving the Container Your Status

You have implemented all the functions necessary to make the dialer complete, but you still need some way to tell the container what you're doing. You do that by creating a couple of OLE events: one to signal when you're dialing, and another to signal when you're disconnecting. (For information on adding events, refer to Chapter 2.)

As you've learned, adding an OLE event to a control is simple. Open the ClassWizard, select the OLE Events tab, and select **A**dd Event. Make sure that you have the CDialerCtrl class selected, and add an event called Dialing (don't worry about adding any parameters). Then add another event called Disconnecting. Visual C++ should create functions called FireDialing and FireDisconnecting. These are private functions declared in the CDialerCtrl class definition.

As you may recall from Chapter 2, you call these two functions to signal the corresponding events. In this case, however, the code that needs to signal the events is in CKeypad. Because FireDialing and FireDisconnecting are both declared as protected members, you can't call them directly from the CKeypad object.

To get around this, create two public members in CDialerCtrl that wrap the two private functions. (You can make the two functions public, but then you interfere with the magic of Visual C++. Microsoft relies on special comment characters in the code to know where to put things.) Add the following two members to the CDialerCtrl class:

```
void CDialerCtrl::CallFireDialing()
{
        FireDialing();
}
void CDialerCtrl::CallFireDisconnecting()
{
        FireDisconnecting();
}
```

Instead of calling `FireDialing` and `FireDisconnecting` directly, you call these two functions. (These two functions might be a good place to put some debugging code.) When you get these members added to the `CDialerCtrl` class, open KEYPAD.CPP, and add a call to `CallFireDialing` in `OnKeypadSnd`, as follows:

```
        .

        .

        if( m_port.OpenPort( "COM3" ) )
        {
                m_port.SetPortSettings( 57600, NOPARITY,
8, ONESTOPBIT );
                wsprintf( szCommand, "ATDT%s\r",
(LPCSTR)m_cszNumber );
                m_port.SendString( szCommand, lstrlen(
szCommand ) );
                ((CDialerCtrl *)GetParent())->CallFireDialing();
        .

        .
```

All you do here is add the call to `CallFireDialing` after the call to `SendString`. To make the call, you have to get a pointer to the `CDialerCtrl` object. `GetParent` returns a `CWnd` pointer to the parent window; then it's cast to `CDialerCtrl` so that you can call members that aren't valid in `CWnd`. Now each time the Snd button is clicked on the keypad, the container is warned. Go ahead and make the changes to `OnKeypadHangup`. Here's what your mods look like:

```
void CKeypad::OnKeypadHangup()
{
        ((CDialerCtrl *)GetParent())->CallFireDisconnecting();
        m_cszNumber.Empty();
        SetDlgItemText( IDC_DISPLAY, m_cszNumber );
        m_port.FlashDTR( 2500 );
        m_port.ClosePort();
}
```

You add the call to CallFireDisconnecting just before emptying the contents of the buffer that stores the telephone number. Before you compile, you need to make sure that DIALERCTL.H is included at the top of your KEYPAD.CPP source file.

Testing Your Dialer Control

In Chapter 2, you learned how to use the Microsoft test container application to test your controls. In this section, you create an application that instantiates the dialer control and use that application to test the control. You get several things by entertaining me on this one. First, you learn how to incorporate your controls into your own applications. (Even if you don't incorporate your controls into applications yourself, you're going to have to explain how to do this to someone else.)

Start by creating an OLE container framework. You can do this by closing the Dialer project and choosing **File, New**. (You should be familiar with the application wizards, so I'll blaze past most of this stuff.) Create a new Project Workspace. Make it an MFC AppWizard project called Tstcon. Choose to build a single document interface and then skip the wizard screens until you get to the Step 3 of 6 dialog box.

In the Step 3 of 6 dialog box, check the OLE controls check box; then click **Finish**, because you don't want to change anything else. When you check the OLE controls check box, MFC includes the stuff necessary for your application to become an ActiveX control container. Now you can use the Component Gallery to plop in the dialer control.

Open the Component Gallery by choosing **Insert, Component**. You see the dialog box shown in Figure 4-6, which opens to the Microsoft tab. Click the OLE Controls tab to get to the dialer control. (I hope that you remembered to compile and link the dialer.) Highlight the dialer control, and click the **Insert** button. Click OK in the Confirm Classes dialog box, and close the Component Gallery dialog box.

Notice that CDialer now shows up as a class in class view. When you drop an ActiveX control into a project by using the Component Gallery, Visual C++ creates a header file and an implementation (.CPP) file. In those files, the dialer control is wrapped with a wrapper class that allows the application to call members and modify properties of the control.

To instantiate the dialer, open the TSTCONVIEW.H header file and add a protected CDialer member called m_dialer. Include the DIALER.H header file at the top of TSTCONVIEW.H. Now go to TSTCONVIEW.CPP and include DIALER.H just

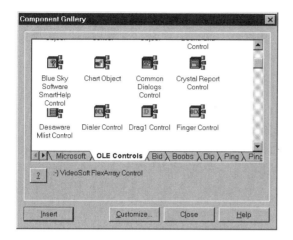

above TSTCONDOC.H. Add a handler for the WM_CREATE message. Edit OnCreate, and make it look like this:

```
int CTstconView::OnCreate(
LPCREATESTRUCT lpCreateStruct)
{
        if (CView::OnCreate(lpCreateStruct) == -1)
                return -1;
        m_dialer.Create( NULL, WS_VISIBLE,
CRect( 0, 0, 320, 200 ), this, 0 );
        return 0;
}
```

The dialer is instantiated when the call is made to the Create member of the CDialer class. Create is a wrapper that calls CreateControl to load and execute the dialer. The WS_VISIBLE flag is specified so that the dialer is visible when the control's window is created. CRect(0, 0, 320, 200) is a rectangle object that tells the framework where to display the control.

At this point, you should be able to compile and run the Tstcon application and use the dialer. Your dialer control is fairly primitive, so about all that you can do is enter a number and dial it. Go ahead and enter the number for a local BBS, and click the Snd button. If you have an external modem, the modem goes off-hook, and the TR light lights up. Click the Hangup button to disconnect the call.

Testing the events that you implemented in the dialer is a bit more complicated. Visual C++ provides an automated mechanism for adding an event handler to your container, through ClassWizard, but it's valid only when the container is a dialog box, so you have to add the handler manually. Open DIALER.H in the TSTCON project directory, and add the following code to your CDialer wrapper class declaration, just below the line that declares AboutBox:

```
protected:
        BOOL OnDialing();
        BOOL OnDisconnecting();
        DECLARE_EVENTSINK_MAP()
```

OnDialing and OnDisconnecting are the handlers that you're going to associate with the dialing and disconnecting events. DECLARE_EVENTSINK_MAP is a macro that declares the map that maps member functions to OLE events. Now go over to the DIALER.CPP file, and create the event map with the following code (below the comment that reads CDialer operations):

```
BEGIN_EVENTSINK_MAP( CDialer, CWnd )
        ON_EVENT( CDialer, 0, 1, OnDialing, NULL )
        ON_EVENT( CDialer, 0, 2, OnDisconnecting, NULL )
END_EVENTSINK_MAP()
```

BEGIN_EVENTSINK_MAP starts the map, and END_EVENTSINK_MAP terminates it. (Semicolons are left out on purpose.) ON_EVENT is the macro that you use to tie member functions to events. The first parameter is the class that's using the map; the second is the control's ID (this one doesn't have one); and the third is the dispatch ID defined in the dialer's type library file. Look at the DIALER.ODL file in the Dialer project to get the dispatch IDs for your events.

> **NOTE:** Windows uses the type library file when generating wrapper classes for your ActiveX controls. It contains information about the members, properties, and events defined in a control, such as names and data types.

The last two parameters in the ON_EVENT calls are the member function to call and a structure that defines the arguments passed by the control. (Don't worry about the argument lists.) OnDialing and OnDisconnecting are the member functions that you added to the

CDialer class definition in DIALER.H earlier. They're defined as member functions that return Boolean values. Examine the following implementations of OnDialing and OnDisconnecting:

```
BOOL CDialer::OnDialing()
{
        ((CFrameWnd *)AfxGetMainWnd())->
SetMessageText( "Dialing..." );
        return( TRUE );
}


BOOL CDialer::OnDisconnecting()
{
        ((CFrameWnd *)AfxGetMainWnd())->
SetMessageText( "Disconnecting..." );
        return( TRUE );
}
```

CFrameWnd has a member function called SetMessageText, which sets the text of an MFC application's default status line. To get to SetMessageText, you call AfxGetMainWnd to get a pointer to the application's mainframe window. You must cast the pointer to a CFrameWnd, because AfxGetMainWnd returns a CWnd *, and SetMessageText is a member of CFrameWnd. Finally, you call SetMessageText and pass it the text that you want to display on the status line. Now you have hooked up the events, and you're ready to see what happens when you dial and disconnect.

Compile and run the Tstcon application. Enter a number, and click the Snd button. Notice that the status line reads Dialing... when you click the Snd button. Now click the Hangup button, and look at the status line. Disconnecting... appears on the status line, and the modem hangs up the phone call.

Now you know what it takes to call the member functions in the ActiveX control, and you know how to implement events. Before you go on with the rest of the book, take some time off to play around and expand the dialer. Maybe you can add member functions to send and receive data.

Nifty Things to Do with the Dialer

While writing this chapter, I dreamed of many applications that you can plug a modem dialer into. I'd like to share those enhancements with you. The idea is to point you in a direction so that you can expand on what you learned in this chapter.

Earlier, you were warned not to hard-code your applications for specific COM ports and port settings if you plan to market your controls. Take some time to remove the hard-coded COM port and port settings in OnKeypadSnd. Tie these settings to properties that can be set in the Properties dialog box. To make your job easier, the controls are already in the default property sheet; all you have to do is implement them.

Detecting the Modem

Many modem applications automatically detect the modem. If you were to build a dialer and market it, you'd want to add some modem initialization code to make sure that the modem is set properly before the dial. You need to do this because there are no standard AT commands for the latest modem technologies, such as data compression and error correction, and you certainly want to support those features.

Modem-detection schemes are simple; they simply loop through the COM ports on the PC and send basic AT commands to the modem. When they get a response, they try to find out what type of modem is attached to the machine. You can do this by looking at the I3 register. To look at the I3 register, send an ATI3? to your modem. I9 may help as well; this is supposed to be the register used for Plug and Play.

Support for Calling Cards

Business travelers often make modem and voice calls from hotels and motels. Because hotels and motels charge an outrageous amount of money for long-distance phone calls, business travelers usually make calls by using a calling card. Building calling-card support into the dialer control makes sense, because unlike a phone number, the calling-card number is not likely to change. (Why force the user to enter that stuff manually each time he or she wants to make a call?)

If you implement calling-card support in your dialer control, make sure that you provide a way to configure how the card number is dialed—the pauses and so on. Procomm Plus, for example, provides a setup screen that lets you configure five or six events. The first event might be to dial 0, followed by the telephone number. The second event might be to pause 5 seconds. The third event would dial the calling-card number, and so on.

> **TIP:** You will save yourself some development and configuration if you make a calling-card call manually and time the sequence of events.

Use the Dialer Indirectly

Indirect use of the dialer opens many doors. By *indirect*, I mean *without an interface*. Wouldn't it be cool if your dialer supported some sort of transparent mode that wasn't visible to the user but could be used by an application for serial-port communications?

Think about the possibilities. An application that doesn't have modem capabilities suddenly gains the capability to connect, send, and receive data. A programmer who is building such an application could write his own interface to the dialer. Such an interface could be a database of names. The user could select a name from the list, and the application would dial that person automatically.

Make Your Dialer TAPI-Compliant

The *Telephony Applications Programming Interface* (TAPI) is a new standard for modem and phone-switch technology that promises to do away with all the stuff that a user has to know before he or she can dial into another computer system. Why should users be forced to know what baud rate, parity, data bits, and stop bits are before they can connect to another computer?

It would be cool to make the dialer in this chapter TAPI-compatible. TAPI compatibility means that the dialer could coexist with other communications applications, such as Microsoft Fax and HyperTerminal. (TAPI allows multiple applications to have access to the port at the same time, basically.) Without TAPI support, you can't use the dialer while Microsoft Fax is set to answer calls. Kind of cheesy, huh?

Chapter Summary

This chapter taught you an easy way to add complex interfaces to your controls, using dialog boxes. At the same time, you learned quite a lot about how programs interact with modems and serial ports. You also learned to take advantage of 32-bit threading to make your modem programs more efficient.

In Chapter 5, "Plug-in Terminal Emulator," you learn to build a terminal control. While building the terminal, you strengthen what you learned about communications in this chapter. You also enhance your interface skills by creating an interface from scratch (without using dialog boxes or subclassed controls).

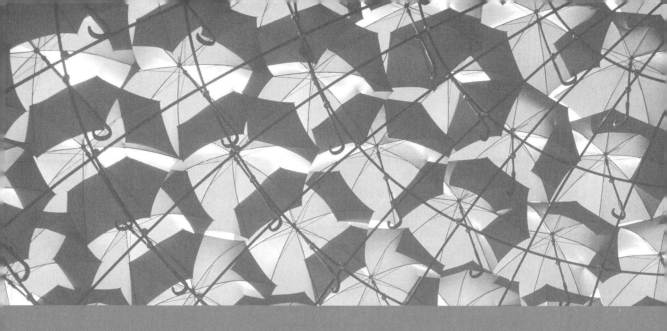

Chapter | 5

Plug-in Terminal Emulator

by Markus Pope

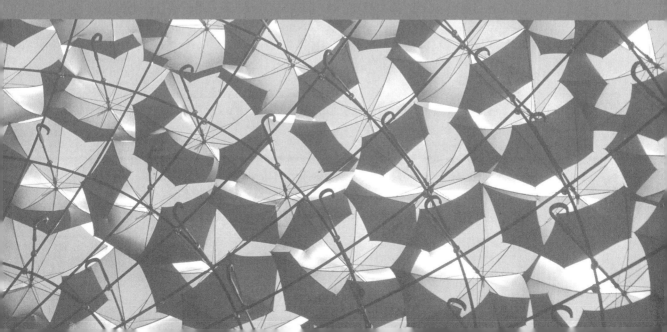

As you can guess from the title, this chapter teaches you how to house a terminal emulation inside an OLE control. You're going to build a TTY terminal—nothing fancy, but it will be well on its way to becoming a full-fledged terminal emulator when you finish. (*TTY* comes from the word *teletype*. Teletypes use a very simple emulation.) You also get a chance to work more with properties and methods in this chapter than you have in previous chapters. The chapter covers the following topics:

♦ What a terminal emulator is

♦ How to write a terminal emulator

♦ What you can do with a terminal emulator

A Terminal Emulator Is Not a Dying Mime

The title of this section describes an emulator fairly accurately. Mimes mimic real-life situations, conveying information through imagination. Similarly, an *emulator* is an object (software or hardware) that mimics the actions of terminals.

In the first section of this chapter, I mention that *TTY* stands for *teletype*. TTY represents the primitive emulation used by the old teletype technology. Teletypes are essentially typewriters with modems. The sender machine sends character after character, which then are typed by the receiving teletype. TTY supports only the most basic of commands.

A carriage return, or ASCII 0x0D, causes the receiving teletype to move the carriage (the apparatus that does the typing) to the beginning of the line. A line feed, or ASCII 0x0A, moves the carriage to the next line. Therefore, a carriage-return and line-feed pair prepare the teletype to type text on a new line. A form feed causes the teletype to advance to the beginning of the next page.

Before you start writing a TTY emulator, I'll give you some terminal-programming background, which involves only a few basic concepts. These concepts have to do mostly with how terminals process incoming data and keep track of the screen. Even though you're creating a software version of a terminal, the concepts are the same.

Introducing the State Machine

The state machine that I'm referring to is the heart of the terminal emulation. A *state machine* is a parser that looks at each byte as it's received and either sets a state based on that character or displays it—whatever needs to be done.

Suppose that a terminal has the capability to display text with variable foreground colors. To change colors, the host system sends a left-bracket character followed by a number. The numbers are 0 through 4, which correspond to black, blue, green, red, and white.

A state is set when the state machine receives a left bracket. That bracket is known as an escape character (don't confuse that with ASCII 0x1B). In this case, the bracket escape character tells the state machine that the character that follows signifies one of the colors listed in the preceding paragraph. When the next character comes in, the state machine checks its current state and sees that it's in "collect-a-color" mode. It then compares the number against 0 through 4. Suppose that it's a 3. From now until another color sequence is received, the terminal displays text with a foreground color of red. Graphically, the whole process looks something like Figure 5-1.

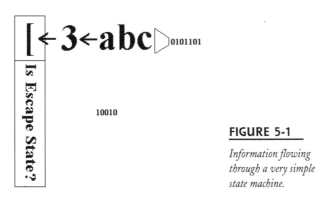

FIGURE 5-1

Information flowing through a very simple state machine.

Of course, you don't need a true state machine to implement a TTY terminal emulation, simply because TTY doesn't support any character sequences that can't be represented by more than one byte. But you'll implement at least one complex sequence so that you can see a state machine in action. (I wouldn't want to deprive you of that.)

Understanding Other Terminal Concepts

State machines make possible other terminal-programming concepts, such as full screen and painted attributes. These are two methods of displaying text that's underlined, bold-faced, dim, highlighted, and/or possibly colored.

When text is painted with full screen attributes, the painting occurs between two attribute characters that are placed at the beginning and end of the text that's painted—that is, the attribute characters that indicate painting take up space in the display area. If they are overwritten for some reason, you can end up with unpainted text or way too much paint, depending on which attribute is stomped on. (*Stomped on* is a technical term that you hear quite a lot around technical support departments. It means that data is corrupted.)

With painted attributes, no space in the display areas is taken up. Instead, two copies of the display area are stored in memory: one for the actual text that's displayed and the other to keep track of how the text is displayed. Painting is turned on and off for specific characters or groups of characters on the screen. Because the first terminals had limited memory and full screen attributes use less memory, it stands to reason that full screen attributes may have come about before painted attributes, but who really knows?

Local echo is another terminal concept that can be attributed to the state machine, although not necessarily. Typically, terminals are used in something called full duplex mode—that is, when a terminal sends characters, it relies on the system it's connected to to send those characters back for display. Why not display the data as it's sent and save yourself some bandwidth? Well, that's valid too. It's called half duplex.

When modems came out, they couldn't send and receive data at the same time, and they were extremely slow. People used half duplex simply because it was faster. Now full duplex is used because it gives the terminal more control. Because of major advances in modem technology, speed is no longer an issue. When a terminal is in half duplex, local echo is said to be on or enabled. You'll implement local echo in your implementation of the TTY terminal emulation.

Create the Emulator Control

You can't start writing code to implement a terminal emulation until you use the OLE ControlWizard to create the framework for the control. Create a new project, using the OLE ControlWizard, and call this one Term. Don't worry about subclassing a Windows control, as you did in Chapter 2. (You could probably base the terminal control on an edit box, but that would be more trouble than it's worth.) After you create the framework for the terminal control, you can build the state machine.

Building the State Machine

Earlier in the chapter, you learned what a state machine is and what it does. The state machine that you're going to build for the terminal control isn't going to be a real state machine at first. To start, you'll examine each character as it's received. If a character does something special, such as carriage return or form feed, you'll call a helper function to perform the corresponding function.

You could have the container pass each character individually to the control's state machine, but in any kind of communications, it's a good idea to do things as efficiently as possible. Passing a character at a time is inefficient because there's some overhead associated with calling a function—more so when that function is in an OLE interface. To save a lot of overhead, you'll pass an array of bytes into your state machine function. Call your state machine function WriteTermText. Here's what it should look like:

```
void CTermCtrl::WriteTermText( LPCSTR lpText, int nMaxBytes )
{
        int i;
        for( i = 0; i < nMaxBytes; i++ )
        {
                switch( lpText[i] )
                {
                        case _TRM_BS:
                                HandleIncomingBS();
                                break;

                        case _TRM_LF:
                                HandleIncomingLF();
                                break;

                        case _TRM_CR:
```

```
                         HandleIncomingCR();
                         break;

            case _TRM_FF:
                         HandleIncomingFF();
                         break;

            case _TRM_ESC:
                         HandleIncomingEsc();
                         break;

            default:
                         HandleIncomingCharacter(
(BYTE)lpText[i] );
                }
        }
        InvalidateControl();
}
```

Take some time to add this function to your terminal control project. Add the function to the protected portion of your CTermCtrl class definition.

WriteTermText's implementation is simple. lpText is a buffer that contains the bytes that the state machine is to analyze. WriteTermText walks through each character in lpText and checks to see if it's an emulation sequence (denoted by _TRM_BS through _TRM_ESC). If a character is an emulation sequence, WriteTermText calls a helper function to perform an emulation function. (You'll implement helper functions here in a minute.) If the character is a display character, it's passed on to a function called HandleIncomingCharacter that takes care of the details of display. After all characters in lpText are handled, WriteTermText calls InvalidateControl to cause the terminal control to repaint.

Before you can implement the helper functions, you have to do a little work on the display mechanism. (After all, without a display mechanism, what would the helper functions do?) The easiest way to do this is to create a buffer that contains the display data. When the control is repainted, transfer the display data in the buffer to the control's device context.

> **NOTE:** I prefer to work with a linear buffer, rather than a two-dimensional one. Although two-dimensional buffers seem to fit the design of terminals well (the display is two-dimensional), linear buffers are easier to work with. You'll see what I mean as you get farther into the implementation of the buffer.

To create a display buffer, add a BYTE * (byte pointer) to your CTermCtrl class definition in the protected section, as shown in the following example. Call the byte pointer m_cbScreen. Also add three integer members: m_nCols, m_nRows, and m_nSize. m_nCols, m_nRows, and m_nSize control the size of the terminal window and the length of the display buffer. Here's what the protected section of your CTermCtrl class definition should look like so far:

```
protected:

       ~CTermCtrl();

       void WriteTermText( LPCSTR lpText, int nMaxBytes );


       int m_nCols;       // Number of columns in terminal.

       int m_nRows;       // Number of rows in terminal.

       int m_nSize;       // Size of screen array.

       BYTE *m_cbScreen;// Array that represents screen.
```

m_cbScreen is a pointer because you're going to allocate the space for it in the OnCreate member of CTermCtrl. OnCreate is called when the framework is ready to create the control's main window. So in the constructor for CTermCtrl, you need to set m_nSize to the total number of bytes needed for the buffer. The length of m_cbScreen is the area of the terminal display area, in bytes. If the terminal is 80 columns by 25 rows, which is typical, you need to allocate a buffer that's 80 * 25 = 2000 bytes long. Make your CTermCtrl constructor look like the following:

```
CTermCtrl::CTermCtrl()

{

       InitializeIIDs(&IID_DTerm, &IID_DTermEvents);


       m_nCols = _DEF_TERM_COLS;

       m_nRows = _DEF_TERM_ROWS;
```

```
    m_nSize = m_nCols * m_nRows;
    m_cbScreen = 0;

}
```

> **NOTE:** In the code examples, defines are used in place of certain values for maintainability. It's much easier to change a bunch of settings in one place than to search through pages upon pages of code to make sure that you've changed all occurrences of something. This is a good habit to get into.

m_nCols and m_nRows are set to the default width and height of the display, in bytes. m_nSize is m_nCols multiplied by m_nRows, or the area of the display in bytes. m_cbScreen is initialized to zero, for safety's sake (so that you can check it to see that it's nonzero before using it). m_cbScreen is actually allocated in the OnCreate member function, so add a handler for WM_CREATE to your project. CTermCtrl::OnCreate looks like this:

```
int CTermCtrl::OnCreate(LPCREATESTRUCT lpCreateStruct)
{
    m_cbScreen = new BYTE [m_nSize];
    if( m_cbScreen )
    {
        if (COleControl::OnCreate(lpCreateStruct) != -1)
            return( 0 );
        delete [] m_cbScreen;
    }
    return( -1 );
}
```

OnCreate tries to allocate the buffer based on m_nSize, which is set to the columns times the rows in the constructor. If the allocation is successful, OnCreate from the base class is called, and the window is created. If the base class OnCreate fails, delete is called to deallocate m_cbScreen and -1 is returned to the framework. (You always want to clean up the memory and resources that you allocate when you're done using it. It's easy to forget to do that when errors occur.)

Now you're allocating the display buffer when the control is created. You should also deallocate the buffer when the control is destroyed. You can do this in either of two ways (or both, if you want to get technical). One way is to add a handler for WM_DESTROY, which is received when the control's window is destroyed. An easier way is to add some cleanup code to CTermCtrl's destructor. The framework provides the destructor, and it's always called when the CTermCtrl object is destroyed. Add the following lines to CTermCtrl::~CTermCtrl:

```
if( m_cbScreen )
        delete [] m_cbScreen;
```

You have more to do before the implementation of the display buffer is complete, but you'll do that stuff as you go along. Right now, let's get back into the state machine. You have used several defines, including _DEF_TRM_COLS and _DEF_TRM_ROWS, to define the width and height of the terminal in columns and rows. Add the following defines to the top of the TERMCTL.H header file:

```
#define _DEF_TERM_COLS          80
#define _DEF_TERM_ROWS          25
#define _TRM_BS                 0x08
#define _TRM_LF                 0x0A
#define _TRM_FF                 0x0C
#define _TRM_CR                 0x0D
#define _TRM_ESC                0x1B
#define _TRM_SPC                0x20
```

The _TRM_ defines give meaning to character code values for backspace, line feed, form feed, carriage return, escape, and space. Your code is difficult to read when it includes *magic numbers*, which are hard-coded values in your code that don't suggest their own context. You may know what they mean when you put the code together, but you'll have no idea what you meant when you come back to change the code a year later.

At this point, the code is at a point where you can start working on the helper functions. Start by adding all the helper functions and prototypes to the CTermCtrl class. (I find it easier to work when all I have to do is fill in functions.) Add the following list of prototypes to the protected section of your CTermCtrl class definition:

```
void HandleIncomingBS();
void HandleIncomingLF();
void HandleIncomingCR();
void HandleIncomingFF();
void HandleIncomingEsc();
void HandleIncomingCharacter( BYTE ch );
```

After you get done with the prototypes, add the functions to the end of TERMCTL.CPP, but leave them empty. You'll fill them in one at a time, starting with HandleIncomingBS.

HandleIncomingBS is the handler for the backspace character. Backspace is the key that a user presses when the user needs to correct something that he or she typed. The key backs up and destroys the character that was typed in the display buffer. To implement the backspace, though, you have to know where on the display text is being added.

Add two more integer member variables to the protected section of the CTermCtrl class definition. Call one of these integers m_nTrackX, and call the other m_nTrackY. m_nTrackX keeps track of the X position of the caret, and m_nTrackY keeps track of the Y position. The current caret position on a terminal denotes the location at which text is displayed when it's received. Its position is moved along the display as data is received, just as a carriage is moved along in a typewriter as data is typed.

Don't forget to initialize m_nTrackX and m_nTrackY to zero in the constructor for CTermCtrl. After doing that, look at this implementation of HandleIncomingBS:

```
void CTermCtrl::HandleIncomingBS()
{
        m_nTrackX—;
        if( m_nTrackX < 0 )
        {
                m_nTrackX = m_nCols - 1;
                m_nTrackY—;
                if( m_nTrackY < 0 )
                        m_nTrackY = m_nRows - 1;
        }
        m_cbScreen[ GlobalToLinearCoord(
m_nTrackX, m_nTrackY ) ] = _TRM_SPC;
}
```

m_nTrackX tracks the current column, and m_nTrackY tracks the current row. HandleIncomingBS decrements m_nTrackX and does some adjustment if the current text location moves to the previous line. If the current text position moves beyond the first position on the screen, m_nTrackX and m_nTrackY are set to the last location on the screen (that's how a real terminal handles it). To make the backspace destructive, you call GlobalToLinearCoord to convert X and Y coordinates to a linear position in m_cbScreen, and you set that byte to a space.

GlobalToLinearCoord uses a simple mathematical equation to convert two-dimensional coordinates to numbers that can be used to reference data in a linear buffer. You can map two-dimensional coordinates in linear space by applying this simple formula:

```
(Row * Width) + Column
```

What does this mean to you? GlobalToLinearCoord gets a pointer into m_cbScreen by multiplying m_nTrackY by m_nCols and then adding m_nTrackX. The result looks something like this:

```
int CTermCtrl::GlobalToLinearCoord( int x, int y )
{
        return( (y * m_nCols) + x );
}
```

Linear to X and Y Conversion

Conversely, although you're not going to use it in this chapter, you may want to convert a linear address back to its X and Y proponents. To do that, you have to apply two equations: one to get the Y value, and another to get the X value. You can get Y by dividing the linear address by m_nCols. As it turns out, X is the remainder of that division. If you put that into a function, you get this:

```
void CTermCtrl::LinearToGlobalCoord(
int nAbsolute, int& x, int& y )
{
        y = nAbsolute / m_nCols;
        x = nAbsolute - (y * m_nCols);
}
```

You could use a linear to global conversion in a print screen or screen-capture algorithm.

That seems like a lot to cover just for the implementation of one helper function, but you'll use GlobalToLinearCoord in several places in the terminal control. Now skip to the HandleIncomingLF helper. A line feed on a teletype or typewriter moves the carriage down one line, and a terminal is no different. Add the following function to your CTermCtrl class:

```
void CTermCtrl::HandleIncomingLF()
{
        m_nTrackY++;
        if( m_nTrackY >= m_nRows )
        {
                ScrollTerminal(1);
                m_nTrackY = m_nRows - 1;
        }
}
```

HandleIncomingLF increments m_nTrackY to advance the current text location to the next line, but it doesn't increment m_nTrackX. I'll show you why in just a little bit. If the current text location moves beyond the bottom of the display, you call a function called ScrollTerminal to scroll the display area up one line. Then m_nTrackY is set to the last line in the display.

ScrollTerminal scrolls the display area by removing the first line on the screen and then moving subsequent lines up by one. The last line is cleared with some kind of character—usually, a space. (Quite a few terminal emulations allow the host to specify the character used to clear lines and screens. Most commonly, space or null is used.) ScrollTerminal looks like this:

```
void CTermCtrl::ScrollTerminal( int nUP )
{
        int i;
        while( nUP- )
        {
                for( i = 1; i < m_nRows; i++ )
                        memcpy( &m_cbScreen[
GlobalToLinearCoord( 0, i - 1 ) ],
&m_cbScreen[ GlobalToLinearCoord(
```

```
0, i ) ], m_nCols );
                memset( &m_cbScreen[ GlobalToLinearCoord( 0,
                      m_nRows - 1 ) ], _TRM_SPC, m_nCols );
        }
}
```

When you write functions, try to make them as flexible as possible. That's why you allow the caller of ScrollTerminal to specify the number of lines that the display is to be scrolled. For each line that is to be scrolled on the display, ScrollTerminal copies all lines in the display to the line before it. Then it uses memset to clear the last line to spaces.

Lines are typically terminated by carriage-return and line-feed pairs. That's why HandleIncomingLF moves the m_nTrackY value and doesn't bother with m_nTrackX. m_nTrackX is adjusted in HandleIncomingCR (when a carriage return is received). The implementation of HandleIncomingCR is incredibly simple. All you have to do is set m_nTrackX to zero, like this:

```
void CTermCtrl::HandleIncomingCR()
{
        m_nTrackX = 0;
}
```

HandleIncomingFF is called when the terminal control receives a form-feed character. A form feed advances the current text location to the beginning of the next page. On a terminal, that's quite simple; it just clears the screen. But you're not going to put the actual code that clears the screen inside HandleIncomingFF. Instead, you're going to make HandleIncomingFF call a function called ClearScreen, which clears the screen to a specified character (a space, in this case). Your implementation of HandleIncomingFF should look like the following.

```
void CTermCtrl::HandleIncomingFF()
{
        ClearScreen( _TRM_SPC );
}
```

Like ScrollTerminal, ClearScreen uses memset to set the contents of m_cbScreen to the specified character. Your implementation of ClearScreen should look like this:

```
void CTermCtrl::ClearScreen( BYTE ch )
{
        memset( m_cbScreen, ch, m_nSize );
        InvalidateControl();
        m_nTrackX = m_nTrackY = 0;
}
```

After calling memset to set the contents of m_cbScreen to the specified character, InvalidateControl is called to force the terminal control to repaint the display area. (You haven't yet made changes to the OnDraw member; you'll do that later in the chapter.) Finally, m_nTrackX and m_nTrackY are both initialized to zero to put the current text location at the beginning of the display.

You may be wondering, at this point, why ClearScreen is separate from HandleIncomingFF. There are several reasons for this, one of which is so that we can call it on the OnCreate member. In fact, go ahead and add a call to ClearScreen in OnCreate, just before the line that returns zero, like this:

```
        .

        .

        if (COleControl::OnCreate(lpCreateStruct) != -1)
        {
                ClearScreen( _TRM_SPC );
                return( 0 );
        }
        delete [] m_cbScreen;

        .

        .
```

After creating the terminal control, the code clears the screen to spaces, giving the user a fresh, clean display.

A second reason is so that we can call it from an exported OLE interface. Exporting an OLE interface that calls this function allows the container to clear the terminal display.

Instead of talking about HandleIncomingEsc (it's the next one in line), I'll skip to HandleIncomingCharacter. Its job is to handle all other characters not handled by the state machine. Look at the sample HandleIncomingCharacter:

```
void CTermCtrl::HandleIncomingCharacter( BYTE ch )
{
        m_cbScreen[ GlobalToLinearCoord(
m_nTrackX, m_nTrackY ) ] = ch;
        m_nTrackX++;
        if( m_nTrackX >= m_nCols )
        {
                m_nTrackX = 0;
                m_nTrackY++;
                if( m_nTrackY >= m_nRows )
                {
                        ScrollTerminal( 1 );
                        m_nTrackY = m_nRows - 1;
                }
        }
}
```

First, HandleIncomingCharacter sets the appropriate character in m_cbScreen to the character passed into the terminal control. Then it increments the text location by one column to prepare for the next character. If the text location moves past the end of the current line, HandleIncomingCharacter advances the caret to the beginning of the next line. If the caret position scrolls off the end of the page, the terminal is scrolled up by one and the new caret position is set to the beginning of the last line. (Can you see how helpful the ScrollTerminal helper function has become?)

Tracking a State in the State Machine

Until now, you have been working on what I'm calling the state machine. But the state machine that you have implemented isn't a true state machine, because it doesn't track any states. To change that situation, add another handler function to your CTermCtrl class definition. Make this one return void, and have it take a BYTE argument. Call it HandleEscapedFunction.

Now add a member variable called m_bEsc to the protected section of CTermCtrl. m_bEsc should be a Boolean value (type BOOL) that's initialized to FALSE in CTermCtrl::CTermCtrl. The object is to set m_bEsc to TRUE when an escape character is received. Then, in

WriteTermText, you check it to see if it's true and call HandleEscapedFunction if it is. Finally, stick some code in HandleEscapedFunction to clear the screen to the character that follows the escape character. Start by adding m_bEsc = TRUE; to HandleIncomingEsc. Then make changes to WriteTermText, as follows:

```
        .

        .

for( i = 0; i < nMaxBytes; i++ )
{
        if( ! m_bEsc )
        {
                switch( lpText[i] )

                .

                .

                .

        } else
                HandleEscapedFunction( (BYTE)lpText[i] );
}

        .

        .
```

When WriteTermText sees an escape, it calls HandleIncomingEsc to set m_bEsc to TRUE. The next character handled by WriteTermText is passed to HandleEscapedFunction, where you check to see that the character is a display character and then clear the screen with that character. Following is the HandleEscapedFunction member for the terminal control example (remember to set m_bEsc back to FALSE):

```
void CTermCtrl::HandleEscapedFunction( BYTE ch )
{
        if( ch >= ' ' && ch <= '~' )
                ClearScreen( ch );

        m_bEsc = FALSE;
}
```

As you can see, HandleEscapedFunction checks the character to see if its character value falls between space and tilde. If the character is a valid display character, it calls

ClearScreen to clear the screen, using that character. If you, for example, send the terminal control ^[., the display is cleared using period characters. The last thing that HandleEscapedFunction does is set the m_bEsc flag back to FALSE.

> **NOTE:** ^[is commonly used by communications software manuals, terminal manuals, instructional books like this one, and modem manuals to denote the escape character. ^ means to subtract 64 from the character value of the character that follows. If you subtract 64 from 91, which is the character value for [, you get 27, the character value for escape. ^M denotes a carriage return, for example.

Now your state machine is a true state machine, because you're setting an escape state and acting on that state. Of course, real terminal emulations take this concept to a whole new level, but the concept is exactly the same.

The following section discusses the terminal display mechanism.

Displaying Data on the Terminal

Even though the preceding section discussed state machines, you had to implement a big part of the display mechanism to finish the state machine. A great deal of the work is already done, but there's enough work left to do to warrant a new section on the subject.

In this section, you're going to do three things:

- ◆ Modify the terminal control so that it displays the data that it receives
- ◆ Add a caret to your terminal so that you can tell where the current text location is
- ◆ Implement local echo

Start by examining the changes that you need to make to the OnDraw function. Here's what I've done with CTermCtrl::OnDraw:

```
void CTermCtrl::OnDraw( CDC* pdc, const CRect&
rcBounds, const CRect& rcInvalid)
{
      POINT ptActual;
      int trm_x, trm_y;
```

```
COLORREF crefForeground;
COLORREF crefBackground;

pdc->SaveDC();
pdc->SelectObject( m_hTermFont );
crefForeground = TranslateColor( GetForeColor() );
crefBackground = TranslateColor( GetBackColor() );
pdc->SetTextColor( crefForeground );
pdc->SetBkColor( crefBackground );
pdc->SetBkMode( OPAQUE );
for( trm_y = 0; trm_y < m_nRows; trm_y++ )
{
        for( trm_x = 0; trm_x < m_nCols; trm_x++ )
        {
                ptActual = GlobalToPixelCoord(
trm_x, trm_y );

                pdc->TextOut( ptActual.x, ptActual.y,
(LPSTR)&m_cbScreen[ GlobalToLinearCoord(
trm_x, trm_y ) ], 1 );
        }
}
pdc->RestoreDC(-1);
}
```

The control framework passes a pointer to a device-context object. A *device context* is the drawing surface of a window. Using that device context, OnDraw sets the foreground and background text colors and the drawing mode. The foreground and background colors are set with the GetForeColor and GetBackColor members of COleControl. GetForeColor and GetBackColor return an OLE_COLOR value that has to be converted to a COLORREF value before you can use it. TranslateColor converts OLE_COLOR values to their COLORREF equivalents. Draw mode is set to OPAQUE so that text is displayed with both the foreground and background colors.

The two nested loops are responsible for displaying data in the terminal control's window. In the inner loop, OnDraw iterates through the characters in each line (lines are controlled by the outer loop) and writes them to the screen with the TextOut function. Notice, though, that the X and Y positions of each character are passed to a function called GlobalToPixelCoord. Similar to GlobalToLinearCoord, GlobalToPixelCoord converts row and column coordinates to actual screen coordinates. This calculation is based on the font width and height. (See the reference to m_hTermFont at the top of OnDraw?)

Before you write GlobalToPixelCoord, implement m_hTermFont. Add m_hTermFont to the protected section of your CTermCtrl class definition, and set its type to HFONT. Then add another variable called m_tmTerm, and give it the type TEXTMETRIC. Now add the following line to CTermCtrl::CTermCtrl, the terminal control's constructor:

```
    m_hTermFont = (HFONT)GetStockObject(
ANSI_FIXED_FONT );
```

This line creates the font used in the terminal display.

Now go to your implementation of the OnCreate member in TERMCTL.CPP and make these changes:

```
    .

    .

    if (COleControl::OnCreate(lpCreateStruct) != -1)
    {
            pdc = GetDC();
            pdc->SaveDC();
            pdc->SelectObject( m_hTermFont );
            pdc->GetTextMetrics( &m_tmTerm );
            pdc->RestoreDC( -1 );
            ReleaseDC( pdc );
            ClearScreen( _TRM_SPC );
            return( 0 );
    }
    delete [] m_cbScreen;

    .

    .
```

In OnCreate, you get the device context for the terminal control, select the font, and then ask for the font measurements. You're going to use the font measurements in GlobalToPixelCoord to convert the row and column positions in the display buffer to coordinates in the terminal control's window.

To convert a row and column value to pixel coordinates, multiply the row by the height of the font and the column by the width of the font. You can get the width and height of the font from the m_tmTerm, TEXTMETRIC, structure. The width of the font is stored in m_tmTerm.tmMaxCharWidth, and the height is stored in m_tmTerm.tmHeight. In the implementation of GlobalToPixelCoord that follows, the converted coordinates are returned in a POINT structure for convenience:

```
POINT CTermCtrl::GlobalToPixelCoord( int x, int y )
{
        POINT pt;
        pt.x = x * m_tmTerm.tmMaxCharWidth;
        pt.y = y * m_tmTerm.tmHeight;
        return( pt );
}
```

> **NOTE:** You don't have to free the font that's pointed to by m_hTermFont, because you used GetStockObject to get a handle to a resource provided by the system: ANSI_FIXED_FONT. Had you used CreateFont to generate a font resource, you would have needed to free the font in the destructor for CTermCtrl.

That just about covers painting the terminal window based on the display buffer. Before you're done with the terminal display, though, you still have to implement caret tracking and local echo. Caret tracking is simple. Windows has only one caret resource, and that resource is shared between all input windows. When your control receives the input focus, you create the caret and adjust its position in the display. When your control loses the focus, you destroy the caret.

Start by creating a function that updates the caret position based on m_nTrackX and m_nTrackY. Call the function UpdateCaretPos. What follows is the CTermCtrl::UpdateCaretPos function from the sample terminal control included with this book:

```
void CTermCtrl::UpdateCaretPos()
{
        if( GetFocus() == this )
        {
                HideCaret();
```

```
                SetCaretPos( GlobalToPixelCoord( m_nTrackX,
    m_nTrackY ) );

                ShowCaret();

        }

    }
```

UpdateCaretPos makes sure that the terminal window has the input focus. This is necessary because you don't want to make calls to HideCaret and ShowCaret unless your window owns the caret. If the terminal window has the input focus, UpdateCaretPos hides the caret, sets the new caret position, and then shows the caret. GlobalToPixelCoord is called to convert m_nTrackX and m_nTrackY to actual window coordinates.

At several places in the code, you're going to call UpdateCaretPos. Before you do, add some code to create and destroy the caret. Add handlers to CTermCtrl for the WM_SETFOCUS and WM_KILLFOCUS messages. Visual C++ should add one member function called OnSetFocus and another called OnKillFocus. Make them look like these:

```
void CTermCtrl::OnSetFocus(CWnd* pOldWnd)
{
        COleControl::OnSetFocus(pOldWnd);
        ::CreateCaret( GetSafeHwnd(), NULL,
    m_tmTerm.tmMaxCharWidth, m_tmTerm.tmHeight );
        ShowCaret();
        UpdateCaretPos();
}
void CTermCtrl::OnKillFocus(CWnd* pNewWnd)
{
        COleControl::OnKillFocus(pNewWnd);
        HideCaret();
        ::DestroyCaret();
}
```

The control framework calls OnSetFocus when the input focus is set to the terminal window and OnKillFocus when it's removed. OnSetFocus creates a caret that's the width and height of a character in the font. (Remember that width and height of the terminal font are stored in m_tmTerm.) Then it shows the caret and calls UpdateCaretPos to adjust its position.

OnKillFocus is even more simple than OnSetFocus. When OnKillFocus is called, the control hides the caret and destroys it, allowing the new input window to create and use the caret. (There's only one caret, because it would get mighty confusing to have more than one window with input focus.)

Now you're ready to add UpdateCaretPos calls to ClearScreen and WriteTermText. Add the following line to ClearScreen after the line that reads m_nTrackX = m_nTrackY = 0;:

```
UpdateCaretPos();
```

Also add this line to WriteTermText, just after the line that reads InvalidateControl();. These are the two places where the caret position is modified. The UpdateCaretPos call in WriteTermText acts for any of the handler functions that happen to modify the caret's position.

Local echo is the last tidbit that you have to implement before you can call the terminal display mechanism complete. Local echo isn't used much anymore. Why implement it, then? Without local echo, the only way you can tell if the terminal is working is to write a container and pump data into it (or use the test container). With local echo, the terminal displays everything that you type as you type it.

To implement local echo, add a BOOL variable called m_bEcho to the protected section of your CTermCtrl class definition. Initialize m_bEcho to FALSE in CTermCtrl's constructor. Next, add a handler to CTermCtrl for the WM_CHAR message. Visual C++ creates a member function called OnChar. The framework calls WM_CHAR any time the user presses a normal key on the keyboard. OnChar isn't called when the user presses keys such as PgUp and PgDn.

All you have to do in OnChar is fill a buffer with the character value of the key pressed and pass that buffer into WriteTermText; WriteTermText takes care of the rest. Your OnChar function should look like this:

```
void CTermCtrl::OnChar(UINT nChar,
UINT nRepCnt, UINT nFlags)
{
    BYTE cbBuff[50];
    memset( cbBuff, nChar, nRepCnt );
    if( m_bEcho )
```

```
        WriteTermText( (LPCSTR)cbBuff, nRepCnt );
    COleControl::OnChar(nChar, nRepCnt, nFlags);
}
```

OnChar uses memset to fill a buffer of 50 bytes with the character value of the key that the user pressed. nRepCnt is the number of times that the key is repeated. (Windows handles repeated keys this way instead of sending multiple WM_CHAR messages.) It's probably not necessary to have a buffer much bigger than 50 bytes, because you're not likely to have a character value repeated that many times.

If m_bEcho is TRUE, WriteTermText is called, passing in cbBuff and the number of bytes in cbBuff (which is the repeat count). Finally, OnChar from the base class is called to finish the key processing. That's all there is to it. If local echo is turned on, characters are echoed to the terminal display through calls to WriteTermText. If local echo is off, the keys are handled normally.

Two Models Direct vs. Indirect

When you get to this point, you can take two different development paths:

- ◆ You can open some interfaces so that the container can pass data to the control (which you probably want to do anyway). In this case, the terminal control doesn't worry about talking directly to the COM port. Instead, the container gets data from the COM port or from another control and feeds the terminal with data to display.

- ◆ You can take the direct path by making the terminal control handle incoming and outgoing data itself.

The indirect model is better than the direct model. Why should the terminal care where the data is coming from? Isolating the terminal in this way gives you some advantages. First, as a separate object, you can connect the terminal to a wide variety of I/O devices. In one application, you can make it talk to a serial port; in another application, you can make it talk to the Internet. Second, when you do want to make it talk to more than one I/O device, you don't have to modify the terminal control, just the container. Even less work is required if you can find a control that's already designed to talk to the I/O device. Figure 5-2 shows a hypothetical indirect terminal object that can plug into a variety of applications.

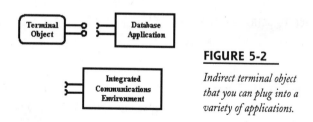

FIGURE 5-2

Indirect terminal object that you can plug into a variety of applications.

Creating an Indirect Version of the Emulator

Because using an indirect model makes the terminal control more modular, you're going to do that first. Then you plug in the CComPort object that you created in Chapter 4 (but not the dialer; I'll leave that for you to do on your own). All the hard work is already done. All you have to do now is create some methods and properties so that the container can interact with the control.

Start by allowing the container to pass in some data for display. To do this, you have to create a wrapper function that's exposed to the container and that calls WriteTermText. Open the ClassWizard, select the OLE Automation tab, and click the Add Method button. Change the external name to WriteTerminalText and the internal name to OCXWriteTerminalText. Create two arguments, one that's an LPCTSTR and another that's a long. Call the LPCTSTR lpText and the long nMaxBytes. Set the return type to void. Click the OK button to add the WriteTerminalText method to your control. Visual C++ creates a function block for OCXWriteTerminalText. Edit that function and make it call WriteTermText, as follows:

```
void CTermCtrl::OCXWriteTerminalText(
LPCTSTR lpText, long nMaxBytes)
{
        WriteTermText( lpText, nMaxBytes );
}
```

Now, when the container receives data from a modem, it can call the exposed WriteTerminalText method in the control and pass the data to be displayed. The control takes that data and passes it to WriteTermText, which checks it for escape sequences and displays it.

That takes care of incoming data. What about outgoing data?

Outgoing data is a bit different. Instead of making the container poll the control for characters that the user typed, you'll notify the container through an OLE event. Open the ClassWizard, select to the OLE Events tab, and click the Add Event button. When the Add Event dialog box appears, change the external name to KeysPressed and make sure that the internal name is FireKeysPressed. Add two arguments, as you did when you added the WriteTerminalText method. Make the first argument an LPCTSTR and the second a long. Call the LPCTSTR lpText and the long nBytes. Click the OK button to create the OLE event. Visual C++ adds a FireKeysPressed method to CTermCtrl.

The body of FireKeysPressed is done by Visual C++, so there's no reason to modify that function. Instead, edit the code for the OnChar member of CTermCtrl. Earlier, you created the OnChar handler for WM_CHAR, which takes the characters typed by a user and writes them to the terminal display if local echo is enabled. Add a call to FireKeysPressed as follows, so that OnChar passes the characters typed by the user to the container application:

```
    .

    .

if( m_bEcho )
        WriteTermText( (LPCSTR)cbBuff, nRepCnt );
FireKeysPressed( (LPCSTR)cbBuff, nRepCnt );

    .

    .
```

That takes care of outgoing data. If local echo is turned on, OnChar calls WriteTermText to display the data locally. Then FireKeysPressed sends an event notification to the client, passing the string to send out and the length.

Although you're done with the interface that makes the container send data to the terminal and the terminal send keys to the container, you have a few things to do before you can call the indirect version of the terminal control complete. You still have to provide a way for the container to enable or disable local echo and change the terminal's display colors. (You make calls to GetForeColor and GetBackColor in OnDraw to get the foreground and background stock properties.)

To add a property that sets local echo on and off, open the ClassWizard, select the OLE Automation tab, and click the Add Property button. When the Add Property dialog box appears, change the external name to LocalEcho, the type to BOOL, and the implementation to Get/Set. Click the OK button. Visual C++ creates two member functions in

TERMCTL.CPP: one called `GetLocalEcho` and the other called `SetLocalEcho`. Following are the `GetLocalEcho` and `SetLocalEcho` functions for the terminal control sample:

```
BOOL CTermCtrl::GetLocalEcho()
{
        return( m_bEcho );
}
void CTermCtrl::SetLocalEcho(BOOL bNewValue)
{
        m_bEcho = bNewValue;
        SetModifiedFlag();
}
```

These functions are straightforward. `GetLocalEcho` returns `m_bEcho`. `SetLocalEcho` sets `m_bEcho` to the new Boolean value passed in and calls `SetModifiedFlag` to indicate that the control properties have changed.

Foreground and background color are stock properties. To add them to your control, open the Add Property dialog box in the ClassWizard. Type **ForeColor** in the **External Name** box and then set the implementation to Stock. Click the OK button. Do the same thing for `BackColor`. That's all you have to do to add stock properties.

Talking Directly to the Serial Port

At this point, you should have a fully functioning terminal emulation control that follows the indirect model described earlier in this chapter. In this section, you take the `CComPort` class from Chapter 3 and make the control talk directly to the COM port. I'll show you how to do this in such a way that you can compile it for both direct and indirect.

The first thing to do is add the COMPORT.CPP and COMPORT.H files, which you created in Chapter 3, to the directory that contains the source for your terminal control. If you didn't create these files in Chapter 3, feel free to grab these files from the Chapter 4 source directory on the CD-ROM that comes with this book. Choose Insert, Files into Project to add COMPORT.CPP to the terminal control project, as you did in Chapter 4.

Use compiler directives when you add code to use the `CComPort` object, so that you can revert to the indirect model. `#ifdef` and `#ifndef` allow you to satisfy conditions before a segment of code is compiled into the control. (Of course, you probably knew that.) Add to COMPORT.CPP a compiler directive that excludes the CComPort member implementations if _TERM_DIRECT is not defined. Add it before the CComPort constructor, as follows:

```
.
.
.
static char THIS_FILE[] = __FILE__;
#endif

#ifdef _TERM_DIRECT
CComPort::CComPort()
{
        m_hComm = INVALID_HANDLE_VALUE;
        m_nTail = 0;
.
.
.
```

Also, add #endif // _TERM_DIRECT as the last line in the file. If _TERM_DIRECT is defined when this module is compiled, the CComPort members are compiled; otherwise, they're excluded.

Do the same thing to COMPORT.H. Open COMPORT.H and add the _TERM_DIRECT compiler directive, as shown in the following code segment:

```
.
.
#define BUFFERSIZE              BUFFER_2K

#ifdef _TERM_DIRECT
class CComPort
{
protected:
        HANDLE m_hComm;                              // Handle to Com Port.
.
.
```

Now go to the end of COMPORT.H and add #endif // _TERM_DIRECT just before the line that reads #endif // _COMPORT_H.

Before you can write code to send and receive data from the COM port, you have to add a `CComPort` object to `CTermCtrl`. To do that, add the COMPORT.H header file to both TERMCTL.CPP and TERMCTL.H. Add the following code segment to the top of both files:

```
#ifdef _TERM_DIRECT
        #include "ComPort.h"
#endif
```

Open TERMCTL.H and add a `CComPort` object to the protected part of the `CTermCtrl` class definition. Modify the file directly instead of using Visual C++, because you need to make inclusion of this stuff conditional, based on `_TERM_DIRECT`. Call the `CComPort` object `m_port`. While you're in there, go ahead and add a character buffer called `szPortName`. Here are the changes that you should make to your source code:

```
        .

        .

protected:

        .

        .

        BOOL m_bEcho;
        BOOL m_bEsc;
#ifdef _TERM_DIRECT
        CComPort m_port;
        char szPortName[10];
#endif
        DECLARE_OLECREATE_EX(CTermCtrl)

        .

        .
```

You'll open the port in `CTermCtrl::OnCreate` by using the name stored in `szPortName`. Somehow, you need to make sure that `szPortName` contains a valid COM port when the terminal control is instantiated. To do that, add the following lines to the `CTermCtrl` constructor after the line that reads `m_bEcho = FALSE`:

```
#ifdef _TERM_DIRECT
        lstrcpy( szPortName, _T( "COM1" ) );
#endif
```

Even though we're not worrying about Unicode, use the _T macro to make sure that the string constant is compiled correctly. Skip to the OnCreate member of CTermCtrl, and make the following changes within the nested conditionals:

```
                    .

                    .
ClearScreen( _TRM_SPC );
#ifdef _TERM_DIRECT
                SetTimer( 42, 55, NULL );
        m_port.OpenPort( szPortName );
#endif
                        return( 0 );

                    .

                    .
```

Because incoming data is stored inside a buffer in the CComPort object, you can use a timer to extract and display the data every 18th of a second without fear of losing data. (In the old days, communications routines were written in assembly so that they could be fast enough to keep up with incoming data. Machines are so fast today that speed is no longer an issue.) The SetTimer call creates a timer that fires every 55 milliseconds. Then the port is opened by calling the OpenPort member of the m_port object, passing the name of the COM port (szPortName).

Don't forget to clean up the port and free the timer. Do that in a handler for the WM_DESTROY message. Add a handler for WM_DESTROY. Visual C++ calls in OnDestroy. Close the port by calling the ClosePort member of the m_port object, and use KillTimer to free the timer resource. Here's what CTermCtrl::OnDestroy looks like:

```
void CTermCtrl::OnDestroy()
{
        COleControl::OnDestroy();
#ifdef _TERM_DIRECT
        m_port.ClosePort();
        KillTimer( 42 );
#endif
}
```

First, OnDestroy calls CComPort::ClosePort to close the port associated with m_port. (ClosePort checks to see that the port is valid before trying to close it.) Then it calls KillTimer to free the timer resource allocated in OnCreate.

You have two changes left to make before the terminal control can talk directly to the COM port (and a few problems that you have to fix before you can compile it). First, you have to change CTermCtrl::OnChar so that it sends keystrokes to the COM port. Then you have to override the OnTimer member of CTermCtrl to handle the timer created on OnCreate. Add the following lines to CTermCtrl::OnChar, just after the FireKeysPressed call:

```
#ifdef _TERM_DIRECT
        m_port.SendString( (LPCSTR)cbBuff, nRepCnt );
#endif
```

m_port's SendString member sends whatever the user types to the port associated with the CComPort object.

Now add a handler for the WM_TIMER message to CTermCtrl. Replace the handler with this OnTimer member for the sample terminal control:

```
void CTermCtrl::OnTimer(UINT nIDEvent)
{
#ifdef _TERM_DIRECT
        int nBytes;

        nBytes = m_port.ReadString( szBuff,
sizeof( szBuff ) );
        if( nBytes )
                WriteTermText( szBuff, nBytes );
#endif
        COleControl::OnTimer(nIDEvent);
}
```

Provided that _TERM_DIRECT is defined, OnTimer calls the ReadString member of the m_port object. ReadString reads data from the CComPort object's receive buffer and returns the number of bytes read. If no data is waiting in the buffer, ReadString returns zero. When ReadString returns a nonzero value, OnTimer passes the contents of the buffer filled by ReadString to WriteTermText. And WriteTermText writes that data to the terminal display.

Notice, though, that szBuff is not defined in CTermCtrl::OnTimer. Add szBuff to the CTermCtrl class definition, just below the declaration of szPortName.

You're finally done with the code that makes the terminal control talk directly to the COM port. But before the terminal control can compile and link, you have to fix the apartment model threading problem that you encountered in Chapter 4 and undefine VC_EXTRALEAN. Fixing the apartment model threading problem is simple. Edit the UpdateRegistry member function of CTermCtrlFactory, which is embedded in the CTermCtrl class (right above the CTermCtrl constructor in TERMCTL.CPP). Change afxRegApartmentThreading in the AfxOleRegisterControlClass call, to 0, just as you did in Chapter 4.

Fixing the VC_EXTRALEAN problem is equally simple. Open the STDAFX.H header file and put conditional compiler directives around the definition of VC_EXTRALEAN, as follows:

```
        .

        .

#ifndef _TERM_DIRECT

        #define VC_EXTRALEAN

#endif

        .

        .
```

As you learned in Chapter 4, the framework excludes the communications functions if VC_EXTRALEAN is defined. Now it's going to be defined only if _TERM_DIRECT is not defined.

To compile the terminal control so that it can access the COM port directly, choose **B**uild, **S**ettings. When the Project Settings dialog box appears, select the C/C++ tab (see Figure 5-3). Add _TERM_DIRECT to the end of the defines in the Preprocessor Definitions list. Click the OK button. Then choose **B**uild, **R**ebuild All to rebuild the terminal control project. If you'd rather have the container handle the COM port, just remove _TERM_DIRECT from the preprocessor definitions and rebuild.

Adding Port Settings to the Properties

The easiest way to handle port settings is to add separate properties for COM port, baud rate, parity, data bits, and stop bits. Then each property is an index in an array of corresponding values. When each property is modified, a call is made to a routine that

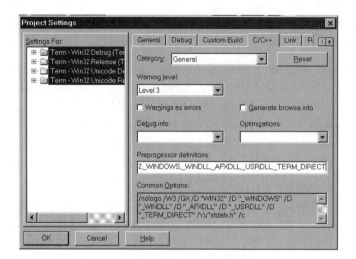

FIGURE 5-3

In the Preprocessor Definitions list, you can define compiler directives, such as `_TERM_DIRECT`.

translates the port settings and calls `CComPort::SetPortSettings`. Because each property is implemented with basically the same code, except for COM port, I'm going to show you how to implement one and let you do the rest. The COM port property is slightly different, so I'll also show you that code.

To implement a COM port property, open the ClassWizard, switch to the OLE Automation tab, and click Add Property. Change the external name to PortName, the type to BSTR, and the implementation to Get/Set. Click the OK button. Visual C++ adds `GetPortName` and `SetPortName` members to your terminal control project. Edit `GetPortName` as follows:

```
BSTR CTermCtrl::GetPortName()
{
        CString strResult;
#ifdef _TERM_DIRECT
        strResult = szPortName;
#else
        strResult = _T( "" );
#endif
        return strResult.AllocSysString();
}
```

Visual C++ puts some code in GetPortName to create a CString object and return a BSTR. Up to now, you've been erasing that code and putting in your own. This time, though, you're adding to it. If _TERM_DIRECT is defined, GetPortName sets the CString, strResult, to the port stored in szPortName. Otherwise, it's set to a blank string. SetPortName, on the other hand, copies the contents of the string passed in to szPortName. Take a look at CTermCtrl::SetPortName:

```
void CTermCtrl::SetPortName(LPCTSTR lpszNewValue)
{
#ifdef _TERM_DIRECT
        lstrcpy( szPortName, lpszNewValue );
        m_port.ClosePort();
        m_port.OpenPort( szPortName );
#endif
        SetModifiedFlag();
}
```

You can't just copy the new port name into szPortName. After you copy in the new port name, you should close the port, using the ClosePort member of m_port, and then open the port again with a call to the OpenPort member. Again, you do this only if _TERM_DIRECT is defined. (Although the properties will be available when you are using an indirect version of the control, they won't do anything.)

To implement a property for baud rate, open the ClassWizard and select the OLE Automation tab. Click the Add Property button. When the Add Property dialog box appears, change the external name to Baudrate, the type to short, and implementation to Get/Set. Click OK to create the property. Edit the GetBaudrate function, making the following changes:

```
short CTermCtrl::GetBaudrate()
{
#ifdef _TERM_DIRECT
        return( nBaudrate );
#endif
        return 0;
}
```

As you can see, it's a piece of cake. If _TERM_DIRECT is defined, GetBaudrate returns a short integer called nBaudrate. If _TERM_DIRECT is not defined, GetBaudrate returns zero.

Don't forget to add a short integer called nBaudrate to your CTermCtrl class definition, within the _TERM_DIRECT conditional compile section that you created earlier. You didn't have to do that for szPortName, because you did it earlier in the chapter.

Following is the corresponding SetBaudrate member:

```
void CTermCtrl::SetBaudrate(short nNewValue)
{
#ifdef _TERM_DIRECT
        if( nNewValue >= 0 && nNewValue <= 9 )
        {
                nBaudrate = nNewValue;
                PortSettingsChanged();
        }
#endif
        SetModifiedFlag();
}
```

SetBaudrate checks to see if the new value is between 0 and 9, because you're going to support 10 valid baud rates: 300, 1200, 2400, 4800, 9600, 7200, 19200, 38400, 57600, and 115200. If the new value is within this range, SetBaudrate sets nBaudrate to the new value and calls a member called PortSettingsChanged. PortSettingsChanged is the function that assembles the port settings and calls the SetPortSettings member of m_port.

Now add the nParity, nDatabits, and nStopbits variables just below nBaudrate in TERMCTL.H. Make them short integers as well. Then use the ClassWizard to add properties called Parity, Databits, and Stopbits. Modify the Get and Set members created by Visual C++ to return and change nParity, nDatabits, and nStopbits.

PortSettingsChanged converts the short integers, which are indexes in lists, into values that you can pass to CComPort::SetPortSettings. Because setting the port settings happens only once in a while and isn't a time-sensitive task, create the lists within the scope of the PortSettingsChanged function, as opposed to creating static lists stored globally or in the CTermCtrl object. Add the following function to the end of TERMCTL.CPP (don't forget to add the prototype to the CTermCtrl class definition):

```
#ifdef _TERM_DIRECT
void CTermCtrl::PortSettingsChanged()
{
        DWORD dwBaudrate[10] = { 300, 1200, 2400, 4800,
                7200, 9600, 19200, 38400, 57600, 115200 };
        BYTE cbParity[4] = { NOPARITY, EVENPARITY,
                ODDPARITY, MARKPARITY };
        BYTE cbDatabits[2] = { 8, 7 };
        BYTE cbStopbits[2] = { 1, 2 };


        m_port.SetPortSettings( dwBaudrate[ nBaudrate ],
                cbParity[ nParity ], cbDatabits[ nDatabits ],
                cbStopbits[ nStopbits ] );
}
#endif
```

dwBaudrate, cbParity, cbDatabits, and cbStopbits are arrays that contain values used to set the port settings. The short integers that you set up earlier are used as indexes in those arrays. You make references directly to the arrays in the call to SetPortSettings because each index is validated as the corresponding property is set, so there's no need to validate here. You need to make sure that the short integer indexes are initialized in the constructor for CTermCtrl.

> **NOTE:** When you add the prototype for PortSettingsChanged to the CTermCtrl class definition, be sure to enclose it in a _TERM_DIRECT conditional. You want to add this function only if you're compiling with _TERM_DIRECT defined.

Modifying the Properties Dialog Box

To finish the terminal control, add some stuff to the properties dialog box. Add a property sheet that allows the user to modify the foreground and background colors, and modify the default property sheet to include port settings. MFC provides a stock property sheet called CColorPropPage to handle the foreground and background properties.

Open TERMCTL.CPP, and find the line that contains the BEGIN_PROPPAGEIDS macro call. Change the number of property pages from 1 to 2. Also, add a line below the definition for the first property page that calls the PROPPAGEID macro, passing CLSID_CColorPropPage—the ID for the CColorPropPage stock property sheet. Your changes should look something like this:

```
BEGIN_PROPPAGEIDS(CTermCtrl, 2)
      PROPPAGEID(CTermPropPage::guid)
      PROPPAGEID( CLSID_CColorPropPage )
END_PROPPAGEIDS(CTermCtrl)
```

That's all there is to it. When the container displays the properties dialog box, a property sheet called Color appears. From this tab, you can set both the foreground and background of the terminal control.

Modifying the default property page is a bit more of a hassle. Switch to resource view, and expand the Dialog folder. Double-click IDD_PROPPAGE_TERM to modify the dialog-box template for the default property page. Add controls for each of the properties supported by the terminal. Use drop-down lists for COM port, baud rate, and parity. Use radio buttons for data bits and stop bits, and use a check box for local echo. Figure 5-4 shows the dialog-box template for the sample terminal control.

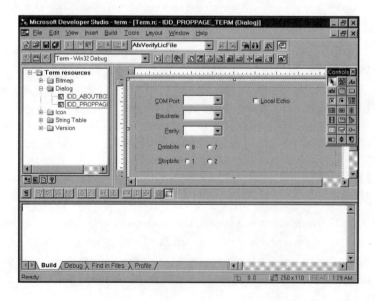

FIGURE 5-4

From this property page, you can change the port, baud rate, parity, data bits, stop bits, and even local echo.

If you double-click a control in the dialog-box editor, the properties for that item are displayed. Do that for the drop-down list that corresponds to the COM port. Visual C++ displays the Combo Box Properties dialog box, shown in Figure 5-5.

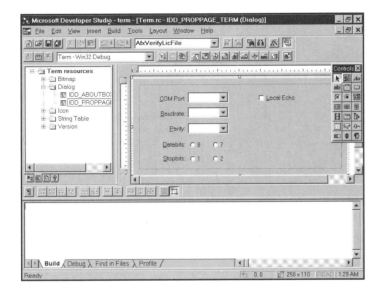

FIGURE 5-5

In the Combo Box Properties dialog box, you can provide a list of items to be contained with the list box.

To keep from having to add code to the CTermPropPage class, you can add the items that will appear in the list boxes to the list box on the right side of the Combo Box Properties dialog box. Press Enter or close the dialog box to continue.

> **TIP:** Pressing Ctrl + Enter when you type in the list-box contents field allows you to enter multiple items. When you are entering baud-rate values, type **300** and then press Ctrl + Enter; type **1200** and press Ctrl + Enter; and so on. The order of the items in your list boxes must correspond to the order of the short integer arrays that you created in CTermCtrl::PortSettingsChanged.

In Chapter 2, you learned how to tie the controls in a property sheet to OLE properties defined in your controls. Hold down the Ctrl key, and double-click the control associated with the COM port. Visual C++ displays the Add Member Variable dialog box. Provide a name for the member variable that you want to associate with the control (it doesn't have to be the same as the variable name used in CTermCtrl). In the Optional **OLE** Property

Name box, type the name of the property that this control should be associated with. Associate the COM port control with the PortName property, as shown in Figure 5-6.

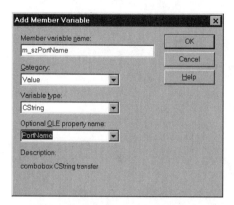

FIGURE 5-6

Using this dialog box, you can easily associate the controls in a dialog box with OLE properties.

Now take some time to tie the rest of the controls in the default property page to the terminal control's properties. When you finish, you're ready to plug the terminal control into a test application.

Testing Your Emulator Control

Use the MFC AppWizard to create a project workspace called TstTerm. Make it a single document interface application support for OLE controls, similar to what you did with the TstCon application in Chapter 4. After you create the framework, open the Component Gallery by choosing Insert, Component. Select the OLE Controls tab, select the Term Control object, and click the Insert button to add it to the TstTerm project. (Click OK in the Confirm Classes dialog box to accept the default settings.) Close the Component Gallery.

Visual C++ creates files called TERM.H and TERM.CPP when you add the terminal control to the TstTerm project. They're the implementation files for the CTerm class generated by the Component Gallery. Add a CTerm object declaration to CTstTermView, and call it m_term. Next, open TSTTERMVIEW.CPP and add a handler for WM_CREATE. Make the following changes in the OnCreate member function:

```
int CTstTermView::OnCreate(
LPCREATESTRUCT lpCreateStruct)
{
        if (CView::OnCreate(lpCreateStruct) == -1)
                return -1;

        m_term.Create( NULL, WS_VISIBLE, CRect(
                0, 0, 640, 480 ), this, 0 );
        m_term.SetPortName( "COM1" );

        return 0;
}
```

To instantiate the terminal control, call the Create member of the m_term wrapper object. Then make a call to SetPortName to close the default port and open the port to which the modem is attached. All you have to do to make the terminal control talk to your modem is change COM1 in the SetPortName call to the port used by your modem.

Now include the TERM.H file at the top of TSTTERMVIEW.H. After you do that, compile and run the TstTerm app. Your TstTerm application should look something like the one shown in Figure 5-7.

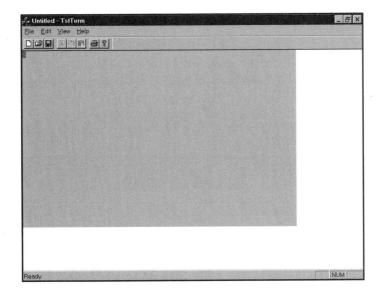

FIGURE 5-7

This TstTerm application instantiates the terminal control object.

To use the terminal control, click in the client area of the TstTerm application, type **AT**, and press Enter. You should see an OK response from your modem. Feel free to dial a local computer bulletin-board number to see how the terminal control works. But bear in mind that this is a simple TTY emulation. You're likely to see some garbage here and there, because most computer bulletin boards use ANSI.

> **NOTE:** Experiment with the TstTerm application. Add a Port Settings menu that allows you to change the baud rate, parity, data bits, stop bits, and local echo. In response to changes in those settings, call the appropriate members of the CTerm wrapper object.

Nifty Things to Do with the Emulator

As I pointed out in previous chapters, I don't like to leave the chapters hanging. I think it's important to give you some direction after you finish a chapter, so that you won't file this information away in the recesses of your mind and never use it. So I'd like to talk a little bit about what you can do with what you've learned in this chapter.

Understanding Attributes

You learned about the differences between full screen and painted attributes earlier. You also learned how to implement the more complicated terminal emulation sequences (those that have more than 1 byte). How hard would it be to add support for color, bold-face, underlining, italics, and reversed text to your terminal control?

The first thing that you want to do is come up with some sequences. You could use the earlier example of a left bracket followed by a number. 0 through 3 could represent the foreground color; 4 through 7 could represent the background color. Then A through D could represent boldface, underlining, italics, and reversed text.

Next, you need to decide whether your attributes are going to be full screen or painted. Painted attributes are more flexible.

To use painted attributes, you have to use three screen buffers. You already have one that stores the text as it's displayed to the end user. The second and third buffers contain bytes that tell your container which attributes affect the characters stored in the first screen buffer. A byte in the second buffer, or color buffer, may look like Figure 5-8.

1	**0**	**Black**
2	**1**	**Lt. Blue**
4	**2**	**Lt. Red**
8	**3**	**Lt. Green**
16	**4**	**Black**
32	**5**	**Blue**
64	**6**	**Red**
128	**7**	**Green**

FIGURE 5-8

A breakdown of a color byte.

A byte in the third buffer is going to look exactly like the byte in Figure 5-8, except that the bits represent boldface, underlining, italics, and reversed text. You can reserve the extra bits in the bytes of the third buffer for future attributes. Alternatively, you can use more bits in the bytes of the second buffer for foreground color; use part of the bits in the third for background color; and use the rest for the text style.

Using ASCII Instead of ANSI

You can use two basic character sets in an emulator. So far, you have been using an ANSI font. (ANSI fonts contain characters approved by the American National Standards Institute.) You can't do this, though, if your emulator is going to be connected to online services and computer bulletin boards. Online services and computer bulletin boards rely on the high-bit characters of the ASCII (or OEM) character set. (*High-bit* means that the 8th bit in a byte is turned on. This includes characters with values from 128 to 255.)

For the most part, the ANSI-vs.-OEM problem affects only high-bit characters, which are used to display graphics such as lines and boxes. Online services and computer bulletin boards rely on the ASCII character set because the high-bit characters include a full set of line-drawing characters, whereas the ANSI character set does not. The challenge is to make the terminal control use an ASCII (or OEM) font, rather than an ANSI font. A related challenge is to modify the terminal control so that the container can specify the font: either ANSI or OEM.

Making a Real Terminal

Throughout the course of this chapter, you have created a simple terminal emulation called TTY. TTY is the most basic type of terminal emulation; it's not good for anything other than basic communication between two computers. To make the control marketable, you have to support (at minimum) the ANSI emulation. To make any money at all, you have to support a wide variety of terminal emulations. A few that come to mind are TVI925, Vidtex, VT100, and Wyse 50, which are common in the mainframe world.

How do you go about turning the terminal control that you've created into a real terminal emulator? In this chapter, you implemented complicated emulation sequences. Get hold of a few manuals for the actual terminals themselves (buy the terminals). Terminal manuals usually outline all the sequences that the terminal supports. Then it's simply a matter of adding support for those sequences to the terminal control's state machine. (You may need to rethink the design of the state machine before you tackle some of the more complex terminal emulations, such as Vidtex.)

> **NOTE:** Your best bet for finding information on terminals is to do a search on the Web. Wyse, for example, has all kinds of information about its terminals at www.wyse.com. To find information on ANSI, search for the ANSI 3.64 standard of the American National Standards Institute (www.ansi.org).

Chapter Summary

Even with the Internet craze, there's still a place for terminal programs—especially in the solutions market. While working through this chapter, you learned how to create a terminal emulator. You wrote code to handle the caret, display text, and scroll the contents of the control's window. In addition, you learned how to create both indirect and direct versions of the terminal emulator control.

Chapter 6, "Talking to the Internet," introduces some important concepts in Internet programming. You're introduced to Windows sockets, and you learn a little bit about the Internet. In addition, the chapter shows you some common Internet programs to jump-start your imagination.

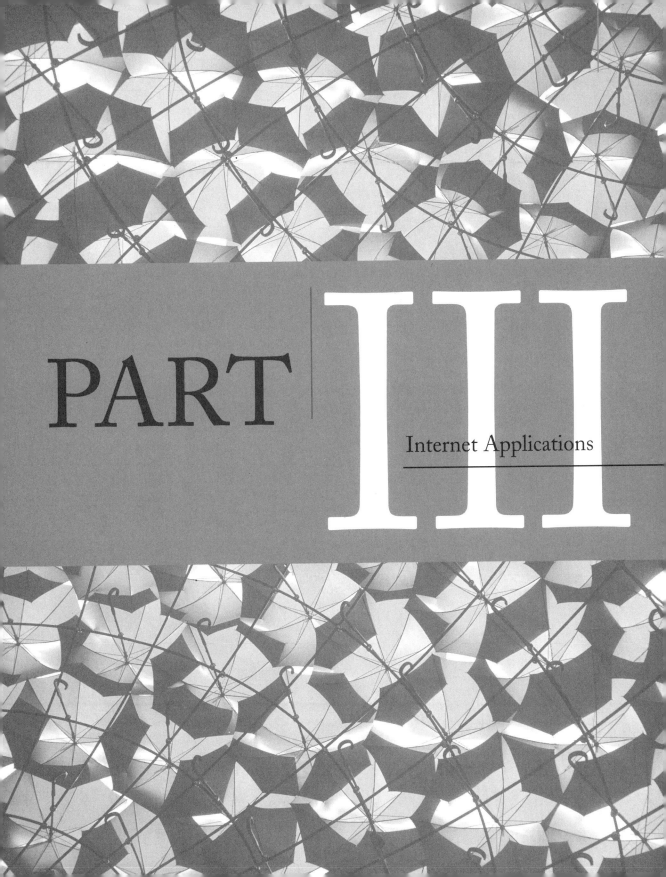

PART III

Internet Applications

Chapter | 6

Talking to the Internet

by Markus Pope

A few years back, the online community took a 90-degree focus swing, from personal computers running bulletin boards, and it has been moving at light speed ever since. Where's it going? It's barreling down what the press likes to refer to as the Information Superhighway. (We call it the Internet.)

In the first part of this book, you learned the basics of modem programming, because (even though the focus has changed) modems still play a big role in how home users connect to the Internet. To get a 24-hour direct connection to the Internet, you'd end up paying close to $700 a month. (That's way too steep for me.) You can get a 28.8 modem for a little more than $100 and an Internet Service Provider for $20 a month. Also, learning modem technology is important, because the principles applied there are also applied in Internet programming.

Although learning the modem technology is important, it's doubtful that you'll make a great deal of money entering the terminal emulator market this late in the game. For that reason, let's spend the rest of the book talking about how to write Internet applications.

As Chapter 3 was an introduction to modem technology, this chapter is an introduction to Internet technology. A billion books cover how the Internet works, though, so I just want to touch on a few concepts that will help you in writing the Internet clients in chapters 7 through 13.

This chapter covers the following topics:

- ◆ An introduction to Windows sockets
- ◆ Communicating with Internet servers
- ◆ Applications used on the Internet

Introducing Windows Sockets

Windows talks to the Internet through an interface known as Windows sockets. *Windows sockets* is an API layer that's sandwiched between the application and TCP/IP services. TCP/IP is the transport protocol used to package data and transport it across the Net. TCP/IP makes sure that the data sent by the client is the same as the data received by the host, or server.

The Windows sockets API is based on the sockets implementation used in BSD UNIX. The Berkeley guys came up with sockets (instead of some other implementation) to both standardize and generalize access to TCP/IP services. But they may not have had any idea that sockets would soon become the de facto way of communicating with TCP/IP networks. Later, Berkeley and Microsoft added asynchronous extensions to implement sockets under Windows.

Berkeley's Implementation of Sockets

Berkeley's implementation of sockets is handled through input and output streams—in other words, the file system. After creating a socket, the programmer has a handle to the socket that can be used with any of the stream I/O functions, such as getc and putc. (This implementation is good because it takes advantage of the standard input and output mechanism of the operating system.) We're not going to spend a lot of time on Berkeley sockets. We'll talk about Berkeley sockets briefly, so that you can understand the differences between it and the Windows implementation.

Even though sockets are implemented in the file system in UNIX, files and sockets are created in different ways. To create a file, you simply call the C standard function open. open prepares a file for I/O and assigns a file descriptor that is tracked by the operating system.

When creating a socket, though, you make a call to a function called socket, which creates a socket, prepares the socket for I/O, and returns a descriptor. File descriptors and socket descriptors are basically the same, except that the operating system stores different data structures for each.

After getting a socket descriptor, you can call connect (another sockets-specific function) to make a connection to a host system. To send and receive data on the socket, you make calls to the standard read and write functions. Then, to close the socket, you simply call close, just as you do to close a file. You use a slew of other functions when you create an Internet client, but this gives you the general idea.

The Windows Sockets API (WINSOCK.DLL)

Windows implements sockets through a DLL called WINSOCK.DLL — WSOCK32.DLL in Windows 95 and Windows NT. For simplicity's sake, I'll refer to both DLLs (16-bit and 32-bit) as *Winsock*. Winsock provides the same functionality as Berkeley's sockets, except that the implementation is adapted slightly to account for

Windowsisms. It's interesting to look at changes made to sockets for the Windows operating system.

In Windows, an application can call a function, have that function return immediately, and then signal the application when the function performed by the application is complete. For that reason, WSAAsync calls were added. To connect to a host system by using a socket, you have to have a HOSTENT structure that describes that host. In Berkeley's implementation of sockets, you call gethostbyname or gethostbyaddr to fill in the HOSTENT structure.

Winsock provides asynchronous versions of those two functions: WSAAsyncGetHostByName and WSAAsyncGetHostByAddr. When WSAAsyncGetHostByName is called, you pass it a HOSTENT structure and a message. It returns immediately and then sends the specified message to your application's window when it's done filling in the HOSTENT structure. gethostbyname is a blocking call. When gethostbyname is called, it doesn't return until an error occurs or it finishes filling in the HOSTENT.

Because the WSAAsync calls are nonblocking calls, the application can call them, go off and do something else, and then handle the results as they arrive. That's the main difference between Winsock's implementation of sockets and Berkeley's. To get this event-driven model in UNIX, you have to spawn, and keep track of, new threads (as you did with the CComPort object in Chapter 4).

MFC's Implementation of Windows Sockets

MFC provides some helpful wrapper classes that take most of the yucky out of programming Winsock. CAsyncSocket is the first layer of abstraction. It wraps the Winsock API and supplies some virtual functions for certain events. (Events for sending and receiving data accept incoming connection, close, connect, and out-of-band data.)

CSocket is the next layer of abstraction. It inherits from CAsyncSocket. There's not much to the CSocket class; most of the work is done in CAsyncSocket. CSocket is provided so that you can associate a socket with a CArchive object. Archives make sending and receiving data easier, as you'll see in later chapters of this book.

So with MFC, you have two ways to write an Internet client:

♦ You can create a class based on CAsyncSocket and handle most of the network details yourself.

♦ You can create a CSocket object, associate it with a CArchive object, and read and write to it by using the standard C++ redirection operators (>> and <<). In the next chapter, you use CAsyncSocket by itself. Then, in Chapter 8, you switch to CSocket and associate the CSocket object with a CArchive.

Connecting to a Host System

Before we go any further, make sure that you understand the roles played by the Internet client, host, and server. When we refer to a *client*, we're talking about an application that creates a socket and tries to connect to another system on the Net. A *host*, on the other hand, is the system that the client application is trying to connect to. Nowadays, *host* and *server* are synonymous. You can see the client–server relationship in Figure 6-1.

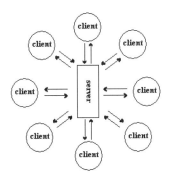

FIGURE 6-1

Shown here is the relationship between clients and their server.

Servers provide services of some kind. FTP servers, for example, allow clients to connect, navigate directories, and download files. Finger servers provide information about users and various other things. I'll explain more about Internet services in "Using Common Internet Applications" later in this chapter. (Most of the example Internet addresses in this chapter are Web addresses, because the Web is the most popular service provided on the Internet.)

Three things happen when a client wants to connect to a server:

♦ A socket is created and associated with a CSocket or CAsyncSocket object.

♦ The server's name (in the form www.microsoft.com) or address (in the form 123.123.123.123) is resolved into a network address that Winsock understands.

♦ The client connects to the server and then begins to send and receive data.

Creating a Socket

Creating a socket in MFC is easy. First, you create a new class that's derived from CAsyncSocket. You derive a new class so that you can override virtual functions (OnConnect, OnReceive, OnClose, and so on) to handle events that occur on the socket.

Suppose that you created a class called CMySocket and derive it from CAsyncSocket. After you create the new socket class, you need to instantiate it. In an MFC application, the view is a good place to put your CMySocket object. That way, if your application supports the multiple document interface (MDI), a new socket can be created for each view. (An MDI app has multiple views.)

Optionally, you can derive your new class from CSocket. If you do that, you should also create a CSocketFile and a CArchive object to associate with the new socket class. I'll get into the details of how to use CSocket in Chapter 8; right now, let's concentrate on the basics of using CAsyncSocket.

Now that the CMySocket object is instantiated, you can create a socket to attach to that CMySocket. You can do that in either of two ways. If you're bent on using the Winsock API to create your socket, you can make a call to the socket API; otherwise, CAsyncSocket::socket creates a socket and returns a descriptor. Then you can call the Attach member of CAsyncSocket to associate the new socket with CMySocket. Here's how you attach a socket to CMySocket:

```
    .
    .
    .
SOCKET hSocket;
CMySocket socket;
hSocket = socket( PF_INET, SOCK_STREAM, 0 );
if( hSocket != INVALID_SOCKET )
{
        socket.Attach( hSocket );
    .
    .
    .
}
    .
    .
    .
```

Alternatively, you can call the `Create` member of `CAsyncSocket`. `CAsyncSocket::Create` creates the socket for you and automatically associates it with the `CMySocket` object. (`CMySocket` inherits the `Create` member from `CAsyncSocket`.) To use the `CAsyncSocket::Create`, you'd do something like this:

```
.
.
.
CMySocket socket;
if( socket.Create( ) )
{
        .
        .

}
.
.
.
```

Understanding Name Resolution

Now that the socket is created, the next step is to connect it to another computer system on the Net. Back in the old days, before Microsoft gave us the `CAsyncSocket` and `CSocket` classes, connecting to a host system wasn't very straightforward unless you already knew the IP address. Typically, though, you don't have those addresses memorized. Instead of using the actual IP address, you specify the domain name of the host (`www.yahoo.com`, for example).

But TCP/IP doesn't know what the heck `www.yahoo.com` means. TCP/IP requires the address of the system to which the domain name is assigned. How do you get the address of a domain? In versions of Visual C++ earlier than 2.1, you made a call to `gethostbyname` or `WSAAsyncGetHostByName` in Winsock. You passed a `HOSTENT` structure to one of those functions, which is filled with the address of a host with the domain specified. Now, thanks to Microsoft, you only have to pass in either the domain name or the IP when you make a connection; `CAsyncSocket` takes care of the details. The following code segment shows how to create a socket and initiate a connection to a server:

```
        .

        .

    CMySocket socket;
    if( socket.Create( ) )
    {
            socket.Connect( "compuserve.com", 23 );

                    .

                    .

    }

        .

        .
```

Even though CAsyncSocket takes care of name resolution for you, it's good to have an idea of what's going on behind the smoke and mirrors. When you call CAsyncSocket::Connect, CAsyncSocket checks to see if what you passed in is an IP address. If not, it calls gethostbyname to resolve the domain name to an address.

gethostbyname looks in your hosts file (there's one included with every stack) and looks for an address that corresponds to the domain name. If you don't have the domain name with a corresponding address in your hosts files, Winsock makes a connection to your domain name server (DNS). The DNS looks up the domain in a database and returns the address.

Sending and Receiving Data

Sending data on a socket is a lot like sending data to a modem by means of the WriteFile function, except that instead of using WriteFile, you use a member of CAsyncSocket called Send. CAsyncSocket::Send takes a buffer and the buffer's size as arguments. (You can also specify some flags, but they're not important.) CAsyncSocket::Send returns the number of characters written to the socket.

Winsock maintains a transmit buffer for you. CAsyncSocket::Send calls the Winsock API function, send. send puts data in the outgoing buffer, and Winsock sends it over the socket. Because the outgoing data is buffered, you can get into a situation in which CAsyncSocket::Send can't send all the data that you requested. In that case, the number of bytes written returned by CAsyncSocket::Send is less than the number of bytes requested.

> **NOTE:** I've never seen a situation in which the transmit buffers are stuffed so full that `CAsyncSocket::Send` or Winsock's `send` writes only part of the data requested. Of course, I've never tried to write a terabyte, or even a gigabyte, to a socket with just one call, so maybe it's possible.

Receiving is a bit more complex. When you send data out in an Internet client, you typically send short command strings; you don't need to do anything fancy. But in response to those commands, you could end up with a lot of data, so you have to come up with a way to receive data and make it useful to the container application.

To receive data, you simply call `CAsyncSocket::Receive`, and pass it a buffer and its length as arguments. But where do you put it? `CAsyncSocket` provides a virtual function called `OnReceive`, and that's where you put your call to `CAsyncSocket::Receive`. Provided that your socket was created with the `FD_READ` flag, `OnReceive` is called any time data is received on the socket. The code segment that follows is a sample implementation of `CMySocket::OnReceive`:

```
void CMySocket::OnReceive( int nError )
{
        char szBuffer[256];
        int nBytes;
        nBytes = Receive( szBuffer, sizeof( szBuffer ) );
        while( nBytes && nBytes != SOCKET_ERROR )
        {
                .
                .
                nBytes = Receive( szBuffer, sizeof( szBuffer ) );
        }
}
```

> **NOTE:** You need to note two things here. First, the flags parameter on `CAsyncSocket::Create` defaults to `FD_READ`, `FD_WRITE`, `FD_OOB`, `FD_ACCEPT`, `FD_CONNECT`, and `FD_CLOSE`. Because there's little overhead in enabling all these events, it's rarely needed to specify flags when calling the `Create` member. Second, read data from the buffer until `CAsyncSocket::Receive` returns 0 bytes read or `SOCKET_ERROR`, which ensures that Winsock's receive buffer is empty.

What you do with the data that you're receiving is most likely a function of the application that you're writing. For a control, where you need to pass that data back to a container, the best way may be to write the data to a file. But you can also apply the buffering technique that you learned in Chapter 4 (in building the CComPort class) and return data to the container as it's received.

You have enough background information that you won't be lost when you start building Internet controls in Chapter 7. Before you start whipping out controls, though, take a break to learn about some common Internet applications. I hope that this discussion will give you a good idea of what your controls need to do.

Using Common Internet Applications

Since the beginning of the Internet explosion at the start of this decade, thousands—maybe even hundreds of thousands—of Internet clients have been written. Some clients talk to vending machines; some provide real-time video from real-time cameras; and others allow you to work robot arms at research facilities. Of all those applications, a handful are used daily by most people. The following sections discuss some of those applications.

Finger and WHOIS

When you want information on someone or something, you're most likely going to use finger or WHOIS clients. Finger clients connect you to host systems and inquire about any topic—anything from a user's name to information about a product to the status of a device connected to the Internet. WHOIS, on the other hand, is used only to retrieve information on a user or domain name.

CFinger, a program written by Charles Wells (a shareware author), is a good example of a combined finger/WHOIS client. Figure 6-2 shows the main window of CFinger version 1.1. You type the search criteria in the [User]@Host field and then click the **F**inger button to do a finger query or **W**HOIS to do a WHOIS query. The only thing odd about this app (and you'll want to avoid doing this yourself) is the fact that the File menu uses *i* as an accelerator instead of *f*.

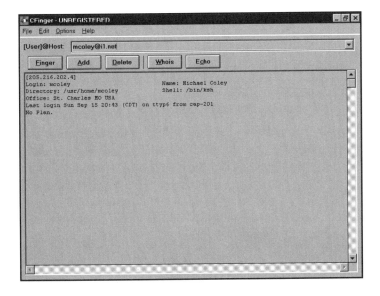

FIGURE 6-2

*Type the name of the user you want to find and the host you want to search; then click the **Finger** button. CFinger 1.1 goes out and grabs the requested information.*

News and Mail

News and mail applications are some of the most frequently used Internet clients of all. These clients are architecturally the same; the differences are in the way that messages are retrieved and responded to (protocol differences). News messages have To and From fields, subjects, date and time stamps, and a message body; so do mail messages. Therefore, most news and mail clients look the same. Figures 6-3 and 6-4 show two popular news and mail applications: News Xpress and Eudora. Notice how similar they are in design.

In a news client, you see a list of topics. After you select a topic, the news reader downloads the headers for the messages. Then you can read and respond to messages under the topic that you selected. News, as opposed to mail, is not private (not as private as mail can be, anyway). News is an open forum, like the message areas on a computer bulletin board.

Mail, on the other hand, is not forum-based. Instead of replying and posting on a newsgroup, you converse one-on-one with someone else on the Net—that is, you send mail to a specific account. (You can send mail to multiple people, though, depending on the mail client that you're using.)

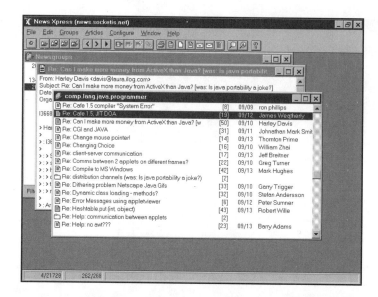

FIGURE 6-3

News Xpress is a public-domain news reader.

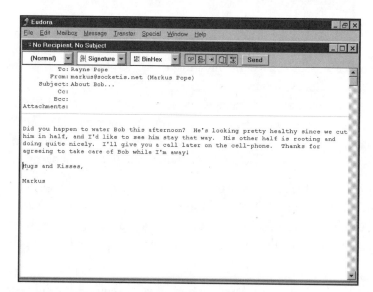

FIGURE 6-4

Eudora, by Qualcomm, is the most popular Internet mail client in use today. Qualcomm has both a freeware version and a commercial version.

FTP and Gopher

FTP and Gopher are grouped together because they are alike in design, but they are still quite different. FTP tends to either be command-line-driven or to use an interface like that shown in Figure 6-5. Gopher, on the other hand, fits a tree-style model, as in the HGopher application shown in Figure 6-6.

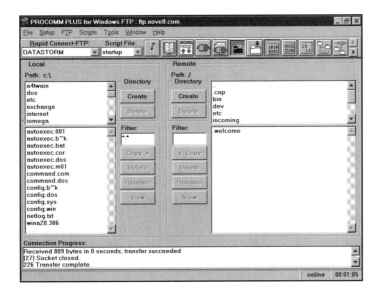

FIGURE 6-5

Although the FTP client that comes with Procomm Plus is not the most popular FTP client used on the Internet, I think it's the easiest to use.

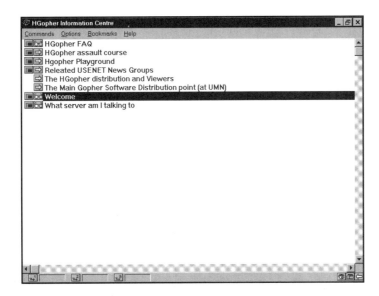

FIGURE 6-6

HGopher, by Martyn Hampson, gives you a nice clean interface for document retrieval.

As you can see in Figure 6-5, FTP is a file-transfer utility. (*FTP* is an acronym for *File Transfer Protocol*.) FTP allows you to connect to a server on the Net and then manipulate the file and directory structure of the host computer. You can move, copy, delete, and view files; you can also remove and create directories, as well as navigate through directory trees.

Gopher is similar to FTP, except that it's geared more toward document search and retrieval. Instead of connecting to a server and allowing you to manipulate a file and directory structure, Gopher gives you structured access to a list of documents. You can easily search for information within the document structure. Many people consider Gopher to be the predecessor of the World Wide Web.

World Wide Web

The latest craze on the Internet is the World Wide Web. Like Gopher, the Web is a document-retrieval system. Documents on the Web, however, can (and almost always do) contains links to other documents, and the links can be for documents that aren't even on the server that you're connected to. It's sort of like a hypertext document (OK, a lot like a hypertext document).

As the Internet gains popularity, new Internet users are becoming more and more computer-illiterate—which isn't bad. Because new users are less technical and the Internet is technical by nature, the Internet needs an interface that's easy to use, nonthreatening, and entertaining. Because the Web is so easy to navigate, and because its document format supports multimedia (sounds, graphics, and so on), the Web has become the standard way of getting information off the Net. Among the most popular Web browsers are Netscape and Microsoft's Internet Explorer (shown in Figure 6-7).

> **NOTE:** You can get the latest versions of the example applications you've seen in this section by querying on their names. Lycos (at www.lycos.com), Yahoo (at www.yahoo.com), and AltaVista (at www.altavista.com) are three places to perform searches.

FIGURE 6-7

Internet Explorer, by Microsoft, ships with Windows 95 Plus!.

Chapter Summary

Internet programming is not difficult to grasp; you only need to understand a few simple concepts. This chapter constructed the foundation for those concepts. You know how Internet programs work, you know the tools needed to build them, and you've seen some example Internet applications. Now you're ready to start working on Internet components.

Chapter 7, "Plug-in Ping," is your first attempt at providing Internet solutions by using the ActiveX controls technology. Chapter 7 builds a Ping utility. Ping is a simple utility that lets you query for servers on the Net (find out whether a system exists). Chapter 7 puts the knowledge that you gained in this chapter to practical use.

Chapter | 7

Plug-in Ping

---

by Edward B. Toupin

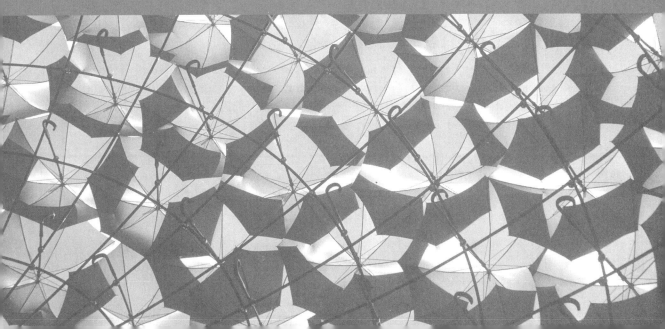

As more and more hosts are added to the Internet, a means of determining the connection status of each host has been developed to determine whether a host is actually communicating. In addition, you may at times simply want to see if a particular host is available for an operation such as FTP, TALK, or WWW browsing. This chapter outlines the well-known Ping utility. Ping allows you to go out onto the Internet and, just like a submarine's sonar, send a message and wait for a response from a target remote host.

Ping is an excellent debugging tool for networks. With Ping, you can query for the status of hosts to determine whether that host or even the subnet is operational. This query operation is performed by means of a simple echo operation, also named a *heartbeat*, which allows the querying node to send a packet and receive a response from a remote host a repetitive number of times.

To provide a foundation for your understanding, this chapter covers the following topics:

- ◆ Overview of Ping and the ECHO protocol
- ◆ Introducing the `CSocket` object
- ◆ Connecting to a Ping-enabled host
- ◆ Requesting a heartbeat
- ◆ Disconnecting
- ◆ Additional features of Ping

What Is Ping?

Ping (Packet Internet Groper) is not a protocol but a simple utility that allows you to test the accessibility of a certain site, as well as to verify the access time of the site. Ping sends out packets of information that go to the system you are Pinging and waits for the remote system to return those packets to your system. The operation of this utility can tell you three things:

- ◆ Whether contact can be established
- ◆ Efficiency of data transfer between the remote site and your site
- ◆ Accuracy of data transfer between the remote site and your site

Using the ECHO protocol, Ping can tell you if a connection is possible, how fast the information can be transferred between sites, and the accuracy of the transfer of the data.

Each of these three elements is essential in optimal performance and communications on the Internet.

The ECHO protocol (RFC 862) itself (see Figure 7-1) is very simple and is based on the master/slave model. In this model, when a query is sent from the master, the slave simply provides a response. With ECHO, the slave simply returns the data that was issued by the originating master.

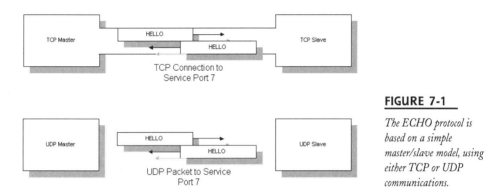

FIGURE 7-1

The ECHO protocol is based on a simple master/slave model, using either TCP or UDP communications.

ECHO has two possible modes of operation: TCP and UDP. The TCP-based echo service is connection oriented via TCP at TCP service port 7. Once a connection is established, any data received is sent back. The echo operation continues until the master terminates the connection.

The UDP-based echo service is a datagram-based UDP operation. A slave listens for UDP datagrams on UDP service port 7 and returns the master's original message to the master.

The *CSocket* Class

Throughout this book, we will be providing examples of protocol implementations, using both Winsock API calls and the CSocket class that has been made part of MFC. The primary purpose of CSocket is to encapsulate the functionality of the Winsock API to provide a simple and robust means of communication on the Internet.

To use a CSocket object, you merely have to call the constructor and then call Create to create the underlying socket handle of type SOCKET. The default parameters of Create create a stream socket, but you can specify a parameter to create a datagram socket instead, or bind to a specific port to create a server socket. Once the specific socket is created, you can begin to send and receive information across the Internet, using calls to Connect, Send, and Receive.

Using a CSocket object involves creating and associating several MFC class objects. As shown in Figure 7-2, a CSocket-based client and server are simple to set up for the establishment of communications, using the encapsulated Winsock API in conjunction with other MFC classes.

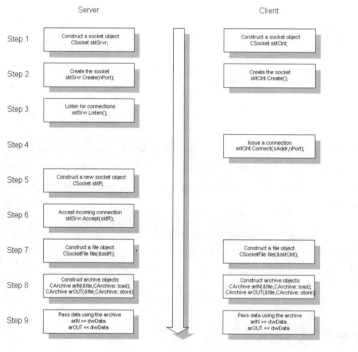

FIGURE 7-2

The CSocket *class allows you to create and communicate via sockets using the encapsulated Winsock API, as well as to combine functionality with other classes of MFC.*

The first step (Step 1) required for communications using the CSocket class is constructing an object of the class. This operation creates an instance of the class for use in establishing a socket and using the members and methods for communications.

Once the object is created, an underlying socket handle of type SOCKET must be created, using the Create method (Step 2). This socket handle is the primary connection through which information will flow between both client and server. Notice the differences in the way that the client and server create the socket. The server creates a socket with a specific port number, whereas the client creates a socket without providing a port number. The port-number assignment of the server provides a common service port, so that the client knows where it needs to connect to access the services of the server.

> **TIP:** At run time, it is customary to have the server side of a prospective connection running first, so that it can be ready and in a listen state when the client application requests a connection.

In preparation for a connection, in Step 3 the server listens for connections being requested by remote clients (Step 4). In this mode, the server merely waits for clients to issue TCP-based connect requests. Notice that since we are using the default parameters in the Create method of Step 2, we are creating a stream (connection-oriented TCP) connection. In this manner, we can have the server wait for connections issued by clients using the Connect method. If we had defined a connectionless (UDP) method of communications, we could not use the Listen method in the server, since single packets would be sent, as opposed to actual connect requests.

> **TIP:** When you are using the Connect method, machine addresses can take several forms. You can provide the name of the host (for example, toupin.com or csn.net) or the dotted notation IP address (for example, 137.62.67.28). The Connect method checks to see whether the address is a dotted number; if not, it assumes a host name.

Once a connect request is received by the server, a new CSocket instance is created (Step 5) and the Accept method is called with that new CSocket instance (Step 6). This operation establishes a connection between a socket handle in the new CSocket instance and the remote client making the connect request. This operation completes the connection establishment between the remote client and the server.

> **NOTE:** The reason that a TCP-based server uses two sockets for connection establishment has to do with the fact that the first socket is primarily for listening. Once the listening socket receives a connect request, the second socket is the one through which actual communications with the remote client occur.

Upon connection establishment, we create a file object of the CSocketFile class (Step 7) and one of two CArchive objects for the client and the server (Step 8). The CArchive objects provide a buffering mechanism for writing or reading serializable objects to or from the CSocketFile or CFile object. Normally, the CFile object represents a disk file, but CSocketFile allows CArchive to write serialized data out of the socket associated with the CSocketFile instance.

> **CAUTION:** Since datagrams are unreliable, they are not compatible with serialization supported by CArchive. This means that CArchive and a datagram CSocket object will not work together.

Upon completion of the operations of exchanging data between the client and the server, all the connections close when the respective objects lose scope or are deleted. This provides a clean way of closing all connections. You must be careful, however, not to simply allow the object's destructors to handle the closing of all connections for all Internet protocols. You will find that in some cases, it is important to close the connections yourself, to ensure that the other end of the connection properly closed its connection first.

Ping Custom Control Architecture

The Ping custom control provides several members and methods (see Listing 7-1) for access by container applications such as Visual Basic, Delphi, and Visual FoxPro. When certain members are assigned values, the associated property procedures create threads that are used to perform the respective operations in a nonblocking, or nonmodal, mode of operation.

Listing 7-1   Dispatch Map for Ping Control

```
BEGIN_DISPATCH_MAP(CPINGCtrl, COleControl)
        //{{AFX_DISPATCH_MAP(CPINGCtrl)
        DISP_PROPERTY_NOTIFY(CPINGCtrl, "RetryCount", m_retryCount, OnRetryCountChanged,
➥VT_I2)
        DISP_PROPERTY_NOTIFY(CPINGCtrl, "CancelEcho", m_cancelEcho, OnCancelEchoChanged,
➥VT_I2)
        DISP_PROPERTY_NOTIFY(CPINGCtrl, "ErrorNumber", m_errorNumber,
➥OnErrorNumberChanged, VT_I2)
        DISP_PROPERTY_NOTIFY(CPINGCtrl, "TimeOut", m_timeOut, OnTimeOutChanged, VT_I2)
        DISP_PROPERTY_NOTIFY(CPINGCtrl, "HostAddress", m_hostAddress,
➥OnHostAddressChanged, VT_BSTR)
        DISP_PROPERTY_NOTIFY(CPINGCtrl, "OutEchoString", m_outEchoString,
➥OnOutEchoStringChanged, VT_BSTR)
        DISP_PROPERTY_NOTIFY(CPINGCtrl, "InEchoString", m_inEchoString,
➥OnInEchoStringChanged, VT_BSTR)
        DISP_PROPERTY_NOTIFY(CPINGCtrl, "EchoHostAddress", m_echoHostAddress,
➥OnEchoHostAddressChanged,
                VT_BSTR)
        //}}AFX_DISPATCH_MAP
        DISP_FUNCTION_ID(CPINGCtrl, "AboutBox", DISPID_ABOUTBOX, AboutBox, VT_EMPTY,
➥VTS_NONE)
END_DISPATCH_MAP()
```

As shown in Figure 7-3, the control itself maintains only one base process and, when activated, one thread. The thread is responsible for connecting to a remote Ping slave, submitting the message to be echoed, receiving the echoed message, and closing its end of the connection.

To initiate a Ping operation, the simple assignment of an IP address to the HostAddress property (see Listing 7-2) initializes the echo thread to begin Pinging the host at the specified address. Upon assignment, the control first checks to see if a thread exists, using the GetExitCodeThread() function. Since the control limits the number of concurrent Ping operations to one, if the echo thread is already active, the code returns an error through the event procedure FireEchoEvent.

Stream
Socket

FIGURE 7-3

*The Ping control consists
of one base thread and the
functional echo thread.*

Listing 7-2 *HostAddress* **Property Procedure**

```
void CPINGCtrl::OnHostAddressChanged()
{
        // TODO: Add notification handler code
        DWORD                   ThreadId;
        DWORD                   ThreadExitCode;

        GetExitCodeThread(m_hThreadHandle ,&ThreadExitCode);
        if(ThreadExitCode!= STILL_ACTIVE)
        {
                m_hThreadHandle = CreateThread(NULL,0,TEcho,this,0,&ThreadId);
        }
        else
        {
                m_errorNumber = 11000;          //Multiple threads not allowed
                m_timeOut = 0;
                FireEchoEvent (m_timeOut,m_inEchoString,m_echoHostAddress,m_errorNumber);
        }

        SetModifiedFlag();
}
```

The echo thread itself (see Listing 7-3) is very straightforward and consists of one simple procedure. This thread connects to a remote Ping slave, issues a message to be echoed, receives the echoed message, and disconnects.

Listing 7-3   Echo Thread Function

```
DWORD WINAPI TEcho(LPVOID pParam)
{
        // TODO: Add your dispatch handler code here
        int             retval = 1, loopcount;
        int             TimeOut = 2000;
        UINT            RemotePort;
        CSocket         sktClnt;
        CPINGCtrl*      thisObject = (CPINGCtrl*)pParam;
        char            OutEchoString[25], InEchoString[25];
        SYSTEMTIME      sys_time1, sys_time2;

        //Initialize error property
        thisObject->m_errorNumber = 0;

        //Open a socket and get a handle
        if(sktClnt.Create(0,SOCK_DGRAM)==0)
        {
                thisObject->m_errorNumber = sktClnt.GetLastError() - WSABASEERR;
        }
        else
        {
                sktClnt.SetSockOpt(SO_RCVTIMEO,(const char *)&TimeOut,sizeof(TimeOut));
                sktClnt.SetSockOpt(SO_SNDTIMEO,(const char *)&TimeOut,sizeof(TimeOut));

                for (loopcount=1; loopcount < thisObject->m_retryCount; loopcount++)
                {
                        GetSystemTime((LPSYSTEMTIME)&sys_time1);

                        strncpy(OutEchoString,thisObject-
>m_outEchoString.GetBuffer(20),20);
                        sktClnt.SendTo((const void*)OutEchoString,strlen(OutEchoString),
                                IPPORT_ECHO,LPCTSTR(thisObject->m_hostAddress));
```

continues

Listing 7-3   Continued

```
                                sktClnt.ReceiveFrom((void*)InEchoString,sizeof(InEchoString),
                                        thisObject->m_echoHostAddress,RemotePort);
                                thisObject->m_inEchoString =
CString(InEchoString,strlen(OutEchoString));

                                GetSystemTime((LPSYSTEMTIME)&sys_time2);

                                thisObject->m_timeOut =
                                (sys_time2.wHour*60*60*1000 + sys_time2.wMinute*60*1000 +
                                        sys_time2.wSecond*1000 + sys_time2.wMilliseconds) -
                                (sys_time1.wHour*60*60*1000 + sys_time1.wMinute*60*1000 +
                                        sys_time1.wSecond*1000 + sys_time1.wMilliseconds);

                                thisObject->m_bPINGEvent = TRUE;
                                thisObject->SendMessage(WM_TIMER,1,0);

                        }

                        thisObject->m_errorNumber = 0;
                }

        thisObject->m_bPINGEvent = TRUE;
        thisObject->SendMessage(WM_TIMER,1,0);

        return(retval);
}
```

To initiate communications, the thread first creates a datagram socket, using the Create method of the sktClnt CSocket object (see Listing 7-4). If successful, we establish a few timeout parameters for the socket to allow the socket to give up waiting on a send and a receive operation if no data arrives from any remote host.

Listing 7-4   Socket Creation

```
if(sktClnt.Create(0,SOCK_DGRAM)==0)
{
        thisObject->m_errorNumber = sktClnt.GetLastError() - WSABASEERR;
}
else
{
        sktClnt.SetSockOpt(SO_RCVTIMEO,(const char *)&TimeOut,sizeof(TimeOut));
        sktClnt.SetSockOpt(SO_SNDTIMEO,(const char *)&TimeOut,sizeof(TimeOut));
```

Once the socket is created, we can begin Pinging remote hosts. This Ping operation, for this simple example, involves simply submitting a message to a remote host repetitively and waiting for the sent message to be echoed back.

As shown in Listing 7-5, we loop for as many times as specified in the m_retryCount (RetryCount) property of the control. Each time we loop, we use the Send method to send a message to be echoed to the host specified by the address in the HostAddress property (thisObject->m_hostAddress). This implementation is a variation on the explanation of CSocket to demonstrate the use of CSocket with datagrams (UDP).

Listing 7-5   Pinging a Remote Host

```
        for (loopcount=1; loopcount < thisObject->m_retryCount; loopcount++)
        {
                GetSystemTime((LPSYSTEMTIME)&sys_time1);

                strncpy(OutEchoString,thisObject-
➡>m_outEchoString.GetBuffer(20),20);
                sktClnt.SendTo((const void*)OutEchoString,strlen(OutEchoString),
                        IPPORT_ECHO,LPCTSTR(thisObject->m_hostAddress));

                sktClnt.ReceiveFrom((void*)InEchoString,sizeof(InEchoString),
                        thisObject->m_echoHostAddress,RemotePort);
                thisObject->m_inEchoString =
```

continues

Listing 7-5   Continued

```
CString(InEchoString,strlen(OutEchoString));

                GetSystemTime((LPSYSTEMTIME)&sys_time2);

                thisObject->m_timeOut =
                (sys_time2.wHour*60*60*1000 + sys_time2.wMinute*60*1000 +
                        sys_time2.wSecond*1000 + sys_time2.wMilliseconds) -
                (sys_time1.wHour*60*60*1000 + sys_time1.wMinute*60*1000 +
                        sys_time1.wSecond*1000 + sys_time1.wMilliseconds);

                thisObject->m_bPINGEvent = TRUE;
                thisObject->SendMessage(WM_TIMER,1,0);


        }
```

Once the remote host responds, the echo string, the remote host's address, and the interval are submitted to the container application. This submission operation occurs in the OnTimer procedure (see Listing 7-6) when signaled by the call to the SendMessage(WM_TIMER,1,0) function.

Listing 7-6   *OnTime* Procedure

```
void CPINGCtrl::OnTimer(UINT nIDEvent)
{
        // TODO: Add your message handler code here and/or call default
        if(m_bPINGEvent == TRUE)
        {
                m_bPINGEvent = FALSE;
                FireEchoEvent (m_timeOut,m_inEchoString,m_echoHostAddress,m_errorNumber);
        }


        COleControl::OnTimer(nIDEvent);

}
```

To perform some interval calculations, we use the `GetSystemTime` function to get the current system time before we submit a Ping and after the remote host responds. This simplistic interval calculation provides an approximate round-trip time, in milliseconds, of the echo message sent from your local host.

The call to the `FireEchoEvent` shown in Listing 7-6 allows the passing of the time interval (`m_timeOut`), the returned echo string (`m_inEchoString`), the IP address of the responding host (`m_echoHostAddress`), and an error number (`m_errorNumber`) identifying any errors that may have occurred during the execution of the Ping operation.

Testing the Ping Control

Now that you have a basic understanding of Ping, the ECHO protocol, and an overview of the OCX implementation, let's look at using the custom control for implementing the protocol in Visual Basic 4.0 under Windows NT 3.51. As shown in Figure 7-4, we have a Ping application running and communicating with a remote Ping slave.

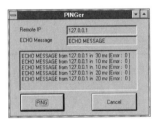

FIGURE 7-4

The Ping Visual Basic test application allows the submission of an echo message to a remote host to perform a Ping operation.

The edit controls at the top of Figure 7-4 allow you to enter the remote host's IP address, as well as a message to be echoed with the remote host. Once the information is entered, clicking the Ping button notifies the application to begin the echo with the remote host. As the Ping operation progresses, the results of the operation are placed in the center edit control of the application window. Clicking the Cancel button at any time cancels the Ping operation.

When you click the Ping button, the application assigns values to the properties of the control in the associated event procedure (see Listing 7-7). The `RetryCount` is the number of times that the control loops while echoing the message `OutEchoString`. The message is echoed with the host whose IP address is specified in HostAddress. Once the address is assigned to the HostAddress property, the Ping control initiates its echo with the remote host.

Listing 7-7   Ping Button Procedure

```
Private Sub Command1_Click()
        PING1.RetryCount = 5
      PING1.OutEchoString = Text4.Text
        PING1.HostAddress = text3.Text
      text2.Text = ""
End Sub
```

As shown in Listing 7-8, every time that an echo is received from the remote host, the event procedure executes. During the execution, the results of the Ping operation are placed in the large edit control located in the middle of the application window (refer to Figure 7-4).

Listing 7-8   Ping Echo Event Procedure

```
Private Sub PING1_EchoEvent(ByVal TimeOut As Integer, ByVal EchoString As String, ByVal
RemoteAddress As String, ByVal ErrorValue As Integer)
  text2.Text = text2.Text + EchoString + " from " + RemoteAddress + " in " +
Str(TimeOut) + _
      " ms" + " (Error : " + Str(ErrorValue) + " )" + Chr$(13) + Chr$(10)
End Sub
```

Nifty Things to Do with Ping

The Ping control presented in this chapter is a very minimal implementation of the Ping utility and the ECHO protocol. You have the capability to expand the functionality of the control considerably by incorporating another network protocol, known as ICMP.

ICMP (Internet Control Message Protocol, RFC 792) is a datagram protocol layered above IP and is the error and control message protocol used by the TCP/IP family of protocols. It is used by the kernel to handle and report errors in protocol processing and may also be accessed by programs using the socket interface or the Transport Level Interface (TLI) for network monitoring and diagnostic functions. Such diagnostic purposes include routing, fault isolation, and congestion control.

For user applications, ICMP messages are sent by means of the standard IP packet, with specially formatted data segments contained within the data portion of the packet. The two primary methods that we will discuss—ECHO and REDIRECT—provide you with the packet formats required to implement the two message types for a higher-level Ping application.

As stated earlier, ICMP can provide the ECHO REQUEST and ECHO REPLY, which are used to find a remote host. You will notice in the following explanations that a Ping utility can be implemented in several ways. You can also use ICMP to retrieve routing information to trace the route a packet travels to reach its ultimate destination.

ECHO and *ECHO REPLY*

The ECHO_REQUEST and ECHO_REPLY messages (see Figure 7-5) provide a means of using ICMP to handle the echoing of information between and remote host and the originating host. This is a variation on the Ping we developed, in which we issued a message to the ECHO service port of a remote host by using UDP. The ICMP version actually issues an ECHO_REQUEST using the ICMP protocol—a different protocol from that of UDP.

FIGURE 7-5

The ECHO_REQUEST / ECHO_ REPLY *message allows you to use ICMP to echo data between two nodes.*

TYPE	CODE	CHECKSUM	IDENTIFIER	SEQUENCE NUMBER	DATA...

The data received by a remote host in the originating echo message must be returned in the ECHO_REPLY message. The identifier and sequence number may be used by the echo sender to aid in matching the replies with the echo requests. For example, the identifier might be used like a port in TCP or UDP to identify a session, and the sequence number might be incremented on each echo request sent.

The TYPE field can contain one of two values. For an originating message, this field should contain the value of 8 to identify an echo message to the recipient. Once the recipient receives the message, it places 0 in the field to identify a reply message, which is then sent to the originating host.

The CODE fields should always be set to 0 when you are issuing ICMP ECHO messages. This is the default value for the operation.

The CHECKSUM field contains the a 16-bit value of the one's complement of the sum of the ICMP message, starting with the TYPE field.

The IDENTIFIER and SEQUENCE NUMBER fields are user fields that can be used in matching echo messages with echo replies. These fields can be any values that you require when issuing echoes between the local and remote hosts to keep track of all echoed information.

REDIRECT

When a host receives a REDIRECT message, the routing table is updated with a new entry or modifies an existing entry. A REDIRECT message is usually sent by a gateway to inform the originator of a shorter path to a destination address.

Consider a scenario. A gateway, GWYA, receives a datagram from a host on its network, NETA. GWYA checks its routing table and finds the address of the next gateway, GWYB, on the route to the datagram's ultimate destination network, NETB. If GWYB and the originating host are on the same network, a REDIRECT message is sent to the host. This message informs the host to send its traffic for NETB directly to GWYB, which is a shorter path to the destination.

In this manner, you can use ICMP and the REDIRECT message to locate all the gateways located between your site and a remote site. By Pinging each consecutive gateway whose IP is returned to you, you will be able to see which gateways a datagram must pass to reach its ultimate destination.

NOTE: If you are dealing with source route options for your datagrams, a REDIRECT message will not be sent, regardless of the existence of a better route to the ultimate destination. With source routing, each successive gateway determines the best path to take in a manner that is transparent to the originating host.

The TYPE field contains a value of 5 to identify to the recipient that the information contained in the packet in Figure 7-6 is a REDIRECT message.

FIGURE 7-6

The REDIRECT *message contains information regarding routing for a given packet to a destination address.*

TYPE	CODE	CHECKSUM	GATEWAY INTERNET ADDRESS	INTERNET HEADER

The CODE field can contain one of the four values shown in Table 7-1. Each of these values informs the recipient of the content of the information within the ICMP REDIRECT message.

Table 7-1   CODE Values for a REDIRECT Message

Value	Description
0	Redirection of datagrams for the network
1	Redirection of datagrams for the host
2	Redirection of datagrams for the type of service and network
3	Redirection of datagrams for the type of service and host

The CHECKSUM field contains the a 16-bit value of the one's complement of the sum of the ICMP message, starting with the TYPE field.

GATEWAY INTERNET ADDRESS is the address of the gateway of the network for the original datagram. Essentially, this is the gateway associated with the original packet's originating network.

INTERNET HEADER is used by the host to match the received ICMP message to the appropriate process running on the recipient host. In many cases, higher-level protocols use port numbers, which are always assumed to be in the header of an datagram. In this type of packet, the INTERNET HEADER actually contains the first 64 bits of data that were in the original datagram, which caused the REDIRECT message to be issued.

Chapter Summary

This implementation of Ping protocol is by no means the full implementation. This implementation can be expanded to provide full Ping support, as well as the capability to trace routes by using the REDIRECT messages. You have the capability to create any other types of applications that you find useful in your intranet or Internet environments. For example, you can implement an application for a real-time critical network that instantly notifies you of network path or host outages. You can develop a wide range of applications by mixing and matching Internet custom controls.

Chapter | 8

Plug-in Finger

by Markus Pope

Finger is an application that people use on the Net to get information. It works like a vending machine—typically, you ask a finger server about a user, and the server responds with all the information it has on the subject. Many times (but not necessarily), that information includes the user's office extension and office location, what the user does, and whether or not the user is signed on.

Finger, though, is used for much more nowadays than getting user information or finding out whether someone is signed onto a host system. If you take a look at the cool finger-sites collection at www.yahoo.com, in the Internet Entertainment section, you'll find a variety of weird contraptions that you can talk to—the hottest of which are Internet-aware vending machines (yes, actual vending machines).

Quite a few Internet-aware Coke and Pepsi machines are connected to finger and Gopher servers on the Net. You can, for example, finger pepsi@cunix.cc.columbia.edu and get the status of the Pepsi machine (which, as of just a few minutes ago, is full). Other devices on the Net include spy cameras, robotic arms, and listening devices. OK, enough about that.

In Chapter 6, you learned how to write code that instantiates a CAsyncSocket object and talks to the Net through a very thin layer of abstraction. In this chapter, you're going to climb up the ethereal totem pole to a much higher level of abstraction, where you don't have to worry about the devilish details of Winsock programming.

Instead of creating a CAsyncSocket object and handling stuff asynchronously, let's look at CSocket and explore synchronous access to sockets through MFC. (Do you remember the difference between asynchronous and synchronous? If not, refer to the discussions of CAsyncSocket and CSocket in Chapter 6.) Here's what you're going to look at:

- What the finger protocol is
- How to make a finger control
- Things to do with the control, once you're done

Quick Overview of the Finger Protocol

As described earlier, finger is a mechanism that people use on the Net to disperse little tidbits of information—not a lot of information, as you'd find on the Web or on a Gopher site; just small tidbits. This doesn't require a really complex protocol. Basically, you just need to be able to send a query-string to the host and get back either a positive or negative response. This, incidentally, is exactly how finger works. Figure 8-1 shows a flow chart of what happens during a finger query.

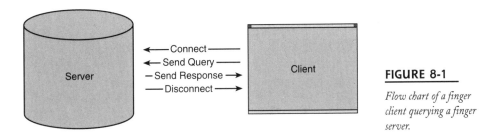

Server

Client

← Connect →
← Send Query →
– Send Response →
– Disconnect →

FIGURE 8-1

Flow chart of a finger client querying a finger server.

> **NOTE:** A protocol simply defines how two entities, things, or objects talk to each other. So finger is considered to be a protocol, even though it's not as complex as something like ZMODEM.

Making the Connection

A client initiates a finger session by making a connection to a finger server on port 79. The finger server accepts the connection request and waits for the query token. We'll get into the query token in about three minutes, but first, let's cover what you do to make the connection.

The primary job of CAsyncSocket is to provide a layer of abstraction between the MFC programmer and the Winsock API. Beyond that, it provides some basic functionality that's in all Winsock-based Internet applications. CAsyncSocket is asynchronous by nature and, thus, difficult to use. CSocket, which you use in this chapter, provides an even higher level of abstraction. It gives you more convenient, synchronous, access to Winsock.

To make a connection to a finger host with a CSocket object, make a call to CAsyncSocket::Connect. "Hey, wait a minute," you say. "We're dealing with a CSocket object, not a CAsyncSocket object." True, but CSocket doesn't have its own Connect member. Connect is actually inherited from CAsyncSocket, the class from which CSocket is derived. Connect, when called within the scope of a CSocket object, blocks until the connection attempt succeeds or fails. Connect returns immediately when called within the scope of a `CAsyncSocket` object. (Remember the discussion of blocking vs. nonblocking calls in "The Windows Sockets API," in Chapter 6?) At this point, the client sends the query token.

Sending a Query and Receiving Results

A *query token* is the part of a command line that tells the finger server what information the user is requesting. Finger originated on the text-based UNIX platform, so the typical command line to do a finger looks something like this: `finger info@nasa.com`. `finger` is the command; the rest is the user or token and the server to query. `info` specifies information to retrieve, and `nasa.com` is the server to connect to.

Your implementation of finger isn't going to be any different. The interface gives users a command line including user and server. You parse the command line, separating the user from the server. Then pass the server in the call to `CAsyncSocket::Connect`, as described in the preceding section. Finally, you send the user (token) to the host.

Finger requires only that tokens be sent followed by a carriage return and line-feed pair. Optionally, `/w` can precede the query to indicate that the client wants to receive "extended" information about the subject. This lets the server present both short and long descriptions of someone or something. (I doubt that this option means much anymore.) And if the token is blank (that is, the client just sends a carriage return and line feed), the finger server should return a list of users signed into the system. Fingering `nasa.com`, for example, with `@nasa.com` gives you a list of who's working weekends.

> **NOTE:** Strangely, the specification for finger requests that the server be able to handle nested references to other servers. For example, `finger user@bob.com@george.com@silly.com` causes the finger server running on `bob.com` to finger `george.com`, who in turn fingers `silly.com`. (Yeah, it seems awfully strange to me, too.)

In response to a query, the finger server returns the information you requested—if it can, of course. (You wouldn't expect to get projected quarterly earnings for Microsoft from that company's finger server, for example.) The response varies depending upon the information you're asking for and the server you're connecting to. `finger` requires that a server respond, but it doesn't specify the format of the information returned.

Disconnecting from the Host

A finger session is terminated just after the finger server sends its response to the client's query. The finger protocol specifies that the finger server initiates the disconnect. That's because the client has no idea how much data the server is sending across. Since the socket connection is terminated when the server is finished sending its data, the client knows at that point that its job is done.

Creating the Finger Control

By now, you've created a control framework at least a billion times. Well, OK, I'm exaggerating, but you've done it enough in the book that I shouldn't have to walk you through it. So before you continue, take some time to use the ControlWizard to create a template for your finger control. Call it Finger. (You just need the basic control framework here—no subclassing.) After you get that done, wake me up, and we'll start adding some code.

Making a Connection

Hey, watch who you're kicking! All right, all right, I'm awake. You've created the framework? Good. Now let's get some work done before we both get fired. Double-click the CFingerCtrl class in the class view to open FingerCtl.h. Insert the following class definition above the definition for CFingerCtrl:

```
class CFingerSocket : public CSocket
{
private:
        CWnd *m_pWnd;
        CSocketFile *m_pSockFile;
        CArchive *m_pArOUT;
        CArchive *m_pArDest;
        struct
        {
                char szHostName[100];
                char szCmdLine[100];
```

```
        } m_condata;
public:
        CFingerSocket();
        ~CFingerSocket();
        BOOL Finger( LPSTR lpszFinger, CWnd
                *pWnd = NULL, CArchive *pArDest = NULL );
        void OnReceive( int nError );
        void OnClose( int nError );
        void InitData();
        void Cleanup();
        void ParseCmdLine( LPSTR lpszCmdLine );
};
```

When you're done, CFingerSocket's going to be in charge of sending the query request and returning the data. CFingerSocket is derived from CSocket instead of CAsyncSocket so that you can associate an archive with outgoing data and also get the benefit of a blocking socket. (As you'll see in a few minutes, blocking sockets are easier to deal with than asynchronous sockets.)

CFingerSocket::Finger is the main entry point for the class (besides the constructor, of course.) It's called by CFingerCtrl to initiate a finger connection. You pass it the finger command line, a pointer to the window that contains the control, and an archive that it'll write the received data to. Here's what the finger member looks like:

```
BOOL CFingerSocket::Finger( LPSTR lpszFinger,
                    CWnd *pWnd, CArchive *pArDest )
{
        ParseCmdLine( lpszFinger );
        if( *(m_condata.szHostName) )
        {
                Create();
                if( Connect( m_condata.szHostName,
IPPORT_FINGER ) )
                {
                        m_pWnd = pWnd;
                        m_pArDest = pArDest;
```

```
                m_pSockFile = new CSocketFile( this );
                m_pArOUT = new CArchive( m_pSockFile,
CArchive::store );
                if( *( m_condata.szCmdLine ) )
                        m_pArOUT->Write( m_condata.szCmdLine,
                                lstrlen( m_condata.szCmdLine ) );
                *m_pArOUT << (BYTE)0x0D << (BYTE)0x0A;
                m_pArOUT->Flush();
                return( TRUE );
            }
        }
        if( pWnd )
                pWnd->PostMessage( WM_FINGER_DONE, 1, 0 );
        Cleanup();
        return( FALSE );
    }
```

> **NOTE:** I chose to add the implementation for CFingerSocket to FingerCtl.cpp. I did that because there's not much to the CFingerSocket implementation, and it was the quick-and-dirty thing to do. You may want to locate both the class definition and the implementation separate from CFingerCtrl, to make it easier to maintain; that's up to you.

Before you can make a connection to the host, you've got to separate the host name from the query-string. Create a member function called ParseCmdLine. ParseCmdLine searches for the @ in lpszFinger. It assumes that everything before the @ symbol is the query-string and the remaining characters make up the host name. After separating the host from the query-string, ParseCmdLine copies both the host and the query into the m_condata structure imbedded in CFingerSocket. The following code shows CFingerSocket::ParseCmdLine:

```
void CFingerSocket::ParseCmdLine( LPCSTR lpszCmdLine )
{
        CString cszStr = lpszCmdLine;
        int nCookiePos;
```

```
        *(m_condata.szHostName) = 0;
        *(m_condata.szCmdLine) = 0;

        nCookiePos = cszStr.Find( '@' );
        if( nCookiePos >= 0 )
        {
                lstrcpy( m_condata.szCmdLine,
cszStr.Left( nCookiePos ) );
                lstrcpy( m_condata.szHostName,
cszStr.Mid( nCookiePos + 1 ) );
        } else
                lstrcpy( m_condata.szHostName, cszStr );
}
```

> **NOTE:** ParseCmdLine copies the contents of lpszFinger into a CString so that it can take advantage of the BASIC-like string-handling member functions.

If CFingerSocket::ParseCmdLine finds a host name in the query-string, CFingerSocket::Finger makes a call to CSocket::Create to create a socket. Then the finger member calls CSocket::Connect to make a connection to the host. Unlike the sample code in Chapter 6, though, CSocket::Connect blocks until the connection is either successful or fails. (Try to make a connection using port 79, represented by IPPORT_FINGER.)

Sending the Query to the Host

After connecting to the host you want to finger, store the pointer to the control's window and the destination archive. (You've got to do that so that you won't lose them when CFingerSocket::Finger goes out of scope.) Next, the finger member creates a CSocketFile object and passes the pointer to CFingerSocket, which associates the socket you created with a file descriptor so that you can use the socket with archives.

Now that the socket is associated with a file object, you create a CArchive and pass the CSocketFile pointer to associate it with the archive. CArchive::store is an enumerator that enables this archive for writing. (You can't use an archive for reading and writing at the same time.)

If there is a query-string to send to the host, found by ParseCmdLine, the finger member writes the query-string to the archive, follows up with a carriage return/line-feed pair, and flushes the archive. (Flushing the archive forces the archive to write its contents to the file it represents.) CFingerSocket::Finger then returns true, indicating that you've gotten as far as the query-string.

If, for some reason, you can't make a connection to the host, the finger member sends a message to the control's main window (which is why you store the window's pointer). For this code to work, put the following line in FingerCtl.h just above the CFingerSocket class definition:

```
#define WM_FINGER_DONE                      WM_APP+1
```

This line defines a custom message. You'll come back and add a handler for this message later on. Right now, let's talk a bit about what to do with the data received from the host.

Receiving the Data from the Query

By this time, the CFingerSocket object has connected to the host and sent the query. This was all done in a synchronous manner, using blocking calls. Receiving data, though, happens asynchronously by nature—that is, data can come in on the socket at any time. Nothing in the finger protocol guarantees that the host responds in a specific amount of time with a specific amount of data.

Because receiving the response from a finger query is asynchronous by nature, you need to override the OnReceive member of the CFingerSocket object. OnReceive is called when there's data in the receive buffer waiting to be sucked out and dealt with. With most Internet protocols, it's most handy to write the incoming information to files. But, of course, you can do this only with something like finger, which doesn't require high-speed data transfer. Take a look at this OnReceive member:

```
void CFingerSocket::OnReceive( int nError )
{
        char buf[256];
        int nBytes;
```

```
nBytes = Receive( buf, sizeof( buf ) );
while( nBytes > 0 && nBytes != SOCKET_ERROR )
{
        if( m_pArDest )
        {
                m_pArDest->Write( buf, nBytes );
                m_pArDest->Flush();
        } else
                TRACE( buf );
        nBytes = Receive( buf, sizeof( buf ) );
}
}
```

buf is a buffer that can hold up to 256 bytes. When OnReceive is called, call the Receive member of CSocket to move the data from the socket to the 256-byte buffer. Then write the data received to the archive passed into CFingerSocket::Finger. When you write data to an archive, the data is buffered until it's absolutely necessary to write it to storage. That means that the data doesn't actually get written to the file until the buffer is flushed. In applications like this one, you should flush the buffer after writing data, because the buffering doesn't really buy you anything. OnReceive loops, receiving data until there's no more data waiting on the socket.

Disconnecting from the Host

Originally, the focus of this section was how to display the data that you get from the socket in the OnReceive member of CFingerSocket. But now that we're here, it seems much more appropriate to talk about how to disconnect from the host. It may seem strange to talk about the CFingerSocket implementation, skip to CFingerCtrl for a bit, and then switch back to CFingerSocket—which is what would happen if we talked about how to display the data that's received. So let's talk about how to disconnect from the host and save the data display for the next section.

Disconnection in the finger protocol is quite simple. Remember the explanation of the finger protocol at the beginning of the chapter? After making the query, the host sends back the response and then disconnects the socket. So really, all you've got to do is add a handler for the OnClose member of CFingerSocket (inherited from CSocket). OnClose gets called after the host sends its response and disconnects the data. Your OnClose should look like this:

```
void CFingerSocket::OnClose( int nError )
{
        if( m_pWnd )
                m_pWnd->PostMessage( WM_FINGER_DONE, 0, 0 );
        Cleanup();
}
```

Most of the work after a disconnect is done by the handler for the WM_FINGER_DONE message. All you have to do in CFingerSocket::OnClose is send the WM_FINGER_DONE message to the control's main window and call a function that cleans up the CFingerSocket object.

In several of the members implemented thus far, you made calls to a Cleanup member. I may have promised at some point that we'd cover its implementation. (Any implementation that's left out, by the way, you can find in the source code on the CD-ROM that accompanies this work, although I've tried very hard to cover every aspect of the samples written for you.) At any rate, here it is:

```
void CFingerSocket::Cleanup()
{
        if( m_pArOUT )
                delete m_pArOUT;
        if( m_pSockFile )
                delete m_pSockFile;
        InitData();
        Close();
}
```

First, CFingerSocket::Cleanup checks to see if there's an archive for outgoing data (you created that archive in CFingerSocket::Finger). If the finger member created the archive correctly, it's deleted; otherwise, it's ignored. Next, you do the same thing with the CSocketFile object, allocated also by CFingerSocket::Finger. Then, before calling CSocket::Close to free the socket's descriptor, make a call to InitData, which resets the values of m_pSockFile, m_pArOUT, m_pArDest, and m_pWnd. Code for InitData follows:

```
void CFingerSocket::InitData()
{
        m_pSockFile = NULL;
        m_pArOUT = NULL;
        m_pArDest = NULL;
        m_pWnd = NULL;
}
```

Displaying the Data from the Query

The code you've written so far has been for the implementation of the CFingerSocket class. You haven't done anything yet to tie the CFingerSocket class to the control (other than hacking out the implementation in the same file as the CFingerCtrl object's implementation). The first thing to do is create a handler for the WM_FINGER_DONE message. Then write a routine that reads the finger reply from an associated archive and puts that info in an edit box. The edit box won't exist until you get to the next section, so let's refer to it as IDC_REPLY for now.

Since WM_FINGER_DONE is a custom message, created based on WM_APP, you must add it to the control's message map manually. Do that with the ON_MESSAGE macro. ON_MESSAGE is similar to the macros such as ON_WM_SIZE and ON_WM_CREATE, except that you specify both the message you want to handle and the name of the handler you want the framework to call, whereas you don't specify anything with ON_WM_SIZE and ON_WM_CREATE. Add an ON_MESSAGE call for WM_FINGER_DONE to your message map in FingerCtl.cpp, as shown here:

```
BEGIN_MESSAGE_MAP(CFingerCtrl, COleControl)
        //{{AFX_MSG_MAP(CFingerCtrl)
        ON_WM_CREATE()
        ON_WM_SIZE()
        ON_MESSAGE( WM_FINGER_DONE, OnFingerDone )
        .
        .
```

The first parameter specified in the ON_MESSAGE macro is, of course, WM_FINGER_DONE—the custom message. The second parameter is the name of a member function to call when the message is received. In this case, you call the function OnFingerDone. Here's CFingerCtrl::OnFingerDone:

```
LONG CFingerCtrl::OnFingerDone(
WPARAM wParam, LPARAM lParam )
{
        if( m_pSock )
        {
                delete m_pSock;
                m_pSock = NULL;
        }
        if( m_pArDest )
        {
                delete m_pArDest;
                m_pArDest = NULL;
        }
        if( m_tempfile.m_hFile != CFile::hFileNull )
        {
                m_pArDest = new CArchive(
&m_tempfile, CArchive::load );
                FillEditBox( *m_pArDest );
                delete m_pArDest;
                m_pArDest = NULL;
                m_tempfile.Close();
        }
if( wParam )
                MessageBox( "Couldn't connect to server.",
                        "Finger Control" );
        return( TRUE );
}
```

CFingerCtrl::OnFingerDone is called when the control framework receives a
WM_FINGER_DONE message. It allows us to do cleanup work that doesn't make sense within
the scope of CFingerSocket. If you look at the first two if conditional blocks, you'll notice
that these blocks are cleaning up two pointers called m_pSock and m_pArDest. m_pSock is a
pointer to a CFingerSocket object that you allocate a little later in the project. m_pArDest is
a pointer to the destination archive that's passed into CFingerSocket::Finger (remember
that code?).

m_tempfile is a CFile object that corresponds to a temporary file. That temporary file is where the finger response is written to. OnFingerDone makes sure that the file is successfully created. If the temporary file is successfully created, OnFingerDone creates and associates a new archive, set to CArchive::load, and passes that archive to a function called FillEditBox.

FillEditBox writes all the response information stored in the temporary file to an edit box in the control's user interface. After FillEditBox is completed, the loading archive is destroyed, and the temporary file is closed. (Code for FillEditBox follows this paragraph.) Notice the check on wParam and the conditional message box just before the return in CFingerCtrl::OnFingerDone. This little code segment allows us to use the WM_FINGER_DONE handler to clean up even when the finger attempt fails. (Recall the PostMessage of WM_FINGER_DONE back in the finger member of CFingerSocket.) To signal a failure, the wParam is simply set to a true value. Here is CFingerCtrl::FillEditBox:

```
void CFingerCtrl::FillEditBox( CArchive& arInput )
{
        CString cszFill;
        CString cszBuf;

        arInput.GetFile()->SeekToBegin();
        while( arInput.ReadString( cszBuf ) )
                cszFill += (cszBuf + "\r\n");

        if( ! cszFill.IsEmpty() )
                m_dlg.SetDlgItemText( IDC_REPLY, cszFill );
}
```

CFingerCtrl::FillEditBox puts the file pointer at the beginning of the temporary file by making a call to CArchive::SeekToBegin. After putting the file pointer at the beginning of the file, it reads through the file a line at a time, adding each line to a CString object called cszFill. Once the contents of the temporary file are read into cszFill, FillEditBox makes a call to SetDlgItemText (passing IDC_REPLY as the control identifier) to set the contents of an edit box to the query received from the finger host.

TIP: Use CString objects in FillEditBox for convenience, so that you don't have to worry about allocating a character array large enough to hold the contents of the temporary file.

Adding a User Interface

At this point, you've completed the code that takes care of connecting to the finger server, queries for information, and displays the results of the query. You could create a control that has no interface—that is, the interface is the responsibility of the control container. However, I like for my controls to provide their own interface so that they are true to the notion of componentware (Plug and Play).

So in this section you create a user interface and tie that interface to the code you've already written. The first step is to create a dialog box to act as a user interface. As you've seen, this hack saves us quite a bit of time. Call the dialog box IDD_FINGER_MAIN. Make it look like the one shown in Figure 8-2.

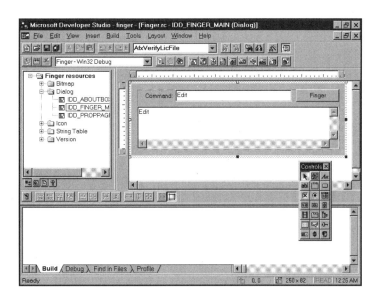

FIGURE 8-2

The IDD_FINGER_MAIN *dialog box provides the user interface for your finger control.*

IDD_FINGER_MAIN contains four controls: a static text, two edit boxes, and a pushbutton. Look at these controls in Figure 8-2. The first edit box is the Command field. The Command field is where you type queries such as **info@bob.com**. That field is followed by a pushbutton that's clicked when the user's ready to perform the query. And the last edit box is where the response from the finger server is displayed. Call the Command edit box IDC_HOSTNAME, the pushbutton IDC_FINGER, and the response edit box IDC_REPLY.

After you've created your IDD_FINGER_MAIN dialog box, open the ClassWizard and associate the dialog box with a new class called CFingerDlg. You're far enough into the book now that I'm going to assume that you know how to add a new class and how to associate that class with a dialog box. Once Visual C++ adds the dialog box and the new class to the project, you can put in the details of the user interface.

The first thing to do is associate IDC_HOSTNAME with a CString variable called m_cszHostName. In case you've forgotten, you can hold down the left Ctrl key and double-click the IDC_HOSTNAME edit box while editing the IDD_FINGER_MAIN dialog box to associate the control with a member variable. Visual C++ creates the member variable and adds code to the dialog box's DoDataExchange member to move data from the control to the member variable and back again.

Now add a handler for the IDC_FINGER pushbutton. Visual C++ creates a handler function called OnFinger. Edit the code for CFingerDlg::OnFinger, and make it look like the handler that follows:

```
void CFingerDlg::OnFinger()
{
        UpdateData( TRUE );
        SetDlgItemText( IDC_REPLY, "" );
        ((CFingerCtrl *)GetParent())->
Finger( m_cszHostName );
}
```

OnFinger is not very complicated. It calls UpdateData to make sure the m_cszHostName member variable contains the contents of the IDC_HOSTNAME edit box. Then it clears the contents of the IDC_REPLAY edit box. Finally, it makes a call to a member function called finger that resides in the CFingerCtrl object.

Go ahead and instantiate a CFingerDlg within the scope of CFingerCtrl. You've done this in several chapters now, so you should be familiar with the process. If not, don't worry—

I'll give you a few hints. First, you've got to add the FingerDlg.h include file to the top of the FingerCtl.h header file. That allows us to put a CFingerDlg member variable in the CFingerCtrl class definition.

Add a CFingerDlg member variable to the CFingerCtrl class definition (I've shown you a variety of ways to do this). Call the CFingerDlg member m_dlg. Also add a rectangle called m_rcMin. Now, in the constructor for your CFingerCtrl class, create the dialog box (as modeless), and set the control's initialize size to the same size as the dialog box. Here's the constructor from the sample finger control included with this book:

```
CFingerCtrl::CFingerCtrl()
{
        InitializeIIDs(&IID_DFinger, &IID_DFingerEvents);

        RECT rcClient;
        m_dlg.Create( CFingerDlg::IDD, GetDesktopWindow() );
        m_dlg.GetClientRect( &rcClient );
        SetInitialSize( rcClient.right, rcClient.bottom );
        m_pSock = NULL;
        m_pArDest = NULL;
}
```

OK, this is good, but you're not off the hook yet. Open the dialog-box template that you created earlier, and make sure that the visible style is *not* set. (I know—it sounds strange.) What you want to do is create the dialog box in the constructor for the control, so that you can set the control's initial size. Later, in the handler for the WM_CREATE message, you set the parent of the dialog box, save the dialog box's size in m_rcMin, and display the dialog box. Add a handler for the WM_CREATE message to your source, like this one:

```
int CFingerCtrl::OnCreate(LPCREATESTRUCT lpCreateStruct)
{
        if (COleControl::OnCreate(lpCreateStruct) == -1)
                return -1;

        m_dlg.SetParent( this );
        m_dlg.ShowWindow( SW_SHOW );
        m_dlg.GetClientRect( &m_rcMin );
```

```
        return 0;
}
```

To tie the user interface back to the CFingerCtrl object, create CFingerCtrl::Finger. This is different from the CFingerSocket::Finger function that you already created. CFingerCtrl::Finger sets up the CFingerSocket and calls the CFingerSocket object's finger member to perform the query. (I realize that it's kind of confusing to have two member functions named the same, but I can't think of a better name, other than CreateCFingerSocketObjectAndPerformFingerQuery. And I'm afraid that you'd get tired of typing that one!) The following code implements the CFingerCtrl::Finger function:

```
void CFingerCtrl::Finger( LPCSTR lpszFinger )
{
        if( m_pSock )
        {
                MessageBox( "Socket already in use.",
"Finger Control" );
                return;
        }

        if( m_tempfile.Open( "temp.txt",
                CFile::modeCreate |       CFile::modeReadWrite ) )
        {
                m_pArDest = new CArchive(
&m_tempfile, CArchive::store );
                m_pSock = new CFingerSocket;
                if( m_pSock )
                {
                        m_pSock->Finger( lpszFinger,
this, m_pArDest );
                } else
                        MessageBox( "Unable to allocate socket.",
"Finger Control" );
        } else
                MessageBox( "Unable to open temporary file.",
```

```
"Finger Control" );
}
```

For this to work, add some member variables to the CFingerCtrl class definition. First, add a CFingerSocket pointer called m_pSock. Then add a CFile object (not a pointer) called m_tempfile and a CArchive pointer called m_pArDest. There are references to these variables in some of the functions that you've already created.

CFingerCtrl::Finger first checks to make sure that m_pSock is invalid. This prevents your code from being re-entrant—that is, the user can't perform a finger query while one is already in progress. If there's not a query in progress, the new finger member creates a temporary file called temp.txt and sets its attributes to CFile::modeCreate and CFile::modeReadWrite.

If you are able to create the temporary file, the finger member creates a storing CArchive object, associates it with m_tempfile, and assigns it to m_pArDest. Then it creates a new CFingerSocket object and assigns it to m_pSock. Assuming that the socket creation is successful, CFingerCtrl::Finger calls the CFingerSocket object's Finger member, passing it the command line from our dialog box, a pointer to the CFingerCtrl object, and a pointer to the archive associated with the temporary file.

As you recall, when the CFingerSocket object is finished performing the query, it sends WM_FINGER_DONE to the control's window. The control's window is represented by the pointer to CFingerCtrl. In response to the WM_FINGER_DONE message, the framework calls OnFingerDone to signal completion of the query. That's where everything comes together.

Whew! At this point, you have everything in the control that's needed for it to function. Now add a few things to pretty up the way the control works. For example, right now, when the control is resized, the user interface controls in IDD_FINGER_MAIN aren't adjusted dynamically.

A user and a developer, using your control, expects to change the size of the user interface and then have the user interface controls reposition and resize themselves to accommodate the change. You can add code to dynamically position and size your controls in the handler for the WM_SIZE message. Add that handler to CFingerCtrl. It looks something like this:

```
void CFingerCtrl::OnSize(UINT nType, int cx, int cy)
{
        COleControl::OnSize(nType, cx, cy);
```

```
// Provide minimum size handling for the control.
BOOL bMinSizeX = cx < m_rcMin.right ? TRUE : FALSE;
BOOL bMinSizeY = cy < m_rcMin.bottom ? TRUE : FALSE;

if( bMinSizeX || bMinSizeY )
{
        SetControlSize( bMinSizeX ? m_rcMin.right : cx,
                bMinSizeY ? m_rcMin.bottom : cy );
        InvalidateControl();
        return;
}

RECT rc;
int dx, dy;
CWnd *pWnd;

// Resize the dialog to fit the window
// and figure the delta of the resize.
m_dlg.GetClientRect( &rc );
m_dlg.SetWindowPos( NULL, 0, 0, cx, cy,
        SWP_NOMOVE | SWP_NOZORDER );
dx = cx - rc.right;
dy = cy - rc.bottom;

// Relocate the Finger pushbutton.
pWnd = m_dlg.GetDlgItem( IDC_FINGER );
pWnd->GetWindowRect( &rc );
m_dlg.ScreenToClient( &rc );
rc.left += dx;
rc.right += dx;
pWnd->MoveWindow( rc.left, rc.top,
        (rc.right - rc.left),
        (rc.bottom - rc.top), FALSE );
```

Send Us
YOUR COMMENTS

Dear Reader:

Thank you for buying this book. In order to offer you more quality books on the topics *you* would like to see, we need your input. At Prima Publishing, we pride ourselves on timely responsiveness to our readers' needs. If you complete and return this brief questionnaire, *we will listen!*

Name (First) _____ (M.I.) _____ (Last) _____

Company _____ Type of business _____

Address _____ City _____ State _____ ZIP _____

Phone _____ Fax _____ E-mail address: _____

May we contact you for research purposes? ❏ Yes ❏ No
(If you participate in a research project, we will supply you with the Prima computer book of your choice.)

---

❶ How would you rate this book, overall?

❏ Excellent   ❏ Fair
❏ Very good   ❏ Below average
❏ Good   ❏ Poor

❷ Why did you buy this book?

❏ Price of book   ❏ Content
❏ Author's reputation ❏ Prima's reputation
❏ CD-ROM/disk included with book
❏ Information highlighted on cover
❏ Other (please specify):_____

❸ How did you discover this book?

❏ Found it on bookstore shelf
❏ Saw it in Prima Publishing catalog
❏ Recommended by store personnel
❏ Recommended by friend or colleague
❏ Saw an advertisement in:_____
❏ Read book review in:_____
❏ Saw it on Web site:_____
❏ Other (please specify):_____

❹ Where did you buy this book?

❏ Bookstore (name):_____
❏ Computer store (name):_____
❏ Electronics store (name):_____
❏ Wholesale club (name):_____
❏ Mail order (name):_____
❏ Direct from Prima Publishing
❏ Other (please specify):_____

❺ Which computer periodicals do you read regularly?_____

_____

_____

_____

❻ Would you like to see your name in print?

May we use your name and quote you in future Prima Publishing books or promotional materials?

❏ Yes   ❏ No

---

❼ Comments & suggestions: _____

_____

_____

8 **I am interested in seeing more computer books on these topics**

- ❏ Word processing
- ❏ Databases/spreadsheets
- ❏ Networking
- ❏ Programming
- ❏ Desktop publishing
- ❏ Web site development
- ❏ Internetworking
- ❏ Intranetworking

9 **How do you rate your level of computer skills?**

- ❏ Beginner
- ❏ Intermediate
- ❏ Advanced

10 **What is your age?**

- ❏ Under 18
- ❏ 40–49
- ❏ 18–29
- ❏ 50–59
- ❏ 30–39
- ❏ 60–over

SAVE A STAMP

Visit our Web site at **http://www.primapublishing.com**

and simply fill out one of our online response forms.

```
    // Resize the command editbox.
    pWnd = m_dlg.GetDlgItem( IDC_HOSTNAME );
    pWnd->GetWindowRect( &rc );
    m_dlg.ScreenToClient( &rc );
    rc.right += dx;
    pWnd->MoveWindow( rc.left, rc.top,
            (rc.right - rc.left),
            (rc.bottom - rc.top), FALSE );


    // Reposition and resize the reply editbox.
    pWnd = m_dlg.GetDlgItem( IDC_REPLY );
    pWnd->GetWindowRect( &rc );
    m_dlg.ScreenToClient( &rc );
    rc.right += dx;
    rc.bottom += dy;
    pWnd->MoveWindow( rc.left, rc.top,
            (rc.right - rc.left),
            (rc.bottom - rc.top), FALSE );


    m_dlg.Invalidate();
}
```

Since this function is so long, I took the liberty of adding a few comments to explain what's going on. That goes against everything I've learned about programming and job security, but what the heck. The first section of the OnSize member performs some ternary operations to determine whether the container has sized the control below its minimum size. Minimum size is controlled by the m_rcMin rectangle, and the m_rcMin rectangle is based on the initial size of the dialog box. If the control was made too small by the container, simply resize it to the minimum size.

The next section of code sizes the dialog box so that it fits into the control's main window. After sizing the dialog box to fit the control's window, compare the new size with the old size to get the delta. Use the delta values to scale the contents of the dialog box.

In the section of code following the dialog-box sizing, OnSize gets a pointer to the IDC_FINGER control, which is the pushbutton we created earlier. Using the pointer, OnSize gets the position and size of the pushbutton. Finally, the delta values are used to reposition the button. The next two sections of code resize the `IDC_HOSTNAME` edit box, and reposition and resize the `IDC_REPLY` edit box. Now when you compile and run this code, as in the test container, and you resize the control, the dialog box is sized to fit, and the controls are scaled appropriately. Pretty cool, eh?

Properties and Methods

You're pretty much done with the guts of the control, and it's about time to top this thing off and get on to something else. The finger control, as it is now, is quite usable as a plug-in, even though you haven't exposed any methods or properties. In fact, you could leave it as it is and not even worry about exposing methods and properties (some controls are like that). But wouldn't it be nice if the container could change the name of the temporary file and the query-string, and finger a host? Also, shouldn't the finger control tell the container when it's finished performing a query?

Open ClassWizard, and add a get/set property called `TempFile` to the finger control project. Set its type to `BSTR`. Visual C++ adds two new members to the `CFingerCtrl` class definition: `GetTempFile` and `SetTempFile`. Edit the code for those two functions, and make them modify the contents of a `CString` called `m_cszTempFile`. You'll have to add `m_cszTempFile` to the `CFingerCtrl` class definition. Following are `GetTempFile` and `SetTempFile` from the sample finger control:

```
BSTR CFingerCtrl::GetTempFile()
{
        return( m_cszTempFile.AllocSysString() );
}
void CFingerCtrl::SetTempFile(LPCTSTR lpszNewValue)
{
        m_cszTempFile = lpszNewValue;
        SetModifiedFlag();
}
```

`CFingerCtrl::GetTempFile` simply returns the `BSTR` returned by the `AllocSysString` member of `CString`. `SetTempFile` is just as simple. It sets the contents of `m_cszTempFile` to the string that's passed in. If you recall, you hard-coded a file name of temp.txt in the Finger member of `CFingerCtrl`. Go back to that code and change the hard-coded reference to `m_cszTempFile`, as follows:

```
            .

            .

        return;

    }


    if( m_tempfile.Open( m_cszTempFile,
        CFile::modeCreate ¦        CFile::modeReadWrite ) )
    {

            .

            .
```

Implementation of the `TempFile` property is completed by initializing `m_cszTempFile` in the constructor for the `CFingerCtrl` object. You can set it to anything you like. If you don't specify a path, the temporary file is created in the current directory. And the current directory changes throughout the course of program execution. So the silly thing moves around on your hard drive (rather annoying). You can fix that by getting the temp directory with `GetTempPath` and appending the file name to it.

> **TIP:** Optionally, you can call `GetTempFileName` to create a name for your temporary file. You could even make the control create a new temporary file each time it performs a query.

A property that corresponds to the query-string is just as easy to implement. Go into ClassWizard, and add a BSTR property called `QueryString`. Use a get/set method, just as you did for the `TempFile` property. Visual C++ adds a member called `GetQueryString`, and another called `SetQueryString`, to your `CFingerCtrl` class. Here's what the code should look like for those two new members:

```
BSTR CFingerCtrl::GetQueryString()
{
    CString cszQuery;
    m_dlg.GetDlgItem( IDC_HOSTNAME )->
GetWindowText( cszQuery );
    return( cszQuery.AllocSysString() );
}
```

```
void CFingerCtrl::SetQueryString(LPCTSTR lpszNewValue)
{
        m_dlg.GetDlgItem( IDC_HOSTNAME )->
SetWindowText( lpszNewValue );
        SetModifiedFlag();
}
```

First, you have probably noticed that the value of this property isn't maintained by the CFingerCtrl object. Instead, the get and set methods for this property talk to the IDD_FINGER_MAIN dialog box to get and set the current query-string. GetQueryString obtains a pointer to the IDC_HOSTNAME edit box and calls GetWindowText to get its contents. Pass a CString to GetWindowText and then return a BSTR by calling the CString's AllocSysString member. SetQueryString gets a pointer to the IDC_HOSTNAME edit box and calls SetWindowText to set its contents to lpszNewValue.

OK, two properties are added to the finger control: one that lets you change the temporary file used to store the reply from the finger server, and another that lets you change the text of the query-string. It's up to you to provide an interface to these properties in the default property sheet provided by the control framework. If you like, you can look at the sample finger control included on the CD-ROM that comes with this book.

Let's take a few minutes and look at adding a method that will invoke the IDC_FINGER pushbutton and initiate a query. What does it take to invoke a pushbutton? It's simple. You just send a WM_COMMAND message to the parent of the pushbutton, passing it the control ID. When the CFingerDlg object receives the WM_COMMAND message (CFingerDlg is the parent of the pushbutton), CFingerDlg::OnFinger is called and the query is initiated. Following is a method called MakeFingerFinger:

```
void CFingerCtrl::MakeFingerFinger()
{
        m_dlg.SendMessage( WM_COMMAND, IDC_FINGER, 0 );
}
```

To notify the container when a query is complete, go into ClassWizard and add an OLE event called FingerDone. Visual C++ automatically creates a new member of CFingerCtrl, called FireFingerDone. Make a call to FireFingerDone in CFingerCtrl::OnFingerDone, just before the return. When OnFingerDone is called by CFingerSocket, OnFingerDone calls FireFingerDone, which in turn notifies the container that a query is complete.

Testing Your Finger Control

Testing the control is simple, as you've seen in previous chapters. All you have to do is create a control container, using the AppWizard. Then, once you have the app created, use the Component Gallery to insert the finger control into the container application. After that, you just instantiate the control, clean up a few things, and you're there!

Open a new instance of Visual C++, and create a new application called FingCon. Make it an SDI (Single Document Interface) application with support for controls. Also, turn off the default toolbar (you really don't need one), and get rid of the print options: Print and Print Preview.

OK, now, go into the Component Gallery, and insert the finger control. (I'm assuming that you've compiled the control and that it's registered with the system registry.) If you choose all the default settings along the way, you'll end up with a new class called CFinger, an implementation file called Finger.cpp, and a header file called Finger.h.

Do you remember how to instantiate the object? It's easy. Include the Finger.h header file at the top of FingConView.h. Adding the header file allows you to add a CFinger member to your CFingConView object (the view object for your container application). After adding the header, add a CFinger member variable to the CFingConView class definition, and call it m_finger.

Edit the FingConView.cpp source file. Add a handler for WM_CREATE, just as you did in the containers of previous chapters. Call the Create member of m_finger. Following is CFingConView::OnCreate, added to handle the WM_CREATE message:

```
int CFingConView::OnCreate(
LPCREATESTRUCT lpCreateStruct)
{
        if (CView::OnCreate(lpCreateStruct) == -1)
                return -1;


        m_finger.Create( NULL, WS_VISIBLE,
                CRect( 0, 0, 640, 480 ), this, 0 );


        return 0;
}
```

Once you get that done, add a handler for WM_SIZE. Make your CFingConView::OnSize function look like this one:

```
void CFingConView::OnSize(UINT nType,
int cx, int cy)
{
        CView::OnSize(nType, cx, cy);
        m_finger.SetWindowPos( NULL, 0, 0, cx, cy,
                SWP_NOMOVE ¦ SWP_NOZORDER );
}
```

The OnSize member changes the size of the control's window, based on the size of the client area of the view. Because you added the special resize and scaling code to the finger control, the finger control sizes itself to fit the view when the view size is changed by the user. (It's cool; check it out!)

At this point, you can compile the container and use the finger control. Instead of leaving the interface bare and unfinished, as you've done in previous chapters, finish the user interface and make a complete application. (Don't worry—it won't take very long.)

You turned off the toolbar and got rid of the printing support, so all that's left to do is change the menus to fit our application. Change to the resource view, and open the IDR_MAINFRAME menu resource. Visual C++ displays the default menu resource, shown in Figure 8-3.

You could argue that there's a use for an Edit menu in a finger application, but I think I'll leave that up to you. Go ahead and delete the Edit menu. After you get that done, change the name of the File menu to Finger, and remove all the contents but the Exit item and the separator above it. Add a menu item to the new Finger menu, call it Connect, and set its ID to IDM_FINGER_CONNECT. The new menu is shown in Figure 8-4.

Save your changes to the IDR_MAINFRAME menu resource, and switch back to the class view. Go back to the FingConView.cpp source file, and add a handler for the IDM_FINGER_CON-NECT menu item. You can do that by choosing it from the CFingConView object ID's drop-down list box. Then choose COMMAND from the Messages drop-down list box. Visual C++ prompts you to add a handler; go ahead and answer Yes to that question. Visual C++ adds CFingConView::OnFingerConnect to your FingConView.cpp source file. Edit that function, and make it look like this:

```
void CFingConView::OnFingerConnect()

{

        m_finger.MakeFingerFinger();

}
```

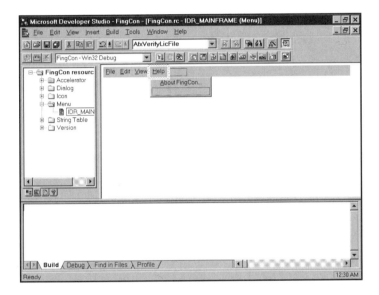

FIGURE 8-3

This figure shows the default menu resource provided by the MFC framework.

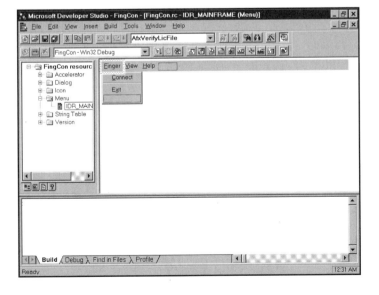

FIGURE 8-4

This is the menu for the finger container sample that accompanies this chapter. There's no Edit menu, and the File menu is fingerized.

OnFingerConnect makes one simple call to the MakeFingerFinger method, exported in the finger control. If you recall, CFingerCtrl::MakeFingerFinger initiates the finger query. This allows the user to fill in the Command edit box and then select the Connect item from the Finger menu to make a connection to the specified finger server.

That's it! You're now ready to compile and run your test container and test the finger control. Take some time to build the project (and get rid of your compiler errors, if you have any). Then I'll run you through a few simple tests.

OK, now that you've compiled the container, press F5 to run it. Play around with it, and have some fun. Type **pepsi@cunix.cc.columbia.edu** in the Command field, and click the finger button. You should get a response that looks something like the output shown in Figure 8–5. Also, resize the app's main window. Do the controls within the view scale to fit the main window?

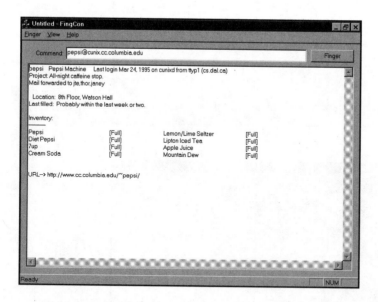

FIGURE 8-5

This figure shows the output that you receive when you finger pepsi@cunix.cc. columbia.edu *with the finger control you've created.*

Nifty Things to Do with Finger

I'm not sure there's anything neat that you can do with the finger control that I haven't already mentioned in the first part of this chapter. We've covered how the technology is used on the Internet—mostly to find information about people and machines. But what's next? How can you extend the finger protocol to make it cutting-edge?

Have you ever come up with some idea but didn't have the capital to bring it to market—and then find it on a shelf at your software store a year later? Yeah, me too. I had this idea to create a finger server that you could query for stock information. I imagined building an enhanced finger client that would read stock data from the queries returned from the finger server. It would have made me millions—probably gergillions.

Needless to say, I saw it running on someone else's machine a few months back, and boy, is it terrific! But there's only one problem (yep, you guessed it): I didn't write it. Don't get me wrong—I'm not complaining about the fact that I didn't follow through with the idea; I'm glad to see that it's out there. My point is that you can do anything you want with the Internet technology.

Looking at PointCast (that's the stock-quote program that I'm talking about), I doubt very seriously that it's based on the finger protocol and talks to a finger server. But it wouldn't be hard to do something like that using finger. You're probably not going to take any market share away from the PointCast folks, because their stuff is darned impressive (not that I don't have faith in you). But there's probably room in the market for a plug-in object that gets stock-type information.

Imagine selling a control that retrieves seismic information from data-collection devices hooked to the Net to research firms across the country. Or imagine a control that keeps tabs on NASA's space programs. The possibilities are limited only by imagination.

Coke, Pepsi, and the Internet

Finger is commonly used to get the status of machines connected to the Internet. Most of these machines are connected by students—that is, the students are the ones who physically connect the machines to the Net; the connection is not actually made up of students.

Coke machines are popular, although a growing variety of devices are connected every day. Wouldn't it be neat to take this a step further, though? Imagine a graphical interface for the Pepsi machine at `cunix.cc.columbia.edu`. Imagine an actual Pepsi machine sitting on your desktop; it tells you what's empty. Maybe you can drop in a quarter and order a soda for one of the dudes on campus.

Information Vending Machines

You don't need me to tell you that the Internet is about information. Just look around you. After many TV shows, on public TV and cable, you get a Web address or an e-mail address. Radio shows have 'em now, too. Heck, you can get everything from information about Twinkies (www.owlnet.rice.edu/~gouge/twinkies.html) to daily Bible readings (www.i1.Net/~mcoley/daily-reading.html).

My two examples are Web addresses, but you can use finger to spread information just as well. Let's say that you have a database of every UFO sighting reported in the United States for the past 50 years. It's a cinch to create a finger server to access that information. And you've already got a finger client control that you can plop into a C++ or Visual Basic interface.

Chapter Summary

This chapter is an important step in learning how to build Internet components. It taught you how to use the CSocket class, along with CArchive, to make your programming easier. You learned an easy way to store incoming information and display that information in an easy-to-use interface. You also learned important concepts of client/server communication.

In Chapter 9, "Plug-in WHOIS," you build a client control that's very similar to the finger control that you built in this chapter. WHOIS is different, though, because it talks to a specific set of servers called NIC servers. You'll strengthen what you've learned so far, as well as learn much more about interfaces and communication between clients and servers.

Chapter | 9

Plug-in WHOIS

by Edward B. Toupin

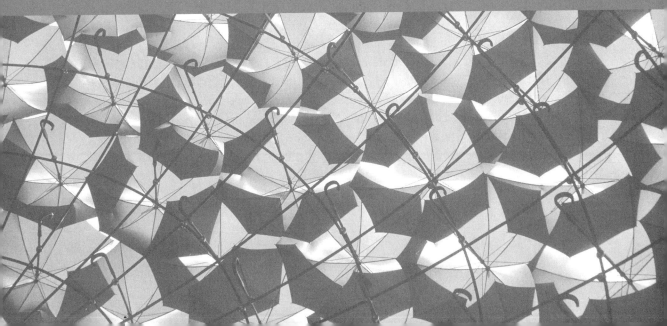

In the past few years, the Internet has grown from a network dedicated to educational institutions, the government, and the military into an enterprise solution for many organizations, as well as a playground for many individuals. Since many of the nearly 20 million users are using Microsoft Windows as a vehicle for Internet access, there is a need for robust Windows-based, Internet-enabled applications.

This chapter outlines the well-known WHOIS protocol. WHOIS allows users to query for information in central repositories regarding users', hosts', and companies' addresses, phone numbers, and contact personnel.

To provide a foundation for your understanding, this chapter covers the following topics:

◆ Overview of the WHOIS protocol

◆ Connecting to a WHOIS server

◆ Sending queries and receiving responses

◆ Closing the connection

◆ Looking for information with WHOIS

What Is the WHOIS Protocol?

The WHOIS service is a TCP-transaction-based query/response service whose primary database resides on the Internet Network Information Center (InterNIC) host (SRI-NIC). This host provides netwide directory service to Internet users for location of user, domain, and host information. It is one of a series of Internet name services maintained by the InterNIC at SRI International on behalf of the Defense Communications Agency (DCA). The service can be accessed across the Internet from user programs running on local hosts to deliver the full name, U.S. mailing address, telephone number, and network mailbox for users registered in the InterNIC database. Primarily, when a query is made, only individuals who administer sites or maintain their own domain have their names registered in the WHOIS database—essentially, anyone who is responsible for creating traffic on the Internet is listed in the database.

The WHOIS Protocol

The protocol itself (see Figure 9-1) is very simple and is based on the query/response model. In this model, when a query is sent, the recipient simply provides a response and drops the connection.

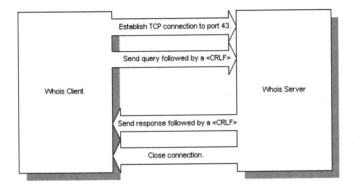

FIGURE 9-1

The WHOIS protocol is based on a simple query/response model.

For WHOIS, the originator of the query connects to service port 43 on the remote WHOIS server via connection-oriented TCP. The originator then sends a command line containing the desired query, terminated with a carriage return/line feed (<CRLF>). The WHOIS server collects the information from its database to satisfy the query and responds with the collected information to the originator of the query. The server closes the connection as soon as all the information has been sent.

WHOIS Commands

The WHOIS command line is generally a single name used as a query string for the remote WHOIS server. You can also send a series of commands to the server for help and general information. Since WHOIS servers, like other technology, advance at a steady pace, you can retrieve the WHOIS commands for a given server by sending a question mark, followed by a carriage return/line feed (?<CRLF>). The response from the server will be a complete list of all possible formats that can be used.

To look up a handle, name, host name, or other field, just type it. WHOIS does a very broad search on your input. To narrow the search or change the behavior of WHOIS, put one or more of the following keywords or characters (shown with their minimum abbreviation in caps) before your input:

To Find Only a Certain Record TYPE:	To Search Only a Specific FIELD:	
DOmain	GAteway	HAndle or !
GRoup	HOst	Mailbox or contains @
NEtwork	ORganization	NAme or leading.
PErson^M	ASn	

Other WHOIS keywords are:

EXPand or *	Shows all parts of display without asking
Full or =	Shows detailed display for each match
HElp	Enters help program for full documentation
PArtial or trailing period (.)	Matches targets starting with given string
Q, QUIT, or press RETURN	Exits WHOIS
SUBdisplay or %	Shows users of host, hosts on Net, and so on
SUMmary or $	Always shows summary, even if just one match exists

Add a trailing period (.) to your input (or use the PArtial keyword) to make it a partial search that matches everything starting with your input. **name mack.**, for example, finds the names *Mack, Mackall, MacKay,* and so on. Arpanet and MIlnet are the same as HOst, except they match only hosts on those networks.

Examples are:

dom root	.smyth.
host nic	full %nic
net 128.15	!lynn^M

To guarantee matching only a single record, look it up by its handle with a handle-only search. **lynn** finds records with the name, handle, mailbox, and other information for lynn, but **!lynn** or **ha lynn** finds only the single record whose handle is lynn. In record summary lines, the handle is shown in parenthesis after the name, which is first in the line.

Type **HELP** for more complete help; press Enter to exit.

The InterNIC registration services host contains only Internet information (networks, ASNs, domains, and POCs). Please use the WHOIS server aty `nic.ddn.mil` for MIL-NET information.

Following is the result of a standard query for the name *TOUPIN*. This query is submitted to InterNIC, and the results are sent back to the originator of the query for output and processing.

```
Toupin, Edward (ET21)      etoupin@TOUPIN.COM      (303) 470-7430

Toupin, Jerry (JT330)      jerryt@jmont.com        (404) 765-0556
```

> **CAUTION:** If a given query has many entries, the operation may take a long time to complete. In some cases, patience is the only thing to have when you are waiting for the results of some queries.

One final query retrieves a list of all WHOIS servers around the world. By sending the query **whois-servers** to `sipb.mit.edu`, you can retrieve a list of all servers and immediately connect to any of them to perform a query. Make sure to request the command set from the connected server in Table 9-1 to know what commands can be sent to the specific server.

Table 9-1   Summary of Internet WHOIS Servers

Host Name	Description
whois.pacbell.com	Pacific Bell (C=US)
whois.sunquest.com	Sunquest Information Systems (C=US)
whois.berkeley.edu	University of California at Berkeley (C=US)
www.binghamton.edu	State University of New York at Binghamton (C=US)
finger.caltech.edu	California Institute of Technology (C=US)
csufresno.edu	California State University—Fresno (C=US)
csuhayward.edu	California State University—Hayward (C=US)
csus.edu	California State University—Sacramento (C=US)

continues

Table 9-1   Continued

Host Name	Description
whois.cwru.edu	Case Western Reserve University (C=US)
cc.fsu.edu	Florida State University (C=US)
gettysburg.edu	Gettysburg College (C=US)
gmu.edu	George Mason University (C=US)
whois.dfci.harvard.edu	Dana-Farber Cancer Institute (C=US)
hmc.edu	Harvey Mudd College (C=US)
indiana.edu	Indiana University (C=US)
who.is.messiah.edu	Messiah College (C=US)
whois.rsmas.miami.edu	University of Miami, Rosentiel School of Marine and Atmospheric Sciences (C=US)
mit.edu	Massachusetts Institute of Technology (C=US)
directory.msstate.edu	Mississippi State University (C=US)
vax2.winona.msus.edu	Minnesota State University—Winona (C=US)
info.nau.edu	Northern Arizona University (C=US)
whois.ncsu.edu	North Carolina State University (C=US)
nd.edu	University of Notre Dame (C=US)
earth.njit.edu	New Jersey Institute of Technology (C=US)
vm1.nodak.edu	North Dakota State University (C=US)
austin.onu.edu	Ohio Northern University (C=US)
ph.orst.edu	Oregon State University (C=US)
osu.edu	Ohio State University (C=US)
whois.oxy.edu	Occidental College (C=US)
info.psu.edu	Pennsylvania State University (C=US)
whois.cc.rochester.edu	University of Rochester (C=US)
whitepages.rutgers.edu	Rutgers University (C=US)
whois.sdsu.edu	San Diego State University (C=US)
stanford.edu	Stanford University (C=US)
camis.stanford.edu	Stanford University (C=US)
whois.slac.stanford.edu	Stanford Linear Accelerator Center (C=US)
stjohns.edu	St. John's University (C=US)
sunysb.edu	State University of New York at Stony Brook (C=US)
whois.bcm.tmc.edu	Baylor College of Medicine (C=US)
whois.ubalt.edu	University of Baltimore (C=US)

Host Name	Description
directory.ucdavis.edu	University of California at Davis (C=US)
uchicago.edu	University of Chicago (C=US)
ucsd.edu	University of California at San Diego (C=US)
weber.ucsd.edu	University of California at San Diego, Division of Social Sciences (C=US)
cgl.ucsf.edu	University of California at San Francisco, School of Pharmacy (C=US)
whois.uh.edu	University of Houston (C=US)
whois.umass.edu	University of Massachusetts at Amherst (C=US)
lookup.umd.edu	University of Maryland (C=US)
umn.edu	University of Minnesota (C=US)
ns.unl.edu	University of Nebraska at Lincoln (C=US)
whois.upenn.edu	University of Pennsylvania (C=US)
x500.utexas.edu	University of Texas at Austin (C=US)
netlib2.cs.utk.edu	na-net (linear algebra on computers) (C=US)
whois.virginia.edu	University of Virginia (C=US)
whois.wfu.edu	Wake Forest University (C=US)
wisc.edu	University of Wisconsin (C=US)
wpi.wpi.edu	Worcester Polytechnic Institute (C=US)
ibc.wustl.edu	Washington University (C=US)
vm1.hqa.dmin.doe.gov	U.S. Department of Energy headquarters (C=US)
wp.doe.gov	U.S. Department of Energy (C=US)
llnl.gov	Lawrence Livermore National Laboratory (C=US)
x500.arc.nasa.gov	NASA Ames Research Center (C=US)
x500.gsfc.nasa.gov	NASA Goddard Space Flight Center (C=US)
larc.nasa.gov	NASA Langley Research Center (C=US)
wp.nersc.gov	National Energy Research Supercomputer Center (C=US)
seda.sandia.gov	Sandia National Laboratories (C=US)
whois.nic.ddn.mil	DoD Network Information Center (Department of Defense and military only)
whois.nrl.navy.mil	Naval Research Laboratory (C=US)
wp.es.net	Energy Sciences Network (C=US)

continues

Table 9-1   Continued

Host Name	Description
ds.internic.net	Network Solutions, Inc. (nonMILNET/non-POC) (C=US)
whois.internic.net	Network Solutions, Inc. (C=US)
whois.lac.net	Latin America and Caribbean WHOIS server (C=EC)
whois.ripe.net	Reseaux IP Europeens (C=NL)
whois.morris.org	Morris Automated Information Network (C=US)
whois.risc.uni-linz.ac.at	Research Institute for Symbolic Computation, University of Linz (C=AT)
archie.au	Australian Academic and Research Network (C=AU)
whois.adelaide.edu.au	University of Adelaide (C=AU)
whois.monash.edu.au	Monash University (C=AU)
uwa.edu.au	University of Western Australia (C=AU)
sserve.cc.adfa.oz.au	University College, Australian Defense Force Academy (C=AU)
whois.kuleuven.ac.be	Katholieke Universiteit Leuven (C=BE)
whois.belnet.be	Belgian National Research Network (C=BE)
whois.camosun.bc.ca	Camosun College, Victoria, B.C. (C=CA)
whois.queensu.ca	Queen's University, Kingston (C=CA)
ac.nsac.ns.ca	Nova Scotia Agricultural College (C=CA)
whois.unb.ca	University of New Brunswick (C=CA)
panda1.uottawa.ca	University of Ottawa (C=CA)
dvinci.usask.ca	University of Saskatchewan, Engineering (C=CA)
whois.usask.ca	University of Saskatchewan (C=CA)
phys.uvic.ca	University of Victoria, Physics and Astronomy (C=CA)
whois.uwo.ca	University of Western Ontario (C=CA)
whois.nic.ch	SWITCH Swiss Academic and Research Network (C=CH)
whois.ci.ucr.ac.cr	University of Costa Rica Computer Center (C=CR)
whois.cuni.cz	Charles University, Prague (C=CZ)
whois.mff.cuni.cz	Charles University, Faculty of Mathematics and Physics (C=CZ)
whois.vutbr.cz	Technical University of Brno (C=CZ)
whois.fh-koeln.de	Fachhochschule Koeln (C=DE)

Host Name	Description
whois.fzi.de	Forschungszentrum Informatik (C=DE)
hermes.informatik. htw-zittau.de	HTW Zittau/Goerlitz Elektrotechnik/Informatik (C=DE)
whois.th-darmstadt.de	Darmstadt University of Technology (C=DE)
whois.tu-chemnitz.de	Technische Universitaet Chemnitz (C=DE)
whois.uni-regensburg.de	Universitaet Regensburg (C=DE)
whois.uni-c.dk	Danish Computing Centre for Research and Education (C=DK)
whois.eunet.es	EUnet, Goya, Spain (C=ES)
whois.dit.upm.es	Tech. Univ. Madrid, Telecommunications High School (C=ES)
cs.hut.fi	Helsinki University of Technology (C=FI)
oulu.fi	Oulu University (C=FI)
vtt.fi	Technical Research Centre of Finland (C=FI)
whois.univ-lille1.fr	University of Sciences and Technologies of Lille, France (C=FR)
isgate.is	Association of Research Networks in Iceland (C=IS)
dsa.nis.garr.it	GARR-NIS c/o CNR-CNUCE (C=IT)
whois.nis.garr.it	GARR-NIS c/o CNR-CNUCE (C=IT)
whois-s.erver.l.chiba-u.ac.jp	Chiba University (C=JP)
whois.cc.keio.ac.jp	Keio University (C=JP)
whois.cc.uec.ac.jp	University of Electro-Communications (C=JP)
whois.nic.ad.jp	Japan Network Information Center (C=JP)
whois.nic.li	SWITCH Swiss Academic and Research Network (C=LI)
whois.canterbury.ac.nz	University of Canterbury (C=NZ)
directory.vuw.ac.nz	Victoria University, Wellington (C=NZ)
waikato.ac.nz	Waikato University (C=NZ)
whois.elka.pw.edu.pl	Faculty of Electronic Engineering, Warsaw University of Technology (C=PL)
whois.ia.pw.edu.pl	Institute of Automatic Control, Warsaw University of Technology (C=PL)
chalmers.se	Chalmers University of Technology (C=SE)

continues

Table 9-1   Continued

Host Name	Description
kth.se	Royal Institute of Technology (C=SE)
sics.se	Swedish Institute of Computer Science (C=SE)
whois.sunet.se	SUNET (Swedish University Network) (C=SE)
whois.uakom.sk	SANET (WAN of Slovak academic institutions) (C=SK)
src.doc.ic.ac.uk	Imperial College (C=GB)
whois.lut.ac.uk	Loughborough University (C=GB)
whois.state.ct.us	Department of Administrative Services, State of Connecticut (C=US)
info.cnri.reston.va.us	Corporation for National Research Initiatives, knowbot interface (C=US)
whois.und.ac.za	University of Natal (Durban) (C=ZA)

WHOIS Custom Control Architecture

The WHOIS control provides several members and methods (see Listing 9-1) for access by container applications such as Visual Basic, Delphi, and Visual FoxPro. When certain members are assigned values, the associated property procedures create threads that are used to perform the respective operations in the background in a nonblocking, or non-modal, mode of operation.

Listing 9-1   Dispatch Map for WHOIS Control

```
BEGIN_DISPATCH_MAP(CWhoisCtrl, COleControl)
    //{{AFX_DISPATCH_MAP(CWhoisCtrl)
    DISP_PROPERTY_NOTIFY(CWhoisCtrl, "WhoisRequest", m_whoisRequest,
➥OnWhoisRequestChanged, VT_BSTR)
    DISP_PROPERTY_NOTIFY(CWhoisCtrl, "ErrorNumber", m_errorNumber,
➥OnErrorNumberChanged, VT_I2)
    DISP_PROPERTY_NOTIFY(CWhoisCtrl, "HostAddress", m_hostAddress,
➥OnHostAddressChanged, VT_BSTR)
    DISP_PROPERTY_NOTIFY(CWhoisCtrl, "Action", m_action, OnActionChanged, VT_I2)
```

```
    DISP_PROPERTY_NOTIFY(CWhoisCtrl, "CurrentState", m_currentState,
➥OnCurrentStateChanged, VT_I2)
    DISP_FUNCTION(CWhoisCtrl, "GetWhoisInformation", GetWhoisInformation, VT_BSTR,
➥VTS_BSTR VTS_BSTR)
    //}}AFX_DISPATCH_MAP
    DISP_FUNCTION_ID(CWhoisCtrl, "AboutBox", DISPID_ABOUTBOX, AboutBox, VT_EMPTY,
➥VTS_NONE)
END_DISPATCH_MAP()
```

As shown in Figure 9-2, the control itself maintains only one base process and, when activated, one thread. The thread is responsible for connecting to a remote WHOIS server, submitting the query, receiving the response, and closing its end of the connection.

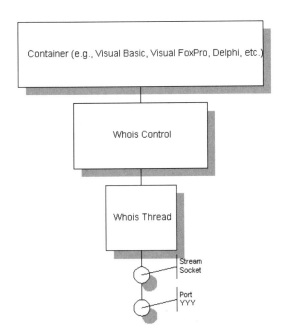

FIGURE 9-2

The WHOIS control consists of one base thread and the functional query thread.

As shown in Listing 9-2, the assignment of a value to the Action property of the control initiates the creation of a thread to perform the WHOIS operation. If a request for information is made, the control first checks to see if a thread exists, using the GetExitCodeThread() function. Since the control limits the number of concurrent requests to one, if the WHOIS thread is already active, the code returns an error through the event procedure FireEndGetWhoisInformation.

Listing 9-2 *Action* **Property Procedure**

```
void CWhoisCtrl::OnActionChanged()
{
        DWORD                ThreadId;
        DWORD                ThreadExitCode;
        CString                  cTempStr;

        switch(m_action)
        {
                case REQUEST_INFORMATION :        //REQUEST
                        GetExitCodeThread(m_hThreadHandle, &ThreadExitCode);
                        if(ThreadExitCode != STILL_ACTIVE)
                        {
                                m_hThreadHandle = CreateThread(NULL, 0, TRequestData, this,
➥0, &ThreadId);
                        }
                        else
                        {
                                m_errorNumber = 11000;
                                cTempStr.Empty();
                                FireEndGetWhoisInformation (cTempStr, m_errorNumber);
                        }
                        break;

                case CANCEL_REQUEST :        //CANCEL
                        GetExitCodeThread(m_hThreadHandle, &ThreadExitCode);
                        if(ThreadExitCode == STILL_ACTIVE) TerminateThread(m_hThreadHandle,
➥0);

                        m_errorNumber = 12050;        //Operation Cancelled
                        m_currentState = WAITING_FOR_ACTION;
```

```
            cTempStr.Empty();
            FireEndGetWhoisInformation (cTempStr, m_errorNumber);
            break;


    default :
            m_errorNumber = 12000;        //Invalid Action Selected
            cTempStr.Empty();
            FireEndGetWhoisInformation (cTempStr, m_errorNumber);
    }


    SetModifiedFlag();

}
```

If the operation is canceled, the thread is terminated, using the TerminateThread() function. A return code for the operation is returned via the FireEndGetWhoisInformation event procedure.

The WHOIS thread itself (see Listing 9-3) is very straightforward and consists of one simple procedure. This thread connects to a remote WHOIS server, issues the query, receives the response, and disconnects.

Listing 9-3   WHOIS Thread Function

```
DWORD WINAPI TRequestData(LPVOID pParam)
{
    CString             s, WhoisStr;
    int                   nListen_sd, nChars, outoffset = 0, offset = 0;
    int                 TimeOut = 10000, retval = 1;
    struct                  sockaddr_in server_addr;
    char                RecvBuff[1500], TempData[1505];
    CWhoisCtrl*             thisObject = (CWhoisCtrl*)pParam;

    //Initialize error property
    thisObject->m_errorNumber = 0;
```

continues

Listing 9-3   Continued

```
        //Open a socket and get a handle
        thisObject->m_currentState = CONNECTING;
        nListen_sd = socket(AF_INET, SOCK_STREAM, 0);
        if(nListen_sd < 0) END_THREAD_WITH_ERROR(WSAGetLastError() - WSABASEERR);

        //Prepare the address structure
        server_addr.sin_family = AF_INET;
        server_addr.sin_addr.s_addr = inet_addr((char*)thisObject-
➥>m_hostAddress.GetBuffer(40));
        server_addr.sin_port = htons(IPPORT_WHOIS);

        setsockopt(nListen_sd, SOL_SOCKET, SO_RCVTIMEO, (const char *)&TimeOut,
➥sizeof(TimeOut));
        setsockopt(nListen_sd, SOL_SOCKET, SO_SNDTIMEO, (const char *)&TimeOut,
➥sizeof(TimeOut));

        //Connect to a remote address
        if(connect(nListen_sd, (struct sockaddr far *)&server_addr, sizeof(server_addr))
➥== -1)
                END_THREAD_WITH_ERROR(WSAGetLastError() - WSABASEERR);

        //Prepare the request for submission
        WhoisStr = thisObject->m_whoisRequest + CString("\r\n", 2);
        thisObject->m_currentState = SENDING_REQUEST;
        if(send(nListen_sd, WhoisStr.GetBuffer(WhoisStr.GetLength()),
➥WhoisStr.GetLength(), 0) == -1)
                END_THREAD_WITH_ERROR(WSAGetLastError() - WSABASEERR);

        s.Empty();
        do
        {
                memset(RecvBuff,0,sizeof(RecvBuff));
```

```
memset(TempData,0,sizeof(TempData));
nChars = recv(nListen_sd,RecvBuff,sizeof(RecvBuff),0);
thisObject->m_currentState = RECEIVING_INFORMATION;


for (offset=0;offset<=nChars;offset++)
{
        switch(RecvBuff[offset])
        {
                case '\n' :
                        TempData[outoffset] = 0x0D;
                        outoffset++;
                        TempData[outoffset] = 0x0A;
                        outoffset=0;
                        s += TempData;
                        memset(TempData,0,sizeof(TempData));
                        break;
                case '\t' :
                        memcpy(&TempData[outoffset],"      ",8);
                        outoffset += 8;
                        break;
                default   :
                        if(isprint(RecvBuff[offset]))
                        {
                                TempData[outoffset]=RecvBuff[offset];
                                outoffset++;
                        }
                        break;
        }
}


if(outoffset)
{
        s += TempData;
```

continues

Listing 9-3   Continued

```
                        outoffset=0;
            }


        }while(nChars >0);



byebye:
        closesocket(nListen_sd);

        if (retval)
        {
                thisObject->m_errorNumber = 0;
        }

        thisObject->m_strWhoisString = s;
        thisObject->m_currentState = WAITING_FOR_ACTION;
        thisObject->m_bWhoisEvent = TRUE;
        thisObject->SendMessage(WM_TIMER, 1, 0);

        return(retval);
}
```

Connecting to a Remote WHOIS Server

The thread function (see Listing 9-4) first creates a stream socket, using the socket()
Winsock API function. The socket handle, nListen_sd, is then used in the connect() API
function to issue a connect request to the remote host specified in the server_addr variable. The server_addr variable is of the sockaddr_in structure, which allows you to specify
the address type (sin_family), remote address (sin_addr.s_addr), and the port to attach to
on the remote host (sin_port).

Listing 9-4   Remote Port and Address Specification

```
server_addr.sin_family = AF_INET;
server_addr.sin_addr.s_addr = inet_addr((char*)thisObject->m_hostAddress.GetBuffer(16));
server_addr.sin_port = htons(IPPORT_WHOIS);
```

For this protocol, we specify that we want to use the standard dot notation Internet address, using the AF_INET define. The address of the remote host with which we want to communicate is specified in the HostAddress (m_hostAddress) property of the control. This property is converted to a standard Internet address, using inet_addr(). The port is identified through the IPPORT_WHOIS define and is assigned to the variable before being passed on to the connect() function.

Sending a Query

Once connected, the thread appends a carriage return and a line feed to the query string in the WhoisRequest (m_whoisRequest) property (see Listing 9-5). The send() Winsock API function is then called to submit the query to the remote connected host. Immediately after the send() function returns, the thread performs a do...loop, using the recv() API function to receive any incoming information from the remote host. Once all the data is received from the remote host, the thread performs some text processing to format properly for tabs and carriage returns/line feeds.

Listing 9-5   Sending a WHOIS Query

```
//Prepare the request for submission
WhoisStr = thisObject->m_whoisRequest + CString("\r\n", 2);
thisObject->m_currentState = SENDING_REQUEST;
if(send(nListen_sd, WhoisStr.GetBuffer(WhoisStr.GetLength()),
➥WhoisStr.GetLength(), 0) == -1)
        END_THREAD_WITH_ERROR(WSAGetLastError() - WSABASEERR);
```

Thread Completion

Upon completion (see Listing 9-6), we perform an assignment to the m_strWhoisString member, as well as set the m_bWhoisEvent to TRUE. The final operation is to send a WM_TIMER message back to the control to signal the completion of the thread's operation.

Listing 9-6   Thread Completion

```
byebye:
        closesocket(nListen_sd);

        if (retval)
        {
                thisObject->m_errorNumber = 0;
        }

        thisObject->m_strWhoisString = s;
        thisObject->m_currentState = WAITING_FOR_ACTION;
        thisObject->m_bWhoisEvent = TRUE;
        thisObject->SendMessage(WM_TIMER, 1, 0);

        return(retval);
```

The reason for the assignment of TRUE to m_bWhoisEvent and the sending of the WM_TIMER message is to allow the control to continue processing the WHOIS operation asynchronously when calling the associated OnTimer event procedure of Listing 9-7. This type of operation allows the thread to complete, exit, and notify the control that it can continue processing the information gathered by the thread. In this case, if the m_bWhoisEvent member is TRUE and the WM_TIMER message is sent, the control calls the FireEndGetWhoisInformation event procedure, which passes the WHOIS information collected, as well as an error value generated, if any, during the WHOIS operation.

Listing 9-7   *OnTimer (WM_TIMER)* **Procedure**

```
void CWhoisCtrl::OnTimer(UINT nIDEvent)
{
        if(m_bWhoisEvent == TRUE)
        {
                m_bWhoisEvent = FALSE;
                FireEndGetWhoisInformation (m_strWhoisString, m_errorNumber);
        }


        COleControl::OnTimer(nIDEvent);

}
```

You may be wondering why we are using go tos and labels in this code. Actually, it was the easiest and most straightforward way to implement the code. A state machine could have been implemented, or a long series of carefully planned if...then statements, but the objective was merely to drop through to the end of the thread when an error occurs. In this way, we can easily reach a point where we could perform cleanup and drop out of the thread completely upon query completion and generated errors.

Testing the WHOIS Control

Now that you have a basic understanding of the WHOIS protocol and an overview of the OCX implementation, let's look at using the custom control to implement the protocol in Visual Basic 4.0 under Windows NT 3.51. As shown in Figure 9-3, we have a WHOIS client running and communicating with a remote WHOIS server.

The edit controls at the top of Figure 9-3 allow you to enter the name of the user about whom you want to query. Once the information is entered, clicking the Query button notifies the application to begin the query to the remote host. Upon completion, the returned information is placed in the larger text control in the center of the figure.

When you click the Query button, the application must first resolve the address for the host name entered in the Remote Host edit control (see Listing 9-8). This address-resolution operation must always be performed to determine the IP address of the specified host. An *IP address* is the value placed in the IP packet sent across the Internet, so that

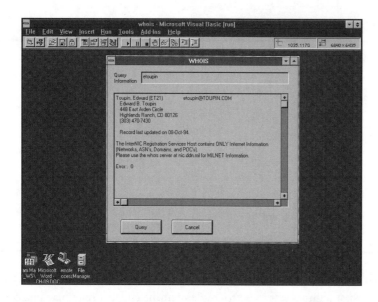

FIGURE 9-3

The WHOIS Visual Basic test application makes queries to WHOIS servers, using the WHOIS control.

the routers, gateways, and bridges can properly direct the packet through the Internet to the appropriate remote host.

Listing 9-8   Address Resolution

```
Private Sub Command1_Click()
   GetAdrs1.HostName = "WHOIS.INTERNIC.NET"
End Sub


Private Sub GetAdrs1_EndGetHostAddress(ByVal IPAddress As String, ByVal ErrorNumber As
Integer)
   Whois1.HostAddress = IPAddress
   Whois1.WhoisRequest = Text3.Text
   Whois1.Action = REQUEST_INFORMATION
End Sub
```

In Listing 9-8, the host name, WHOIS.INTERNIC.NET, is passed to a member of the GetAdrs1 control. This control is part of the GetHost control, which allows you to easily perform address resolution on any host name found on the Internet or an intranet. Once the operation is complete, the EndGetHostAddress event procedure is called, passing the resolved IPAddress and an ErrorNumber.

The IPAddress is assigned to the HostAddress property of the Whois1 control and the text of the Text3 control, the query, is assigned to the WhoisRequest property. Once REQUEST_ACTION is assigned to the Action property, the thread is initialized, and the WHOIS query begins.

In Listing 9-9, the WHOIS event procedure is called upon completion of the WHOIS query and after the thread exits. The application takes the WhoisInformation, which is the returned information from the WHOIS query, and assigns it to the Text2 control (the larger of the controls in Figure 9-3). At this point, the WHOIS information from the query is displayed and the application waits for additional queries to a remote host.

Listing 9-9   WHOIS Event Procedure

```
Private Sub Whois1_EndGetWhoisInformation(ByVal WhoisInformation As String, ByVal
ErrorNumber As Integer)
  Text2.Text = WhoisInformation + Chr(13) + Chr(10) + "Error : " + Str(ErrorNumber)
End Sub
```

Nifty Things to Do with WHOIS

A useful function of the WHOIS protocol is the capability to locate people on the Internet. By entering the person's name or a substring thereof, you can locate anyone who is registered in a WHOIS database. As mentioned earlier, the requirement for being listed in the database is that an individual or organization be responsible for creating traffic on the Internet. You can also locate companies and domains on the Internet easily by submitting queries to a WHOIS server for information.

To locate an individual, you can precede his or her name with the PE command, as shown in Listing 9-10. For this command, you receive the address, e-mail address, and phone number of the company or individual.

Listing 9-10   WHOIS Query for PErson Toupin

```
QUERY : PE Toupin, Edward


RESPONSE :


Toupin, Edward (ET21)          etoupin@TOUPIN.COM
   Edward B. Toupin
   448 East Arden Circle
   Highlands Ranch, CO 80126
   (303) 470-7430


   Record last updated on 08-Oct-94.


The InterNIC Registration Services Host contains ONLY Internet Information
(Networks, ASN's, Domains, and POC's).
Please use the whois server at nic.ddn.mil for MILNET Information.
```

If we perform another query for Toupin, but this time precede the name with DO (for *domain*), we receive domain-related information about the entire Toupin domain (see Listing 9-11). In this instance, we receive the name and address of the domain, the name and e-mail address of the administrator, and the domain name servers on which the Toupin domain is originally located. Notice the differences in the two types of requests; each request returns a different set of information.

Listing 9-11   WHOIS Query for DOmain Toupin

```
QUERY : DO Toupin


RESPONSE :


Edward B. Toupin (TOUPIN-DOM)
   448 East Arden Circle
   Highlands Ranch, CO 80126
```

```
Domain Name: TOUPIN.COM

Administrative Contact, Technical Contact, Zone Contact:
 Toupin, Edward (ET21) etoupin@TOUPIN.COM
 (303) 470-7430

Record last updated on 08-Oct-94.
Record created on 08-Oct-94.

Domain servers in listed order:

NS-1.CSN.NET            199.117.27.21
NS1.WESTNET.NET        128.138.213.13


The InterNIC Registration Services Host contains ONLY Internet Information

(Networks, ASN's, Domains, and POC's).

Please use the whois server at nic.ddn.mil for MILNET Information.
```

A final example is multiple hosts under a particular domain—in this case, Colorado Supernet, Inc. (CSN). We requested a query on the DOmain for CSN and received four entries for the domain, as shown in Listing 9-12.

Listing 9-12   WHOIS Query for DOmain CSN

```
QUERY : DO CSN
RESPONSE :
CSN (CFR-CSN-RAC-DOM)                    CFR-CSN-RAC.COM
Colorado SuperNet, Inc. (CSN-DOM)           CSN.ORG
Colorado Supernet, Inc. (CSN1-DOM)          CSN.COM
Colorado Supernet, Inc. (CSN2-DOM)          CSN.NET


The InterNIC Registration Services Host contains ONLY Internet Information

(Networks, ASN's, Domains, and POC's).

Please use the whois server at nic.ddn.mil for MILNET Information.
```

If you want to retrieve information that is specific to any of the four locations for CSN's domain, simply use the unique identifier for the specific host or domain. Listing 9-13 demonstrates the display for a search on DOmain CSN1-DOM to access the details of the specific domain.

Listing 9-13   WHOIS Query for DOmain CSN1-DOM

```
QUERY : DO CSN1-DOM
RESPONSE :
Colorado Supernet, Inc. (CSN1-DOM)
   999 18th Street, Suite 2640
   Denver, CO 80202

   Domain Name: CSN.COM

   Administrative Contact, Technical Contact, Zone Contact:
    Colorado Supernet, Inc. (CSN-NOC) hostmaster@csn.net
    voice (303) 296-8202 fax (303) 296-8224


   Record last updated on 28-Sep-95.
   Record created on 15-Dec-91.

   Domain servers in listed order:

   NS-1.CSN.NET            199.117.27.21
   NS1.WESTNET.NET         128.138.213.13


The InterNIC Registration Services Host contains ONLY Internet Information
(Networks, ASN's, Domains, and POC's).
Please use the whois server at nic.ddn.mil for MILNET Information.
```

WHOIS is not only simple to use, but also can provide rich information on people, domains, and organizations available on the Internet. This is one of the easiest and least expensive methods available for searching the yellow pages of the Internet.

Chapter Summary

The implementation of the WHOIS protocol in the WHOIS control does not limit you to developing only specific WHOIS clients. You have the capability to create any other types of applications that you find useful in your intranet or Internet environments. For instance, you can implement a query mechanism to locate a particular user and then automatically extract the e-mail address to send e-mail to or issue a TALK request to that user, using an application that supports the NTALK protocol. The applications of Internet protocols in custom controls are virtually limitless, since you can instantly Internet-enable your applications for communications on the Internet or your internal intranet.

Chapter | 10

Plug-in News

by Jose Mojica

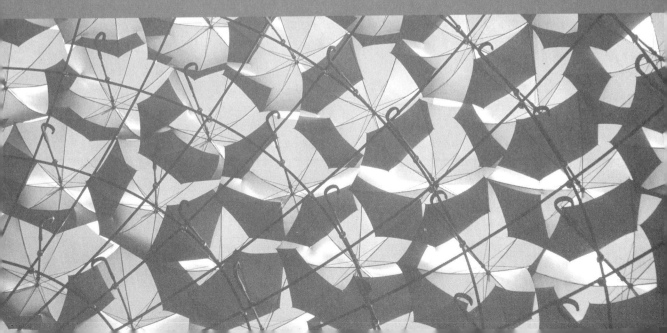

This chapter shows you how to make an OLE control that acts as a foundation for a news reader. A *news reader* is a program that allows you to access and reply to articles in a newsgroup. Your control will allow you to:

- Connect to a news server on the Internet
- Send commands to the server
- Receive and analyze server responses
- Fire events that are specific to each response

Background

Before you create a news reader, however, you may find it helpful to learn more about the network containing the newsgroups and the command protocol used to communicate with news servers.

Usenet

If you have ever connected to the Internet, chances are that you are now newsgroup-aware. You may have heard all the buzz words (such as Usenet, netnews, and newsgroups), and even though you might be able to use them correctly in sentences when you're talking to other computer initiates, you may not be very sure of what you are saying. Did you know, for example, that newsgroups are not really part of the Internet?

The Internet is a network. Newsgroups are a part of a separate network called Usenet. The word *Usenet* stands for "user's network." The user's network is an international network devoted to the distribution of information in the form of postings or articles, which people refer to as news. This news is not exactly like the news you read in a newspaper; it consists of announcements and opinions presented by other users of the server. News is not edited or monitored in any way. If you choose to post your own news, there is no guarantee that anyone will comment on your article.

A large number of newsgroups exist, grouped in seven standard Usenet categories (see Table 10-1). There are also several other categories, referred to as non-Usenet categories; they may or may not be present, depending on the news server that you are logged into. Below the main categories are numerous subcategories. One newsgroup, for example, discusses third-party add-on tools for the computer language Visual Basic. The name of this group is `comp.lang.basic.visual.3rdparty`.

Table 10-1   Usenet Categories

Category	Description
comp	Computers
misc	Miscellaneous
news	News (concerning the Usenet system)
rec	Recreation
soc	Social
sci	Science
talk	Talk (general debate)

Although it is not necessary to have Internet access to reach Usenet, you can reach Usenet through the Internet, and most Internet providers offer access to a news server. Other network services also offer access to Usenet, including bulletin-board services, CompuServe, and America Online. In general, it is safe to say that if you have access to the Internet, you have access to Usenet.

Network News Transfer Protocol (NNTP)

Another set of buzz words that you need to learn before creating your control relate to the protocol used in communicating with the news servers. These buzz words allow you to understand the basics of a news reader, and even if you decide to go no further, you can use them to impress your peers and supervisors.

The main term to know is NNTP. *NNTP* stands for *Network News Transfer Protocol*, which is the standard protocol used to read news via an Internet server. You may be familiar with the term TCP/IP from previous chapters. TCP/IP is a set of protocols; one of these protocols is NNTP.

In the next chapter, you learn about two other protocols: *SMTP* (Simple Mail Transfer Protocol), which allows you to send mail; and *POP* (Post Office Protocol), which allows you to retrieve mail. You reach these protocols through numbered ports. You transfer news articles, for example, by using TCP/IP via NNTP, using port 119. Port 119 is standard for all computers using TCP/IP.

A *protocol* is a set of predefined commands and responses. This chapter covers several of those commands for NNTP, but not all. For a complete list, download "Network News Transfer Protocol" (RFC 977), which is the official reference document for the NNTP, published in February 1996 by Brian Kantor and Phil Lapsley. You can find the document at http://www.academ.com/academ/nntp/index.html.

Building the Base Control

In this section, you learn how to create a tool that uses TCP/IP to connect to a news server. Then you add the capability to send commands and receive responses by using NNTP protocol. Finally, you add parsing routines that allow you to interpret the responses from the news server and route them to different OLE events.

In previous chapters, you learned how to use the ProjectWizard to create the foundation for your control, as well as how to use the ClassWizard to add properties, methods, and events. This chapter, therefore, assumes that you are familiar with these procedures.

Start by running the ProjectWizard and choosing to create an OLE control. Because of the complexity of this control, I recommend that you pace yourself, adding one feature at a time, and compiling and testing before adding the next feature.

Names in the Example

In the example code, I chose to name the directory NewsOCX. I also edited the names of my source files, as well as the name and description of the control itself. I named the source-code file that contains the control's functionality NewsCtl.cpp.

Visible vs. Invisible

Making this control invisible at run time makes sense. When you are deciding whether a control should be invisible at run time, a good practice is to determine whether the control has a single possible interface that encompasses all the control's functions. If you can think of several mutually exclusive possibilities for the interface, by selecting one, you may be attempting to design an application rather than a reusable object.

Because the control has a great deal of functionality, and because having a single interface for all the functions is impossible, I therefore chose to make it invisible at run time.

Supporting TCP/IP

After the ProjectWizard creates the necessary files, you need to add support for TCP/IP. Remember that the Internet uses TCP/IP to transfer information between remote computers. To write a program that uses TCP/IP, you need to use the TCP/IP API called *sockets*. The sockets that are specific to Windows operating systems are called *Windows sockets*. Therefore, you need to add the Windows sockets component to your control.

To add the Windows sockets container, choose the component option from the Insert menu in the Developer Studio. One of the components is Windows sockets. Click the Insert button. You will notice that the following code has been added to the file NEW-SOCX.CPP:

```
    // CG: The following block was added by the Windows sockets component.
    {
#ifndef _MAC
        if (!AfxSocketInit())
        {
            AfxMessageBox(CG_IDS_SOCKETS_INIT_FAILED);
            return FALSE;
        }
#endif // _MAC
    }
    BOOL bInit = COleControlModule::InitInstance();
```

At this point, you might think that you are ready to start using the TCP/IP API—and if you do, you are wrong. You still need to open the file stdafx.h and add the header files afxsock.h and windowsx.h. *Then* you'll be ready.

Establishing a Connection

The first task that your control needs to accomplish is to establish a connection with a news server. To connect, you will need to add some properties, a method, and an event to your control. You also need a member variable to hold a method's return value and a window handle. Finally, of course, you need to add code to handle the connection itself.

Adding Properties, Methods, and Events

Your control must know the name of a news server to which to connect. Therefore, using the ClassWizard, add the property HostName. This property will contain the name of the news server. (The news server that I connect to, for example, is news.emi.net.) Choose type CString and the implementation member variable for the property.

The user of the object issues the Connect method to make a connection to the server. Add this method as type Boolean.

It is important to realize that just because the user requests to be connected to the server, there is no guarantee that the connection will be successful. For this reason, add the event Connected. Fire this event when the news server responds favorably to a connection request.

You also need to add a property called IsConnected. The purpose of this property is to inform the programmer using the control whether the control is connected to the server before he/she issues a command. This property is useful in case the server decides to terminate the connection for no apparent reason. For this property, use the Boolean type and the Get/Set methods of implementation.

Table 10-2 shows the properties, methods, and events that your control should have at this point.

Table 10-2   Properties, Methods, and Events

Control Attribute	Type	Implementation
Property HostName	CString	Member variable
Property IsConnected	Boolean	Get/Set methods
Method Connect	void	—
Event Connected (with no parameters)	—	—

Adding a Member Variable

When you are done using the ClassWizard, you need to add a member variable to store the status of the connection that will be returned from the property IsConnected. In this example, I named the variable m_bConnected.

Adding a Window Handle

Even though you may be getting impatient to connect to the news server, you have one more preparation to make. Earlier, we decided that it made sense to make the control invisible at run time. Well, this plan has one small flaw. Later, you will see that some of the functions require the control to have a window handle. Invisible controls, however, are not automatically provided a window handle, because when the container discovers that the control is never going to be visible, it does not execute the code that creates a window handle. For this reason, you need to force the container to create the window handle. You do so by using the OLE control function RecreateControlWindow(), as in the following code:

```
void CNewsCtrl::OnSetClientSite()
{
        RecreateControlWindow();
}
```

Place that code in the file NEWSCTL.CPP, and place the declaration for the function in the file NEWSCTL.H.

Coding the Connection

Now you are ready to add code to the Connect method. I chose to separate the functions that are specific to this control from the functions that deal with Windows sockets. In the example code, I created the file SOCKSUPP.CPP. In that file, I stored all the functions that deal with Windows sockets directly. I also adopted the naming convention of placing the prefix WS before all the functions that deal with Windows sockets.

Obtaining a Socket Handle

The first step in connecting to the news server is obtaining a socket handle. This socket handle will be used in nearly every call made to the Windows sockets thereafter. See the following code:

```
BOOL CNewsCtrl::WSCreateSocket()
{
        m_hSock = ::socket(AF_INET, SOCK_STREAM, 0);

        if (m_hSock <= 0)
            return FALSE;
        else
        return TRUE;

}
```

Notice that the code declares a member variable, m_hSock. This variable will contain the value of the Windows socket handle.

The statement socket(AF_INET, SOCK_STREAM, 0) allocates the socket. The first parameter, AF_INET, is the address format. Only one address format is supported: AF_INET, which is the Internet format. The second parameter is the socket type. Currently, two socket types are available; only one type, SOCK_STREAM, is reliable for transferring large amounts of data. The third parameter is the protocol number. Given the first two parameters, only one protocol number is possible. Therefore, set this parameter to zero. Zero means that you allow the Windows socket library to find the protocol number that corresponds to the first two parameters.

Notice also that the code tests the value of m_hSock after the call has been made to see whether the statement was executed successfully. A value greater than zero means that the statement was successful.

Determining the Correct Port

The second step in making a connection to any remote server is determining the correct port. You may recall from the discussion earlier in this chapter that to use the NNTP protocol, you use port 119. If you were not sure of the value of the port, however, you could obtain this information by querying Windows sockets, as the following code shows:

```
BOOL CNewsCtrl::WSGetNewsPort()
{
        LPSERVENT servent;

        servent = ::getservbyname("nntp", "tcp");
        m_Port = servent->s_port;

        if (m_Port <= 0)
            return FALSE;
        else
            return TRUE;
}
```

The line that you are mostly interested in is servent = ::getservbyname("nntp", "tcp");. This function gets information about a particular service by querying TCP/IP directly for information. The code returns a structure that contains the following members:

Members	Use
s_name	Official name of the service
s_aliases	Null-terminated array of alternative names
s_port	Port number at which the service may be connected
s_proto	The name of the protocol to use when contacting the service

The code obtains the port number from the s_port member. Notice also that the code stores the value in a member variable, m_Port, to be used in later function calls.

Locating the Server

The next step is a little more complex. TCP/IP communicates with a server by finding a unique numeric address for that object, called an *IP address*. Many times, the user has a string representation of the server (in my case, news.emi.net). This server name needs to be located in the network and translated to a numeric address.

Locating a server can be time-consuming. You do not want to tie up the TCP/IP port while you are searching for this server and, thus, prevent other applications from using it. Therefore, you issue the locating function asynchronously—that is, issue the command in such a way that control immediately returns to the calling function.

At the point at which control is returned, the locating function may not be finished processing. Thus, you need to set up what is called a *callback function*—a function that the Windows socket calls when it is finished processing your request.

You may recall from the discussion earlier in this chapter that the control needs a window handle. The reason that the control needs that window handle is to implement the callback function. The following code shows the locating function:

```
BOOL CNewsCtrl::WSGetHostFromName()
{
        m_szBuf = (LPBYTE) GlobalAllocPtr(GHND, 2048);


    m_hTask = WSAAsyncGetHostByName(m_hWnd, WSCB_GETHOST, m_HostName, (char FAR *)
➡m_szBuf, 2048);
        return TRUE;
}
```

This function locates a host, given a host name. The name of the host is set by the user through the control's property HostName and is stored in the member variable m_HostName.

The heart of the preceding procedure is the call to the function WSAAsyncGetHostByName. This function is used to retrieve the host address that corresponds to a host name. The first three parameters set up the callback functionality. The first, m_hWnd, is the window handle. The second parameter is a custom message identifier. The following declaration should be placed in the file NEWSCTRL.H:

```
#define WSCB_GETHOST  (WM_USER + 100)
```

The third parameter is the host name that you are attempting to locate. The fourth parameter is a pointer to the data area that will receive the host data. You use this address to obtain the IP address.

In the preceding code, the Windows socket sends the WSCB_GETHOST message back to the control when it is done retrieving the address of the host. To capture this event, you need to add an entry to the message map macro for the control, as follows:

```
BEGIN_MESSAGE_MAP(CNewsCtrl, COleControl)
      //{{AFX_MSG_MAP(CNewsCtrl)
      // NOTE - ClassWizard will add and remove message map entries
      //   DO NOT EDIT what you see in these blocks of generated code !
      //}}AFX_MSG_MAP
      ON_OLEVERB(AFX_IDS_VERB_PROPERTIES, OnProperties)
      ON_MESSAGE(WSCB_GETHOST, OnGetHostCB)
END_MESSAGE_MAP()
```

Here is the callback function itself:

```
afx_msg LONG CNewsCtrl::OnGetHostCB(UINT wParam, LONG lParam)
{
      HANDLE hTask = (HANDLE) wParam;
      UINT  wserr = HIWORD(lParam);
      UINT  uCode = LOWORD(lParam);

      LPVOID lphe;

      // If the call didn't return an error do the connection.
      if (wserr == WSANOERROR)
      {
            lphe = (LPVOID) GlobalAllocPtr(GHND, sizeof(hostent));
            memcpy(lphe, (LPVOID) m_szBuf, sizeof(hostent));
            WSDoConnection(lphe);
      }
      return TRUE;
}
```

Because you are doing things asynchronously, you do not perform all the steps within the Connect method. You divide the method into parts. When you receive notification that one of the parts is complete, you begin executing the next part. This situation will be clearer later in this chapter, when I summarize the connection process.

Connecting to the Server

Now look at the code in the preceding section. Notice that if no errors resulted from locating the server we execute the function WSDoConnection. Following is the code for that function:

```
BOOL CNewsCtrl::WSDoConnection(LPVOID phostent)
{
        hostent he;
        u_long addr;
        sockaddr_in ca;


        // Copy the hostent data handle from the container to a real
        // hostent structure.


        memcpy((LPVOID) &he, phostent, sizeof(hostent));


        // Get the IP address from the hostent.


        addr = (*(u_long FAR *) he.h_addr_list[0]);


        // Fill in the sockaddr_structure so we can connect to
        // the specific port and IP address
        ca.sin_family   = AF_INET;
        ca.sin_port          = m_Port;
        ca.sin_addr.s_addr = addr;


        // Make the control watch for connections
        WSAAsyncSelect(m_hSock, m_hWnd, WSCB_ASELECT, FD_CONNECT );


        // Call the API connect() function, returning immediately.
        // The container will get a Connect event when the
        // connection is complete.


        return (::connect(m_hSock, (LPSOCKADDR) &ca, sizeof(sockaddr_in)) != NULL);

}
```

This function is really the heart of the connection process, where the actual Connect statement takes place. To connect to the news server, you see, you really need only three things:

- A handle to the Windows sockets library
- A port number for the protocol that you want
- The IP address of the server

All the other functions that you issued before this one were merely used to gather these three pieces of information.

Two of the pieces of information are stored in a sockaddr_structure. The first several lines extract the server's IP address, which is stored in an array of bytes. The code obtained the location of this array from the function WSAAsyncGetHostByName in the procedure WSGetHostFromName.

Notifying Completion

You are almost done with the connection, but not entirely. I probably was not able to keep you from seeing the call to the function WSAAsyncSelect. If you think that this function looks like another of those asynchronous functions that needs a callback function, you are correct.

This function call is very important. The connection statement is going to occur asynchronously, and you need to set up a way to notify the control when it is done. You do this before issuing the Connect event. WSAsyncSelect sets up a callback function to receive notification that the news control was connected successfully. The last parameter in the call FD_CONNECT informs the Windows sockets that you are interested only in obtaining notification of the status of the connection. It is possible to receive several other notifications in the same callback function, and you will expand that statement later in the chapter to enhance your control.

Firing the Connected Event

Here is the final step in connecting to the news server:

```
afx_msg LONG CNewsCtrl::OnASelectCB(UINT wParam, LONG lParam)
{
```

```
HANDLE hTask = (HANDLE) wParam;
UINT  wserr = HIWORD(lParam);
UINT  uCode = LOWORD(lParam);

switch (uCode)
{
    // If a connect message comes back, fire the Connect event
    case FD_CONNECT:
    {
        FireConnected();
        m_Connected=TRUE;
        break;
    }
    default:
    break;
}

return TRUE;
}
```

In this code, you see that if you receive the code FD_CONNECT from the Windows sockets library, your connection attempt was successful, and you are in. Therefore, you fire the Connected event to notify the user that he can continue issuing of other news commands. Also, you set the m_Connected value to TRUE to allow the user to query the status of the connection through the method IsConnected.

Summary of Connecting

This section summarizes what you have done so far.

When the user issues the Connect command, the following code executes:

```
void CNewsCtrl::Connect()
{
    WSCreateSocket();
    WSGetNewsPort();
    WSGetHostFromName();
}
```

The first function creates the handle to the Windows sockets library. The next statement finds out the port number for the NNTP service. The third statement gets the IP address of the news server from the given host name. After that command is issued, the code waits for the `OnGetHostCB` to gain control. From there, the code calls `WSDoConnection`. This function takes place immediately; then the code waits for the Windows sockets to invoke the callback function `OnASelectCB`. There, the code tests to see whether you have received an `FD_CONNECT` flag; if so, the `Connected` event fires.

> **TIP:** In creating a news reader, the programmer may disable the user's capability to invoke other commands while connecting. These command buttons need to remain disabled until the connection has been established. You do not enable the buttons after issuing the `Connect` statement, because control returns to the calling program immediately and does not imply that the connection has been set. Rather, wait until the `Connected` event is fired and then enable all the other functions.

You are done with the connection phase and are ready to get into NNTP. Therefore, take a breather, compile your project, go to the bathroom, and grab a snack before continuing.

Sending Commands, Receiving Responses

NNTP is a protocol—a language. It is a set of commands with a predefined set of responses. To make an OLE control that can understand NNTP, you simply need to be able to send commands to the NNTP port and interpret the answers.

There are 15 basic NNTP commands, which are described in Table 10-3.

Table 10-3   NNTP Commands

Command	Description
ARTICLE	Displays the header and then a blank line, followed by the text of the specified article.

continues

Table 10-3 Continued

Command	Description
BODY	The same as ARTICLE, except that it returns only the text of the article.
GROUP	Allows you to look at a particular newsgroup.
HEAD	The same as ARTICLE, except that it returns only the header of the article.
HELP	Returns a list of commands, along with the parameters that they accept.
IHAVE	Stands for *I have*; informs the news server that you have an article with a certain ID number. The server responds with a request for the article or a refusal for the article. If the article is requested, you can proceed to transmit it.
LAST	Every time you read an article, the server maintains a current article pointer. This command sets the pointer to the preceding article.
LIST	Returns a list of valid newsgroups.
NEWNEWS	Returns a list of message IDs of articles posted or received to the specified newsgroup since a particular date.
NEWSGROUPS	Returns a list of newsgroups created since a certain date.
NEXT	Moves the current article pointer to the next article.
POST	Submits an article to the server.
QUIT	Closes the connection with the news server.
SLAVE	Indicates that the connection to the server is from another server (called a slave server) rather than from an user.
STAT	Returns the message ID of a certain article.

Individual servers may have more commands, but they need to support these 15. Generally, these extra commands have x as the first letter.

The Format of Commands

These commands are sent to the server in the form of ASCII text. To be accepted by the server, the text needs to start with one of the words in Table 10-3, followed by a space and then by any parameters that the command may accept. These parameters are separated by spaces. The command concludes with a carriage return (character 13) and a line feed (character 10): <CR-LF>.

That's it! Having received your command, the happy little server might reply in the ways described in the following sections.

The Format of Responses

Each command has predefined responses. These responses can be divided into two categories: plain text and status lines. An example of a plain-text response is the answer generated from the command LIST. The server answers with a list of newsgroups in text format. The only rule with text is that any time it is transmitted, a line with a period (.) immediately followed by <CR-LF> indicates the end of the text transmission—that is, the server responds to the LIST command by sending a large amount of text with all the names of all the newsgroups. The last line in the text will be . followed by <CR-LF>.

Status lines are another kind of response. These lines are also sent in the form of ASCII text, but they are formatted in a special way. Status lines consist of three-digit numbers known as the *status codes*, followed by text that describes the status code (known as the *status description*). Sometimes, these codes denote completion of a command; sometimes, they denote error status. The LIST command, for example, has one possible status response:

```
215 list of newsgroups follows
```

Sample Command-Response Dialogue

Let's look at the typical conversation with the news server in plain English:

1. Establish connection.
2. Request list of newsgroups.
3. Open a newsgroup.
4. Get a list of articles.
5. Read an article.

In NNTP, this conversation would translate to the following once a connection is established. Assume that each line has a <CR-LF> at the end.

Command	Response
LIST	215 list of newsgroups follows
	comp.cool.sites 00543 00501 y
	comp.basic.visual.3rdparty 01010 00200
	(more newsgroups)
GROUP	comp.basic.visual.3rdparty
	211 104 00200 01010 comp.basic.visual.3rdparty group
	selected.
HEAD	221 00200 article retrieved - head follows.
	(header for the article)
NEXT	223 00201 article retrieved - statistics only.
BODY	222 00210 article retrieved - body follows.

Adding Command Methods and Response Events

You have endured several pages of reading without coding, and now you should reward yourself. From the preceding discussion, you know what you are trying to accomplish; you are going to add to your OCX the capability to send commands and retrieve responses. The type of OCX that you are developing is sometimes referred to as a *wrapper*—that is, it is a layer on top of the low-level commands that facilitate the building of programs. Many people make the mistake of creating wrappers that are too close to the low-level commands. When this happens, programmers who are using the tool must needlessly memorize a series of commands that are not in plain English, and they become frustrated—especially because in their minds, the reason that the tool was created in the first place was to simplify the instruction set.

What's my point? Instead of simply creating methods in your OCX that correspond word for word to the NNTP commands, you're going to use high-level commands that will be easier to remember. Instead of using a LIST method in the OCX, for example, why not have a GetNewsgroups method?

Using the ClassWizard, add the method GetNewsgroups. Add the following code to the method:

```
BOOL CNewsCtrl::GetNewsgroups()
{
    return WSSendCommand("LIST");
}
```

Sending a Command

I know that the preceding code really does not tell you how to send a command; it just tells you how to call a routine that sends a command. Following is the actual function that sends the command:

```
BOOL CNewsCtrl::WSSendCommand(CString sCommand)
{
    sCommand=sCommand+ "\r\n";
    if (send(m_hSock,sCommand,sCommand.GetLength(),0) != 0)
        return TRUE;
    else
        return FALSE;
}
```

As soon as the code executes, you will notice that nothing really happens. Why? Remember that when you were handling the receipt of any type of response from the server, all the calls that you were making were asynchronous. Therefore, before executing a command, you had to inform the Windows sockets library of your callback function so that it could inform you when it finished executing your command. You need to do the same thing before sending these commands. For that reason, you need to modify one of your earlier statements.

Recall the function WSConnect. Locate the following line:

```
WSAAsyncSelect(m_hSock, m_hWnd, WSCB_ASELECT, FD_CONNECT );
```

Now modify the line to appear like the following:

```
WSAAsyncSelect(m_hSock, m_hWnd, WSCB_ASELECT, FD_CONNECT | FD_READ | FD_WRITE |
➥FD_CLOSE);
```

This line informs the Windows sockets library that any time anything happens, it should send your window handle the message WSCB_ASELECT. See the following table for an explanation of the flags:

Flag	Description
FD_CONNECT	A connection has been achieved.
FD_READ	The server has sent some data, and the data is ready to be read.
FD_WRITE	The server is ready to accept commands.
FD_CLOSE	The connection has been terminated.

Enhancing the Callback Function

Now that your callback function is going to handle all these extra messages, it is time to enhance that function, as follows:

```
afx_msg LONG CNewsCtrl::OnASelectCB(UINT wParam, LONG lParam)
{
    HANDLE hTask = (HANDLE) wParam;
    UINT   wserr = HIWORD(lParam);
    UINT   uCode = LOWORD(lParam);

    switch (uCode)
    {
        // If a connect message comes back, fire the Connect event
        case FD_CONNECT:
        {
            FireConnected();
            break;
        }


        // Not yet handling a close message
        case FD_CLOSE:
        break;


        // When data is incoming, call the RecvData event
        case FD_READ:
        {
            char msg[10240];
```

```
        recv(m_hSock, msg, 10240, 0);
        FireRecvData(msg);
        break;
    }


    // Not yet handling a ready to write message
    case FD_WRITE:
    break;


    // Not yet handling an accept message
    case FD_ACCEPT:
    break;


    default:
    break;
    }


    return TRUE;
}
```

Now the callback function is capable of handling all the messages. The one that you are mostly concerned with is the FD_READ message, which tells you that the server has sent you some data. A word of caution: It is best to read the data and not ignore this message. The Windows sockets library will not send you another FD_READ message until you have read the data from the first message. To read it, simply use the recv statement. In the preceding example, you are reading the information from the port 10KB at a time.

Adding Methods and Events for Each Command/Response

You have enough information to finish your OCX right now. You have made a connection to the news server. You have sent a command to the server and have captured the information that it sent back. If you do not want to provide higher-level functions, you could have an OCX that has one method (SendCommand) and one event (RecvData), which gets fired each time data gets transmitted from the server. In fact, the example shows you how to fire this event.

It would be nice, however, to have at least one method per NNTP command. It also would be nice to have a routine that parses the server responses and fires an event that is specific to that response.

Take the LIST command. After you execute the LIST command, the response should be a status line, followed by a flood of text responses (about 16,000 lines, to be exact)—one per newsgroup. According to NNTP specifications, the list of newsgroups is formatted in the following way:

```
215 list of newsgroups follows
comp.cool.sites 00543 00501 y
```

The fact that the parameters are separated by spaces makes it easy to parse the line. In this case, it would be nice to have an event called ServerStatus that has two parameters: status code and description. Immediately after the LIST command is issued, the first line received will be the status. The next lines received will be a newsgroup entry, which contains the name, the number of the last article, the number of the first article, and y or n (to indicate whether posting to this newsgroup is allowed).

Overlapping Commands

Because commands are sent to the server asynchronously and control returns to the program immediately, what happens if you issue another command before the first is done? Fortunately, the Windows sockets library handles this situation rather nicely. If a second command is issued while text responses are flowing from the first command, the first command is paused while the second command takes place. Then, when the second command finishes, the text following is a continuation of the first command. This switch between command responses makes it a little more difficult to analyze text. A way to handle the situation is to maintain an array of the commands that have been issued, so that when you are analyzing a response, you know which command the response belongs to. To do this, modify the function WSSendCommand, as follows:

```
BOOL CNewsCtrl::WSSendCommand(CString sCommand)
{
    Call AddCommandToList(sCommand);
    sCommand=sCommand+ "\r\n";
    if (send(m_hSock,sCommand,sCommand.GetLength(),0) != 0)
        return TRUE;
```

```
          else
                return FALSE;
}
```

The function `AddCommandToList` adds the last command to the list of commands and increments an internal member variable, `m_LastCmdNumber`. This variable informs you that the received text belongs to the `m_LastCmdNumber` item in the command array. When the server informs you that it is finished with that command (it does that by sending you a line that contains only a period), you call the function `DeleteCommandFromList`, which removes it from the list and decrements the variable `m_LastCmdNumber`.

With that in mind, look at the text-parsing routine:

```
void CNewsCtrl::WSParseText(CString sServText)
{
      int iCurrCmd = m_LastCmdNumber;
      BOOL bDone=FALSE;

      int iMarker = sServText.Find("\r\n");
      if (iMarker < 0)
            bDone=TRUE;

      while (!bDone)
      {
            CString sNextLine = sServText.Left(iMarker);

            if (m_StatusFound[iCurrCmd]==FALSE)
            {
                  FireServerStatus(sNextLine.Left(3),sNextLine.Mid(4));
                  m_StatusFound[iCurrCmd]==TRUE;
            }

            else
            {
                  if (m_sCommand[iCurrCmd] == "LIST")
                  {
```

```
                    iMarker = sNextLine.Find(" ");
                    CString sGroupName = sNextLine.Left(iMarker+1);
                    sNextLine = sNextLine.Mid(iMarker + strlen(" "));

                    iMarker = sNextLine.Find(" ");
                    CString sLastArticle = sNextLine.Left(iMarker+1);
                    sNextLine = sNextLine.Mid(iMarker + strlen(" "));

                    iMarker = sNextLine.Find(" ");
                    CString sFirstArticle = sNextLine.Left(iMarker+1);
                    sNextLine = sNextLine.Mid(iMarker + strlen(" "));

                    iMarker = sNextLine.Find(" ");
                    CString sCanPost = sNextLine.Left(iMarker+1);
                    sNextLine = sNextLine.Mid(iMarker + strlen(" "));


                    FireNewsgroupEntryRecvd(sGroupName,sLastArticle,sFirstArticle,
➥sCanPost);
                }
            }

        sServText = sServText.Mid(iMarker + strlen("\r\n"));
        iMarker = sServText.Find("\r\n");
        if (iMarker < 0)
                bDone=TRUE;
        }


}
```

This function examines one line at a time by finding a <CR-LF> marker, and it proceeds to examine each line until the text is exhausted. Notice that the OCX control maintains another internal array: m_StatusFound. This array has entries that match the command-list array, and it keeps track of whether a status line has already been found for that command. If not, the array treats the first line received as a status line and marks the array element as received. The lines of code that follow simply divide the lines into the appropriate parameters by finding where the spaces are.

As described earlier in this chapter, the LIST command has four parameters. Also notice that you have created an OLE event NewsgroupEntryRecvd, which you fire to indicate to the user of the OLE control that a newsgroup entry has been received from the server.

To complete your OCX, you simply need to add OLE methods to your OCX to transmit the other NNTP commands, and add code to the function WSParseText to handle the other responses.

Nifty Things to Do with Your News Reader

This section gives you an idea of how to go where no news OCX has gone before. Many news readers allow you to subscribe to a certain newsgroup. Subscribing is not a function of the news server. No file is changed in any way over on the server side. Subscribing to a newsgroup is simply saving a list of the user's favorite newsgroups. How about letting the OCX do that for the person who uses it? You can store the user's subscription information by using OLE Structured Storage.

Another chapter could be written on this subject alone, but briefly, OLE Structured Storage allows you to save in a single file information that generally is stored in separate files. In an OLE Structured Storage file, you divide the information that you store into tables. So in this case, your file might have a subscription table. Then you create a structure that defines a record in the subscription table. For example, you might have a structure that contains a character array to store the name of the newsgroup that the user is subscribing to, as illustrated in the following code:

```
typedef struct _OBJECTSUBSCRIPTION {
        char NewsgroupName[255];
} OBJECTSUBSCRIPTION, FAR *POBJECTSUBSCRIPTION;
```

To manipulate your file, you need to use the OLE Structured Storage functions. These functions are explained in detail in the Books Online help that is included with Visual C++ 4.2. I'll give you a hint: Search for StgCreateDocfile, StgOpenStorage, or OpenStream. Do not be intimidated by the number of parameters and long-named constants these functions have. The majority of the time, you will just use the default values.

Once you have created functions to manipulate the OLE Structured Storage file, you can provide a method called Subscribe that takes two parameters: a user identifier and a comma-delimited list of groups to subscribe to. Then you can create an OLE Structured Storage file in the same directory as the OLE control (with the name NewsOCX.stg, for example) and keep the information there.

Another suggestion is to use the OLE Structured Storage file to store the list of available newsgroups. Because there are about 16,000 newsgroups in Usenet, displaying the complete list of newsgroups every time you want to find a newsgroup is both time-consuming and annoying. Instead, you could write a program to store this list after accessing it one time from the server. The next time that the user wants to find a newsgroup, you could read the list from the OLE Structured Storage file, and read from the server a list of new newsgroups since the last time that the list was read.

Chapter Summary

A few pages ago, you thought that Usenet was part of the Internet; now you can write your own news reader. You have come a long way.

To summarize what this chapter covered, you learned the following things:

- ◆ NNTP is a protocol that TCP/IP uses to access information in a news server.
- ◆ To connect to a news server, you communicate with TCP/IP port 119 by using the Windows sockets API.
- ◆ To establish communication, you need to determine the IP address of the server that you are communicating with.

You also learned how to do the following:

- ◆ Send commands to the news server
- ◆ Capture the information received from the server
- ◆ Parse the information received from the server
- ◆ Fire events that are specific to each command

In Chapter 11, "Plug-in Mail," you learn a set of TCP/IP protocols to read mail from a server, and you use this knowledge to create a mail-reader control.

Chapter | 11

Plug-in Mail

by Edward B. Toupin

The Internet has evolved into an important medium for communications between individuals and organizations throughout the world. As an enterprise solution for many organizations, electronic mail (aka e-mail) has become a very important part of the entire Internet community, in that it allows individuals and organizations to exchange ideas, information, and even full documents and applications inexpensively and easily.

This chapter details the two main e-mail protocols for the Internet—the Simple Mail Transfer Protocol (SMTP) and the Post Office Protocol (POP). The chapter takes the details of the protocols and examines how to implement them in a simple-to-use 32-bit custom control for communications on the Internet. On the Internet, SMTP is used to send mail and attachments to individuals on the Internet, and POP allows you to retrieve e-mail from your post office box on the Internet.

To provide a foundation for your understanding, this chapter covers the following topics:

◆ Overview of the SMTP and POP protocols

◆ Connecting to SMTP and POP servers

◆ Sending and receiving e-mail

◆ Closing the connection

◆ Encoding and decoding attachments

What Is Electronic Mail?

Electronic mail is a simple and efficient means of transferring information between users on a network—in this case, the Internet. E-mail systems provide a means of allowing an originating user to write a message and to address that message for a destination user. This message usually consists of standard text, but with the MIME (Multipurpose Internet Mail Extensions or Multimedia E-Mail) standard, originating users can attach documents from applications such as Microsoft Word for Windows and Microsoft Excel, or even entire applications, sounds, and images.

Many of us who communicate on the Internet connect via dial-up SLIP or PPP connections. When we connect, we use an account that has been assigned to us by an Internet Service Provider (ISP). This account provides us with access to an SMTP server for sending e-mail and a POP server for receiving e-mail.

As shown in Figure 11-1, when we connect to our account, we can send e-mail by submitting the e-mail directly to our SMTP server, using a desktop client e-mail application (such as Eudora, Pegasus, and so on). This server then uses the destination addresses you provide in the header of the e-mail to determine how to route the e-mail to the appropriate remote SMTP server to which your mail is destined.

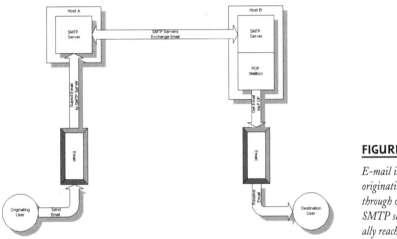

FIGURE 11-1

E-mail is relayed from an originating user and through one or more SMTP servers to eventually reach its destination.

The POP server that is available with your account provides a means of storing e-mail relayed by SMTP until you decide to retrieve it from your mailbox. E-mail is extracted from the mailbox and delivered directly to your desktop e-mail client application (such as Eudora or Pegasus).

What Is the SMTP Protocol?

SMTP (RFC 0821), or Simple Mail Transfer Protocol, is a mechanism used to transfer e-mail from an originating user machine across a network to a remote destination user machine. SMTP's functionality allows for communications with simple e-mail clients for the submission of e-mail to an SMTP server. To transfer the e-mail from your SMTP server across the Internet, SMTP servers can communicate with one another to provide a means of relaying e-mail across the network to eventually reach a designated SMTP server and user.

SMTP communicates over a TCP (stream-oriented) connection established between the sender process and the receiver process on service port 25. This connection can be between two SMTP servers for relaying or between a user's SMTP client machine and an SMTP server for submission of e-mail.

The primary objective of Simple Mail Transfer Protocol is to transfer mail across a communications medium, regardless of the host or intermediate operating system. The communications medium is the mechanism over which an interprocess communications (IPC) channel is established between two or more or hosts or over several networks. In this manner, mail can be transferred between processes in different environments by being relayed through a process connected to two (or more) IPC channels. Specifically, hosts can forward, or relay, e-mail across a network between hosts on different transport systems or networks.

SMTP Model

SMTP is based on the model depicted in Figure 11-2. As the picture demonstrates, the Sender-SMTP establishes a two-way transmission channel to a Receiver-SMTP, which may be either the ultimate destination or an intermediate relay SMTP server. SMTP commands are generated by the Sender-SMTP and sent to the Receiver-SMTP, whereas SMTP replies are sent from the Receiver-SMTP to the Sender-SMTP in response to the commands.

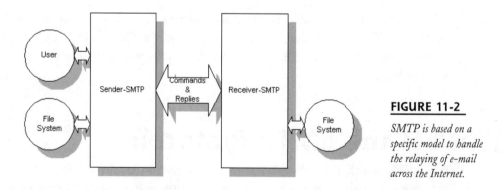

FIGURE 11-2

SMTP is based on a specific model to handle the relaying of e-mail across the Internet.

Once a communications channel is established, the Sender-SMTP sends a MAIL command, which is used to indicate the sender of the e-mail. If the Receiver-SMTP is able to accept mail, it responds with OK. Upon receipt of an OK, Sender-SMTP sends a RCPT command, identifying the recipient of the mail. If the Receiver-SMTP can accept mail for that recipient, it responds with OK; otherwise, it responds with a reply rejecting that recipient. The Sender-SMTP and Receiver-SMTP may negotiate several recipients.

When the recipients have been negotiated, the Sender-SMTP sends the mail data, terminating with a special sequence. If the Receiver-SMTP successfully processes the mail data, it makes an OK reply.

If the originator and ultimate destination hosts are not immediately connected, the message must be relayed through a series of hosts for delivery to the ultimate destination. to accomplish this task, the SMTP server must be supplied with the name of the ultimate destination host, as well as the destination mailbox name. The argument to the MAIL command is *reverse-path*, which specifies the originator of the mail. The argument to the RCPT command is *forward-path*, which specifies the destination user of the mail. The *forward-path* is a source route, whereas the *reverse-path* is a return route that may be used to return a message to the sender when an error occurs with a relayed message.

Mail Transactions

To effectively send e-mail across the Internet, SMTP performs several transactions for submission of e-mail from a user and between SMTP servers. This small section briefly overviews some of the basic transactions of an SMTP server to bring you into the actual implementation of an SMTP custom control. The section first discusses the establishment and termination of e-mail exchanges; next, it discusses the submission of e-mail to an SMTP server. The remaining segments of this section describe verifying mailbox names and expanding mailing lists.

Opening and Closing an SMTP Connection

Before you can initiate e-mail transactions, you have to open a channel for the transaction. As noted earlier, you can establish a stream-oriented connection to port 25, over which communications can occur. Once this stream is established, the originator of the communications can begin a transaction with the SMTP server to which it is connected.

The first set of transactions to occur involve the acknowledgment that the hosts are communicating properly and are available. This is accomplished with the simple HELO command, as in the following example:

```
HELO <domain> <CRLF>
```

In the HELO command, the host sending the command identifies itself, using its domain name. For example, my SMTP client software would submit HELO TOUPIN, which can be interpreted as saying, "Hello, I am TOUPIN."

Upon completion of all transactions and before the termination of the TCP connection, the Sender-SMTP should send the QUIT command. This command tells the Receiver-SMTP to close the transaction channel and forward the mail to each of the recipients specified. The command is quite simple, as shown in the following example:

```
QUIT <CRLF>
```

Sending Mail

Submitting e-mail to an SMTP server consists of four very simple steps. The first part of the transaction is to submit a MAIL command, which provides the SMTP server with the identification of the originator, or sender, of the e-mail. Immediately following the MAIL command are one or more RCPT commands, which inform the SMTP server of the desti-nation users' e-mail addresses. The final command to be issued as part of a mail transac-tion is the DATA command, which provides the mail data. Finally, the end-of-mail data indicator confirms the end of the transaction.

As discussed in the preceding paragraph, the first operation performed is the transmission of the MAIL command. The *reverse-path* contains the originating user's mailbox in stan-dard form (for example, etoupin@toupin.com), as follows:

```
MAIL FROM:<reverse-path> <CRLF>
```

The purpose of this command is to allow the Sender-SMTP to tell the Receiver-SMTP that a new mail transaction is starting and to reset all its state tables and buffers, includ-ing any recipients or mail data. The *reverse-path* contains a reverse source routing list of hosts, showing the path that the e-mail traversed. The first host in the *reverse-path* should be the host sending this command; it is usually used for error reporting back to the originator of the e-mail.

Once the originating mailbox is designated, the originator must specify the destination mailbox for the e-mail. This is accomplished with the RCPT command, as shown in the following example:

```
RCPT TO:<forward-path> <CRLF>
```

The RCPT command provides the mechanism for submitting a *forward-path* that identifies a recipient of the e-mail in standard form (such as etoupin@toupin.com). This operation can be performed as many times as necessary to forward the e-mail to all the appropriate mailboxes. If, during transmission, any of the recipients is unknown, the Receiver-SMTP returns an error, notifying the originator that there is no such recipient.

Like the *reverse-path*, the *forward-path* is a source routing list of hosts and the destination mailbox, with the first host in the list being the host receiving this command. This list of hosts can be used to trace the path that the e-mail traversed.

Once the origination and destination mailboxes have been specified, the next step is to submit the e-mail data itself. This operation is accomplished with the DATA command, as shown in the following example:

DATA <CRLF>

All memo header items and related information (Date, Subject, To, Cc, From, and so on) are submitted as part of the segment of data following the DATA command. In this way, you have a bit of flexibility as to what additional information you want to add in the header of the e-mail.

Once DATA is submitted, the Receiver-SMTP assumes that all subsequent lines of data contain the text of the e-mail message. Since the mail data is sent on the transmission channel, the end of the mail data must be indicated so that the command-and-reply dialogue can be resumed. SMTP indicates the end of the mail data by sending a line that contains only a period.

The end-of-mail data indicator also confirms the mail transaction and tells the Receiver-SMTP to process the stored recipients and mail data. The DATA command should fail only if the mail transaction was incomplete (if no recipients were found, for example), or if resources are not available.

Now that we have examined each of the three commands required to send data, review Figure 11-3 to see the protocol with a typical set of transactions. As you can see, we have initiated a mail transaction to submit e-mail to toupieb@nipuot.com. The Receiver-SMTP receives the e-mail and, once the QUIT command is sent, initiates a conversation with the SMTP server at nipuot.com to transfer the e-mail to the destination mailbox.

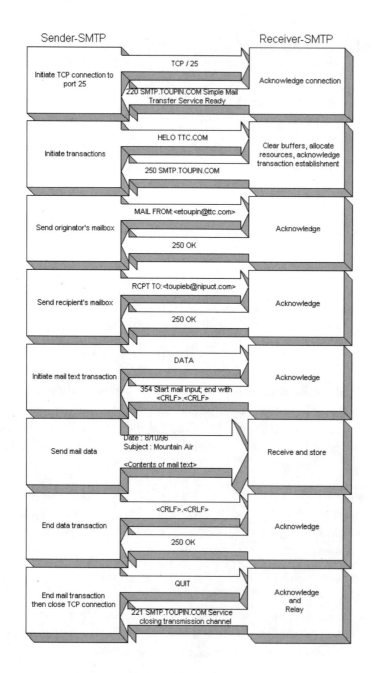

FIGURE 11-3

SMTP receives and relays e-mail, using a series of transactions.

Relaying E-Mail

To effectively deliver e-mail to its ultimate destination, an e-mail message might go through numerous intermediate SMTP servers (see Figure 11-4). The `forward-path` from the RCPT command may be a source route of the form @SMTP-A.COM,@SMTP-B.COM:ED@ SMTP-C.COM, where SMTP-A, SMTP-B, and SMTP-C are hosts through which the e-mail should travel before reaching the mailbox for ED on SMTP-C. This form is used to differentiate an address and a route in the e-mail, where the mailbox itself is an absolute address and the route is information regarding the path that should be taken to get there.

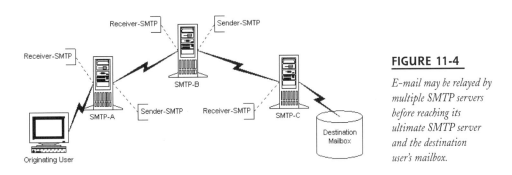

FIGURE 11-4

E-mail may be relayed by multiple SMTP servers before reaching its ultimate SMTP server and the destination user's mailbox.

Using source routing, the Receiver-SMTP receives mail to be relayed to another Sender-SMTP. The Receiver-SMTP may accept or reject the task of relaying the mail in the same way it accepts or rejects mail for a local user. The Receiver-SMTP transforms the command arguments by moving its own identifier from the `forward-path` to the beginning of the `reverse-path`. The Receiver-SMTP then becomes a Sender-SMTP, establishes a transmission channel to the next SMTP in the `forward-path`, and sends it the mail.

The first host in the `reverse-path` should be the host sending the SMTP commands, and the first host in the forward-path should be the host receiving the SMTP commands. For each part of the relay operation in Figure 11-4, notice that each SMTP host along the relay route changes its role to relay the mail to the ultimate destination mailbox.

To perform the e-mail relaying, role reversals between SMTP servers are initiated with the TURN command. Issuance of this command causes a role reversal of the two programs communicating over the transmission channel. For example, if SMTP-A is currently the Sender-SMTP, and if it sends the TURN command and receives an OK reply, SMTP-A becomes the Receiver-SMTP. Likewise, if SMTP-B is currently the Receiver-SMTP, and if it receives the TURN command and sends an OK reply, SMTP-B becomes the Sender-SMTP.

> **NOTE:** The TURN command is not a necessary command for submitting e-mail to an SMTP server from a client machine; it is discussed here to show you how e-mail is relayed across the Internet.

What Is the POP Protocol?

The Post Office Protocol, or POP3 (RFC 1725), allows a client machine to query a server's mailbox for mail that was previously delivered by SMTP. POP3 is important for e-mail communications, in that it is often difficult to have a large message transport system, such as SMTP, on most end-user or client machines. For example, a workstation may not be able to provide enough resources to host an SMTP server and a local mail delivery system. Also, it is difficult and expensive to maintain a dial-up connection for long periods of time, which prohibits the capability to dynamically receive mail from other SMTP servers.

To tend to some of these resource and connectivity problems, it is more efficient to manage mail on a central server and provide a means for smaller nodes to retrieve mail from a mail server, using a mail agent such as Eudora or Pegasus. The server node maintains a full mail transport system, such as SMTP, and provides a mailbox service to give these smaller nodes a place to retrieve their e-mail. The primary objective of POP3 is to permit a workstation to dynamically access a mailbox on a server host. This means that a POP3 server is used to allow a workstation to retrieve mail that the server is holding for it.

In Figure 11-5, a sender of Host A is submitting e-mail to an SMTP server. Once the e-mail is submitted, the server relays the e-mail to the destination host, Host B. Host B's Receiver-SMTP then delivers the e-mail to the destination user's mailbox for storage until the user connects to his mailbox to retrieve the e-mail. The destination user on Host B connects to the server via POP3, and through a series of commands from the e-mail user, POP3 delivers the e-mail from the user's mailbox to the user's machine.

Basic Operation

A POP3 server host providing mail services to mail clients begins its function by listening for connections from remote mail client applications on TCP port 110. When users want to request e-mail from their mailboxes, their e-mail client applications establish a

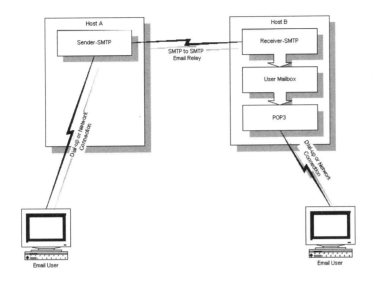

FIGURE 11-5

SMTP and POP work together to deliver e-mail to the ultimate-destination user.

TCP connection with the server host to port 110. Once a connection is established between the client application and the POP3 server, the server sends a short greeting to the e-mail client. The client and POP3 server then begin to exchange commands and responses to download the e-mail located in the mailbox on the POP3 server for the respective user.

From connection establishment to connection termination, a POP3 session progresses through various states to accomplish the task of transferring e-mail to a requesting client (see Figure 11-6). Once the TCP connection has been opened and the POP3 server has sent the greeting, the session enters the AUTHORIZATION state. In this state, the client must identify itself to the POP3 server. Once the client has successfully done this, the server acquires resources associated with the client's mailbox, and the session enters the TRANSAC-TION state. In this state, the client requests actions on the part of the POP3 server. When the client has issued the QUIT command, the session enters the UPDATE state. In this state, the POP3 server releases any resources acquired during the TRANSACTION state and terminates the connection at TCP port 110.

The *AUTHORIZATION* State

Once the TCP connection has been established between the POP3 server and client, the POP3 server issues a one-line greeting, terminated by CRLF. Such a greeting might be:

```
+OK The TOUPIN.COM POP3 server is ready!
```

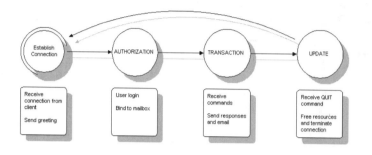

FIGURE 11-6

A POP server goes through several states from the time when a client logs on and retrieves mail to the time when the client logs off.

Notice that this greeting is a POP3 reply, which should always receive a positive response from the client.

At this point, the POP3 session is in the AUTHORIZATION state, awaiting identification from the client. The POP3 server must use that identification to authenticate the client on the POP3 server.

To authenticate, the client must first issue the USER command with the POP user name as the argument. If the POP3 server responds with a positive status indicator (+OK), the client may issue the PASS command to complete the authentication. If the POP3 server responds with a negative status indicator (-ERR) to the USER command, the client may either issue a new authentication command or QUIT. When the client issues the PASS command, the POP3 server uses the argument pair from the USER and PASS commands to determine whether the client should be given access to the appropriate mailbox. At any point during authentication, the client may issue a QUIT command to end the session.

Once the POP3 server has authenticated the user and determined that the client should be given access to the appropriate mailbox, the POP3 server acquires an exclusive-access lock on the user's mailbox to prevent messages from being modified or removed before the session enters the UPDATE state. If the lock on the mailbox is successful, the POP3 server responds with a positive status indicator and enters the TRANSACTION state. If the mailbox cannot be opened for some reason, the POP3 server responds with a negative status indicator and may close the connection.

NOTE: If the mailbox lock is successful but the connection is broken for some reason, the lock remains in place for a definite period of time, as determined by the POP3 server. Any attempt to reconnect and reauthenticate will result in a negative response from the POP3 server until the lock is released for the user's mailbox.

The *TRANSACTION* State

Once the client has successfully identified itself to the POP3 server and the POP3 server has locked and opened the appropriate mailbox, the POP3 session is in the TRANSACTION state. The client may now issue POP3 commands repeatedly to list, retrieve, and delete e-mail messages in the mailbox. After each command, the POP3 server issues a response to the client, containing status information and e-mail data. After all the required commands are issued, the client issues the QUIT command, and the POP3 session enters the UPDATE state.

Table 11-1 shows some of the basic commands sent to a POP3 server in the TRANSACTION state.

Table 11-1   POP3 *TRANSACTION* State Commands

Command	Description
STAT	Retrieves the status of the mailbox associated with the authenticated user. The returned status message includes the number of messages in the mailbox and the accumulated size of all messages.
LIST	Lists all the e-mail messages in receipt order, with a message number and size for each message.
RETR *msg*	Retrieves the message designated by the number in *msg*.
DELE *msg*	Deletes the message designated by the number in *msg*.
RSET	Unmarks all messages marked for deletion by the DELE command.
TOP *msg n*	Provides the top *n* lines of the body of the message designated by the number in *msg*.
UIDL *[msg]*	Retrieves the Unique ID Listing number for all messages or the message specified by the number in *msg*.

The *UPDATE* State

Upon completion of the commands in the TRANSACTION state, the client can issue the QUIT command to end the session and place the POP3 server in the UPDATE state. If the client should issue the QUIT command from the AUTHORIZATION state, the POP3 session terminates but does not enter the UPDATE state. If a session terminates for some reason other than a client-issued QUIT command, the POP3 session does not enter the UPDATE state and does not remove any messages from the mailbox.

In the UPDATE state, the POP3 server removes all messages marked for deletion from the mailbox. The server then releases any exclusive-access lock on the user's mailbox and replies to the client with the corresponding status of these operations. Upon completion, the TCP connection is closed for port 110 between the client and the POP3 server.

Sample POP3 Transaction

In Figure 11-7, the POP3 commands and related states are submitted to the POP3 server in the same manner as that of the aforementioned SMTP server. As shown in the figure, the AUTHENTICATION state involves the connection and user authentication operation. Immediately after a successful authentication, the POP3 server is in the TRANSACTION state, and the client machine can send commands and receive responses, status information, and e-mail text. Upon completion of all desired client operations, the client can send a QUIT command to the server to make the server change states to the UPDATE state.

Mail Custom Control Architecture

The MAIL custom control contains two separate controls to manage both the SMTP and POP3 protocols. The MAIL control provides several members and methods for access by container applications such as Visual Basic, Delphi, and Visual FoxPro. Since the control is multithreaded, when certain members are assigned values, the associated property procedures create threads that are used to perform the respective operation in a nonblocking, or nonmodal, mode of operation.

Since multithreaded controls with event notification operate nicely under Windows NT and Windows 95, the functionality of the SMTP and POP modules had to be broken out into several functions, each of which cumulatively adds to the overall functionality of the custom control. Each of the threads made part of the control is based on the *worker-thread* architecture, wherein each worker thread is an instance of a procedure from within the main process that operates concurrently with other threads and within the context of the main process or container.

As shown in Figure 11-8, the control consists of two modules, each consisting of multiple threads of operation. Each of the threads performs a specific operation that complements the overall functionality of the MAIL control. The SMTP module has only one thread to

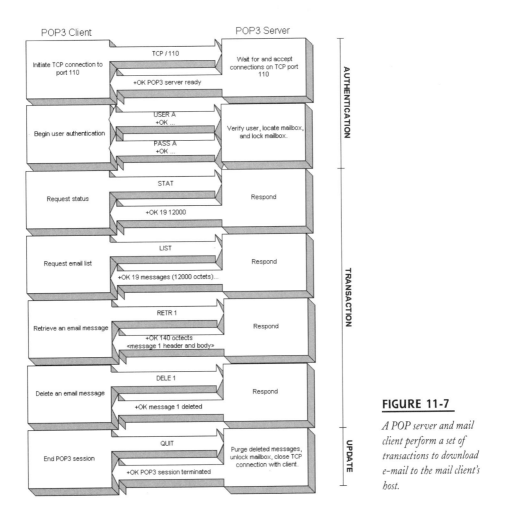

FIGURE 11-7

A POP server and mail client perform a set of transactions to download e-mail to the mail client's host.

handle all its functionality. This thread takes information provided via properties and sends the mail to a designated SMTP server. Once the thread is initialized, e-mail is submitted to the server and exits. Upon completion, an event is fired, notifying the container application of the success or failure of the operation. The POP3 module is a bit more complex than the SMTP module, since it is responsible for authentication, e-mail transfer, and mailbox-status-related information.

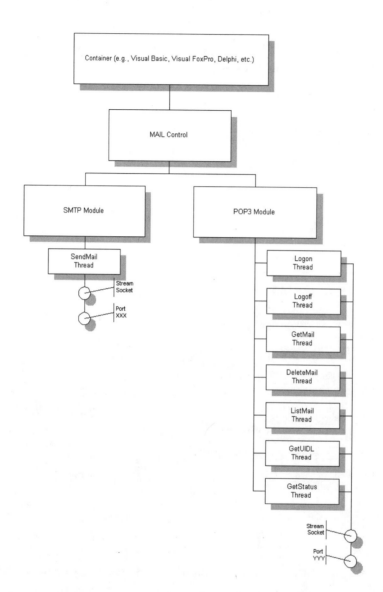

FIGURE 11-8

The MAIL *custom control consists of two modules, each of which may spawn several threads of execution.*

SMTP Module

The SMTP module consists of several properties and one function to provide a means of preparing an e-mail message for transmission to a destination user. The property values appear in the header and the body of the e-mail message, and provide a mechanism for the submission of the e-mail message to a designated SMTP server. As you see in Listing

11-1, the base class for the SMTP module is `CSmtpCtrl`. Each of the properties of this class provides a means of storing the values required for sending e-mail across the Internet.

Listing 11-1   Properties and Functions of the SMTP Module

```
BEGIN_DISPATCH_MAP(CSmtpCtrl, COleControl)
        //{{AFX_DISPATCH_MAP(CSmtpCtrl)
        DISP_PROPERTY_NOTIFY(CSmtpCtrl, "DomainName", m_domainName, OnDomainNameChanged,
➡VT_BSTR)
        DISP_PROPERTY_NOTIFY(CSmtpCtrl, "MailDate", m_mailDate, OnMailDateChanged,
➡VT_BSTR)
        DISP_PROPERTY_NOTIFY(CSmtpCtrl, "CCUserList", m_cCUserList, OnCCUserListChanged,
➡VT_BSTR)
        DISP_PROPERTY_NOTIFY(CSmtpCtrl, "MailTime", m_mailTime, OnMailTimeChanged,
➡VT_BSTR)
        DISP_PROPERTY_NOTIFY(CSmtpCtrl, "TotalSendBytes", m_totalSendBytes,
                OnTotalSendBytesChanged, VT_I4)
        DISP_PROPERTY_NOTIFY(CSmtpCtrl, "CurrentState", m_currentState,
➡OnCurrentStateChanged,
                VT_I2)
        DISP_PROPERTY_NOTIFY(CSmtpCtrl, "ErrorNumber", m_errorNumber,
➡OnErrorNumberChanged, VT_I2)
        DISP_PROPERTY_NOTIFY(CSmtpCtrl, "TotalEncodedBytes", m_totalEncodedBytes,
                OnTotalEncodedBytesChanged, VT_I4)
        DISP_PROPERTY_NOTIFY(CSmtpCtrl, "DestinationUserList", m_destinationUserList,
                OnDestinationUserListChanged, VT_BSTR)
        DISP_PROPERTY_NOTIFY(CSmtpCtrl, "OriginatingAddress", m_originatingAddress,
                OnOriginatingAddressChanged, VT_BSTR)
        DISP_PROPERTY_NOTIFY(CSmtpCtrl, "OriginatingName", m_originatingName,
                OnOriginatingNameChanged, VT_BSTR)
        DISP_PROPERTY_NOTIFY(CSmtpCtrl, "RetryCount", m_retryCount, OnRetryCountChanged,
➡VT_I2)
```

continues

Listing 11-1   Continued

```
        DISP_PROPERTY_NOTIFY(CSmtpCtrl, "Action", m_action, OnActionChanged, VT_I2)
        DISP_PROPERTY_NOTIFY(CSmtpCtrl, "HostAddress", m_hostAddress,
➡OnHostAddressChanged,
            VT_BSTR)
        DISP_PROPERTY_NOTIFY(CSmtpCtrl, "MailSubject", m_mailSubject,
➡OnMailSubjectChanged,
            VT_BSTR)
        DISP_PROPERTY_NOTIFY(CSmtpCtrl, "MailBody", m_mailBody, OnMailBodyChanged,
➡VT_BSTR)
        DISP_PROPERTY_NOTIFY(CSmtpCtrl, "MailAttachment", m_mailAttachment,
            OnMailAttachmentChanged, VT_BSTR)
        DISP_PROPERTY_NOTIFY(CSmtpCtrl, "MailPriority", m_mailPriority,
➡OnMailPriorityChanged,
            VT_I2)
        DISP_PROPERTY_NOTIFY(CSmtpCtrl, "MailApplication", m_mailApplication,
            OnMailApplicationChanged, VT_BSTR)
        DISP_PROPERTY_EX(CSmtpCtrl, "Version", GetVersion, SetVersion, VT_BSTR)
        DISP_FUNCTION(CSmtpCtrl, "SendMail", SendMail, VT_BOOL, VTS_BSTR VTS_BSTR
➡VTS_BSTR
            VTS_BSTR VTS_BSTR)
    //}}AFX_DISPATCH_MAP
        DISP_FUNCTION_ID(CSmtpCtrl, "AboutBox", DISPID_ABOUTBOX, AboutBox, VT_EMPTY,
➡VTS_NONE)
END_DISPATCH_MAP()
```

In addition to the properties created with the ControlWizard, we have added a few methods to the class to encapsulate some of the functionality of the basic Winsock API. These methods, shown in Listing 11-2, provide a simple means of handling communications over the Internet that conforms to the requirements of communications for SMTP. I will be discussing each of the methods in Listing 11-2 throughout this chapter.

Listing 11-2   Winsock API-Encapsulated Methods

```
int GetSendTime();

int OpenSocket();

int RecvRemote(CString& buffer);

int SendRemote(CString buffer);

int ConnectRemote(CString IPAdrs);

int SendHeaderInfo(CString from, CString to, CString cc);

int StartData();

int SendData(CString buffer);

int CloseRemote();

int UUENCODE(CString);

BOOL CheckMsg(CString msg);

void GenerateUIDL(short, char*);
```

As shown in listings 11-3, 11-4, and 11-5, the SendMail function, the Action property procedure, and the TSendMail thread procedure work together to transfer the mail to the SMTP server. When the value of *SEND_MAIL* is assigned to the Action property of the control, the property procedure checks to see whether the associated thread is already active. If active, an error is returned by a call to the EndSendMail event procedure via FireEndSendMail(*m_errorNumber*), where the container receives the value of any errors passed as the argument. If the thread is not already active, the procedure attempts to start the TSendMail procedure as a thread.

Listing 11-3   *Action* Property Procedure

```
void CSmtpCtrl::OnActionChanged()

{
        DWORD                           ThreadId;
        DWORD                           ThreadExitCode;


        // TODO: Add notification handler code
        switch(m_action)
        {
```

continues

Listing 11-3 Continued

```
                case SEND_MAIL :
                    if(m_mailPriority == 6 || m_mailPriority == 0)
                    {
                            GetExitCodeThread(m_hSendMailThreadHandle,
➥&ThreadExitCode);

                            if(ThreadExitCode == STILL_ACTIVE)
                                    TerminateThread(m_hSendMailThreadHandle, 0);
                            m_currentState = CLOSING_CONNECTION;
                            CloseRemote();
                            m_currentState = WAITING_FOR_ACTION;
                            m_errorNumber = 12050;
                            FireEndSendMail(m_errorNumber);
                    }
                    else
                    {
                            GetExitCodeThread(m_hSendMailThreadHandle,
➥&ThreadExitCode);

                            if(ThreadExitCode != STILL_ACTIVE)
                            {
                                    m_hSendMailThreadHandle = CreateThread(NULL, 0,
➥TSendMail,
                                            this, 0, &ThreadId);
                            }
                            else
                            {
                                    m_errorNumber = 11000;
                                    FireEndSendMail(m_errorNumber);
                            }
                    }
            }

        SetModifiedFlag();
}
```

The only public function available within the control is the SendMail function (see Listing 11-4). This function uses each of the properties from Listing 11-1 to format the message, encode any attachments, and send the e-mail to the SMTP server. The SendMail function provides a means of bypassing the threaded nature of the control to provide a blocking-style call for sending the e-mail. This method is very useful if you desire to have your application wait for the completion of e-mail submission to the SMTP server. This function is available only for those programmers who want to stay with a structured programming approach, as opposed to the thread-oriented, event-based approach.

> **TIP:** To make the operation of the control, in conjunction with its container, more efficient, use the thread-oriented operation from Listing 11-3. The SendMail method simply assigns the appropriate values to properties and calls the thread procedure directly without creating a thread first. The threaded operation keeps the container application from appearing to lock up, since the thread is operating separately from the base container thread.

Listing 11-4 *SendMail* **Function**

```
BOOL CSmtpCtrl::SendMail(LPCTSTR ServerIPAddress, LPCTSTR Subject, LPCTSTR DestUserList,
➥LPCTSTR CCUserList, LPCTSTR MailBody)
{
        // TODO: Add your dispatch handler code here
        m_hostAddress = ServerIPAddress;
        m_mailSubject = Subject;
        m_destinationUserList = DestUserList;
        m_cCUserList = CCUserList;
        m_mailBody = MailBody;
        if(!TSendMail(this))
                return(FALSE);
        else
                return(TRUE);

}
```

Whether a blocking or nonblocking style of sending e-mail is desired, the `TSendMail` function of Listing 11-5 is called. When called as either a function or a thread function, it is responsible for connecting to the SMTP server, submitting e-mail, checking for response errors from the server, and closing the connection.

Listing 11-5   *TSendMail* **Thread Function**

```
DWORD WINAPI TSendMail(LPVOID pParam)
{
        CString         msgbuffer;
        CSmtpCtrl*         thisObject = (CSmtpCtrl*)pParam;
        int             retval = 1;
        char            tempstr[100];
        char            drive[5], dir[30], fname[35], ext[10];
        CString          FName;

        thisObject->m_errorNumber = 0;

        if(!thisObject->OpenSocket()) END_THREAD(0);

        thisObject->m_currentState = CONNECTING;
        if(!thisObject->ConnectRemote(thisObject->m_hostAddress)) END_THREAD(0);

        thisObject->m_currentState = ESTABLISHING_SESSION;
        if(!thisObject->SendHeaderInfo(thisObject->m_originatingAddress,
                thisObject->m_destinationUserList, thisObject->m_cCUserList))
➥END_THREAD(0);

        if(!thisObject->StartData()) END_THREAD(0);

        thisObject->m_currentState = SENDING_HEADER;
        thisObject->GetSendTime();

        msgbuffer = "Date: " + thisObject->m_mailDate + " " + thisObject->m_mailTime + "
➥GMT";
```

```
if(!thisObject->SendData(msgbuffer)) END_THREAD(0);


msgbuffer = "From: " + thisObject->m_originatingAddress + " (" +
        thisObject->m_originatingName + ")";
if(!thisObject->SendData(msgbuffer)) END_THREAD(0);


msgbuffer = "To: "+ thisObject->m_destinationUserList;
if(!thisObject->SendData(msgbuffer)) END_THREAD(0);


msgbuffer = "Subject: "+ thisObject->m_mailSubject;
if(!thisObject->SendData(msgbuffer)) END_THREAD(0);


msgbuffer = "Cc: " + thisObject->m_cCUserList;
if(!thisObject->SendData(msgbuffer)) END_THREAD(0);


msgbuffer = "Reply-To: " + thisObject->m_originatingAddress;
if(!thisObject->SendData(msgbuffer)) END_THREAD(0);


if(thisObject->m_mailAttachment.GetLength()>0)
{
        msgbuffer = "Content-Type: multipart/mixed; boundary=\""+
                thisObject->m_boundary+"\"";
        if(!thisObject->SendData(msgbuffer)) END_THREAD(0);


        msgbuffer = "X-Attachments: "+ thisObject->m_mailAttachment;
        if(!thisObject->SendData(msgbuffer)) END_THREAD(0);
}


msgbuffer = "X-Mailer: "+ thisObject->m_mailApplication;
if(!thisObject->SendData(msgbuffer)) END_THREAD(0);


if(thisObject->m_mailAttachment.GetLength()>0)
{
```

continues

Listing 11-5   Continued

```
                        msgbuffer = "Mime-Version: 1.0";
                        if(!thisObject->SendData(msgbuffer)) END_THREAD(0);
          }


        sprintf(tempstr, "%d", thisObject->m_mailPriority);
        msgbuffer = "Priority: ";
        msgbuffer += tempstr;
        if(!thisObject->SendData(msgbuffer)) END_THREAD(0);


        //Generate X-UIDL
        if(thisObject->m_mailAttachment.GetLength()>0)
                        thisObject->GenerateUIDL(1, tempstr);
        else
                        thisObject->GenerateUIDL(0, tempstr);
        msgbuffer = "X-UIDL: ";
        msgbuffer += tempstr;
        if(!thisObject->SendData(msgbuffer)) END_THREAD(0);


        msgbuffer = "\xD\xA";
        if(!thisObject->SendData(msgbuffer)) END_THREAD(0);


        //Check for attachment name
        if(thisObject->m_mailAttachment.GetLength()>0)
        {
                        msgbuffer = "—"+thisObject->m_boundary+"\xD\xA";
                        msgbuffer += "Content-Type: text/plain;
➥charset=\"us-ascii\"\xD\xA\xD\xA";
                        msgbuffer += thisObject->m_mailBody;
                        msgbuffer += "\xD\xA\xD\xA";
                        if(!thisObject->SendData(msgbuffer)) END_THREAD(0);

                        thisObject->m_currentState = ENCODING_ATTACHMENT;
```

```
            _splitpath(thisObject->m_mailAttachment.GetBuffer(
                    thisObject->m_mailAttachment.GetLength()), drive, dir, fname,
➥ext );

            FName = fname;
            FName += ext;


            //MIME Header
            msgbuffer = "—"+thisObject->m_boundary+"\xD\xA";
            msgbuffer += "Content-Type: application/octet-stream; name=\"" +
                    FName + "\";\xD\xA";
             msgbuffer += " x-mac-type=\"42494E41\";
➥x-mac-creator=\"6D646F73\"\xD\xA";
            msgbuffer += "Content-Transfer-Encoding: x-uuencode\xD\xA";
            msgbuffer += "Content-Disposition: attachment; filename=\"" +
                    FName + "\"\xD\xA\xD\xA\xD\xA";
            msgbuffer += "begin 777 " + FName;
            if(!thisObject->SendData(msgbuffer)) END_THREAD(0);


            //UUENCODE
            if(!thisObject->UUENCODE(thisObject->m_mailAttachment))
            {
                    thisObject->m_errorNumber = 927;
                    thisObject->m_mailAttachment.Empty();
                    retval = 0;
                    goto byebye;
            }


            msgbuffer = "end\xD\xA\xD\xA";
            msgbuffer += "—"+thisObject->m_boundary+"\xD\xA\xD\xA";
            if(!thisObject->SendData(msgbuffer)) END_THREAD(0);
        }
        else
        {
```

continues

Listing 11-5   Continued

```
                 msgbuffer = thisObject->m_mailBody;
                 if(!thisObject->SendData(msgbuffer)) END_THREAD(0);
         }


         retval = 1;

byebye:


         if (retval)
                 thisObject->m_errorNumber = 0;


         //Close sockets
         thisObject->m_currentState = CLOSING_CONNECTION;
         thisObject->CloseRemote();
         thisObject->m_currentState = WAITING_FOR_ACTION;
         thisObject->m_bSendMailEvent = TRUE;
         thisObject->SendMessage(WM_TIMER, 1, 0);


         return(retval);
}
```

Two very important elements to note in the thread function are the parameter *LPVOID*
pParam and the variable definition *CSmtpCtrl*thisObject = (CSmtpCtrl*)pParam*. This
information allows you to pass a pointer to an object so that you can access the members
and methods of the object within the context of the thread. In this way, you can execute
the methods of an object asynchronous to the primary thread of the module.

WARNING: Threads and multithreaded applications are wonderful—except when
threads interfere with threads. This thread architecture allows for only one major
thread of execution at any given time. If multiple threads could be executed, the
possibility exists that the threads, accessing the same object, could overwrite information. In this case, semaphores could easily handle such a critical section; their use
is recommended for a situation in which multiple threads of execution exist.

Connecting to an SMTP Server

Once the thread is initialized, the TSendMail function attempts to open a new socket to retrieve a handle for communications over the Internet. The OpenSocket method of the CSmtpCtrl class (see Listing 11-6) is used to encapsulate the socket() Winsock API function for this operation. In this method, we are opening a stream socket to (in the next step) establish connection-oriented communications with the remote SMTP server.

Listing 11-6 *OpenSocket* **Method**

```
int CSmtpCtrl::OpenSocket()
{
        skt = socket(AF_INET, SOCK_STREAM, 0);
        if(skt < 0)
        {
                m_errorNumber = WSAGetLastError() - WSABASEERR;
                return 0;
        }
        return 1;
}
```

Once the socket is opened, we attempt to connect to the remote SMTP server by submitting a connect request via the Winsock API connect() function, using the ConnectRemote procedure shown in Listing 11-7. In this procedure, we populate a *sockaddr_in* structure with information regarding the remote address (*IPAdrs*), the port to connect to (*IPPORT_SMTP*), and the type of address to use for issuance across the Internet (*AF_INET*).

Listing 11-7 *ConnectRemote* **Method**

```
int CSmtpCtrl::ConnectRemote(CString IPAdrs)
{
        struct          sockaddr_in server_addr;
        CString         msgbuffer;
```

continues

Listing 11-7   Continued

```
server_addr.sin_family = AF_INET;
server_addr.sin_addr.s_addr = inet_addr(IPAdrs.GetBuffer(60));
server_addr.sin_port = htons(IPPORT_SMTP);

//Connect to remote address
if (connect(skt, (struct sockaddr far *)&server_addr, sizeof(server_addr)) == -1)
{
        m_errorNumber = WSAGetLastError() - WSABASEERR;
        return 0;
}

if(!RecvRemote(msgbuffer)) return 0;
if(!CheckMsg(msgbuffer))
{
        m_errorNumber = 210;
        return 0;
}

//Send HELO to setup a conversation
msgbuffer = "HELO " + m_domainName;
msgbuffer += "\xD\xA";
if(!SendRemote(msgbuffer)) return 0;
if(!RecvRemote(msgbuffer)) return 0;
if(!CheckMsg(msgbuffer))
{
        m_errorNumber = 213;
        return 0;
}

return 1;
}
```

One important thing to note in the connection operation is in the actual assignment of the IP address to the *sockaddr_in* variable. In this operation, we must take a standard dot-notation IP address (for example, aaa.bbb.ccc.ddd) and convert it to a numeric representation. The use of inet_addr in this assignment performs that conversion for us to take the dot-notation string representation and turn it into the numeric value required for routing on the Internet.

Another point to note is the use of htons in the port assignment. This operation converts the format of the local host's numeric representation of the TCP port to a network representation for transmission to the remote host.

> **NOTE:** The reason for the transformation of numeric values via htons has to do with the compatibility of numeric representations on different hosts. Many hosts do not store their numeric values in the same way, which means that an IBM PC *may not* be able to send a numeric value to an RS6000. Since all hosts convert their numeric values to a common representation on a network, all hosts can take that common format and convert it to their local numeric representation for storage.

Upon a successful connection, we wait for the greeting message from the remote SMTP server with a call to RecvRemote. If successful, we issue a HELO command to the SMTP server to identify ourselves, using SendRemote. The resulting response from the server is verified, using CheckMsg to determine success or failure. This operation is the first step in establishing communications with the SMTP server to submit e-mail to the server.

Notice the use of RecvRemote and SendRemote throughout Listing 11-5 and in Listing 11-6. These two functions, from Listing 11-8, encapsulate and enhance the functionality of the send and recv Winsock API functions for sending and receiving messages between the SMTP module and the remote SMTP server. The RecvRemote procedure primarily adds the capability to handle retries from busy remote servers, based on a value entered in the RetryCount property of the module.

Listing 11-8   *RecvRemote* and *SendRemote* **Methods**

```
int CSmtpCtrl::RecvRemote(CString& buffer)
{
        int             NumOfChars;
        char             inbuff[1500];
        int             TimeOut = 2000;
        int             loopcount = 0;


        m_errorNumber=0;
        setsockopt(skt, SOL_SOCKET, SO_RCVTIMEO, (const char *)&TimeOut,
➡sizeof(TimeOut));


        do
        {
                buffer.Empty();
                memset(inbuff, 0, sizeof(inbuff));
                NumOfChars = recv(skt, inbuff, sizeof(inbuff), 0);
                switch(NumOfChars)
                {
                        case -1     :       m_errorNumber = WSAGetLastError() -
➡WSABASEERR;
                                        if (m_errorNumber == 60)
                                                loopcount++;
                                        else
                                        {
                                                m_errorNumber=0;
                                                return 1;
                                        }
                                        break;
                        case 0      :       return 1;
                        default     :       buffer = CString(inbuff, NumOfChars);
                                        if(atoi(buffer.GetBuffer(4)) > 0)
                                        {
                                                m_errorNumber = 0;
```

```
                                        return 1;
                                }
                                else
                                        loopcount++;
                                break;
                        }
                }while(loopcount<m_retryCount);

                return 0;
        }


        int CSmtpCtrl::SendRemote(CString buffer)
        {
                int                     TimeOut = 5000;

                m_errorNumber=0;

                setsockopt(skt, SOL_SOCKET, SO_SNDTIMEO, (const char *)&TimeOut,
        ➥sizeof(TimeOut));

                if (send(skt, buffer.GetBuffer(buffer.GetLength()), buffer.GetLength(), 0)<0)
                {
                        m_errorNumber = WSAGetLastError() - WSABASEERR;
                        return 0;
                }
                return 1;
        }
```

As mentioned earlier, the CheckMsg method (see Listing 11-9) examines the incoming
response from the SMTP server to determine whether an error condition exists or
whether the operation was successful. For SMTP, any message that is returned whose
code begins with 1, 2, or 3 is noted as a success, whereas 4 or 5 is an error.

Listing 11-9 *CheckMsg* **Method**

```
BOOL CSmtpCtrl::CheckMsg(CString msg)
{
        if(msg.GetAt(0) == '1' || msg.GetAt(0) == '2' || msg.GetAt(0) == '3')
        {
                m_errorNumber = 0;
                return(1);
        }


        if(msg.GetAt(0) == '4' || msg.GetAt(0) == '5')
        {
                m_errorNumber = atoi(msg.GetBuffer(4));
                return(0);
        }


        return 1;
}
```

Sending a Message

Once the SMTP module is connected to an SMTP server, the module can transfer e-mail to the server. The transfer begins with a call to the SendHeaderInfo method, shown in Listing 11-10. In this method, all the information on the origination and destination users is submitted to the SMTP server. This information is used to relay the e-mail to the appropriate SMTP server, as well as to inform the recipient of the originator of the e-mail. This procedure provides a means of allowing the container application to submit multiple destination addresses. As the listing shows, two loops exist to allow the procedure to loop through the CCUserList and DestinationUserList properties of the module to send the mail to multiple destination users.

Listing 11-10   *SendHeaderInfo* **Method**

```
int CSmtpCtrl::SendHeaderInfo(CString from, CString to, CString cc)
{
        CString         msgbuffer;
        int         offset, prevoffset;

        //Send MAIL FROM to prepare message send
        msgbuffer = "MAIL FROM:<" + from + ">\xD\xA";
        if(!SendRemote(msgbuffer)) return 0;
        if(!RecvRemote(msgbuffer)) return 0;
        if(!CheckMsg(msgbuffer))
        {
                m_errorNumber = 211;
                return 0;
        }

        //Send TOs
        prevoffset = 0;
        for(offset = 0;offset<to.GetLength();offset++)
        {
                if(offset == to.GetLength()-1)
                {
                        msgbuffer = "RCPT TO:<" + to.Mid(prevoffset, offset-prevoffset+1) +
                                ">\xD\xA";
                        prevoffset = offset;
                        if(!SendRemote(msgbuffer)) return 0;
                        if(!RecvRemote(msgbuffer)) return 0;
                        if(!CheckMsg(msgbuffer))
                        {
                                m_errorNumber = 212;
                                return 0;
                        }
                }
```

continues

Listing 11-10   Continued

```
        if(to.GetAt(offset) == ', ')
        {
                msgbuffer = "RCPT TO:<" + to.Mid(prevoffset, offset-prevoffset) +
                        ">\xD\xA";
                prevoffset = offset+1;
                if(!SendRemote(msgbuffer)) return 0;
                if(!RecvRemote(msgbuffer)) return 0;
                if(!CheckMsg(msgbuffer))
                {
                        m_errorNumber = 212;
                        return 0;
                }
        }
}


//Send CCs
prevoffset = 0;
for(offset = 0;offset<cc.GetLength();offset++)
{
        if(offset == cc.GetLength()-1)
        {
                msgbuffer = "RCPT TO:<" + cc.Mid(prevoffset, offset-prevoffset+1) +
                        ">\xD\xA";
                prevoffset = offset;
                if(!SendRemote(msgbuffer)) return 0;
                if(!RecvRemote(msgbuffer)) return 0;
                if(!CheckMsg(msgbuffer))
                {
                        m_errorNumber = 217;
                        return 0;
                }
        }
```

```
            if(cc.GetAt(offset) == ',')
            {
                    msgbuffer = "RCPT TO:<" + cc.Mid(prevoffset, offset-prevoffset) +
                            ">\xD\xA";
                    prevoffset = offset+1;
                    if(!SendRemote(msgbuffer)) return 0;
                    if(!RecvRemote(msgbuffer)) return 0;
                    if(!CheckMsg(msgbuffer))
                    {
                            m_errorNumber = 217;
                            return 0;
                    }
            }
        }

        return 1;
}
```

Once the header information is sent to the SMTP server, the client can start sending all the data information related to the body of the message. To start the transmission of the message body, the client sends the DATA command and waits for a response from the remote SMTP server (see Listing 11-11). If a positive response is received by the client, the client begins to transmit the date, subject, To list, cc list, attachment information, and related header information.

Listing 11-11 *StartData* **Procedure**

```
int CSmtpCtrl::StartData()
{
        CString         msgbuffer;

        //Send DATA to prepare message send
        msgbuffer = "DATA\xD\xA";
```

continues

Listing 11-11   Continued

```
        if(!SendRemote(msgbuffer)) return 0;
        if(!RecvRemote(msgbuffer)) return 0;
        if(!CheckMsg(msgbuffer))
        {
                m_errorNumber = 214;
                return 0;
        }


        return 1;
}
```

During the transmission of the mail message body, the SMTP module will uuencode any attachments specified in the m_mailAttachment property (see Listing 11-12). This operation takes a binary file and converts it to ASCII printable characters for transmission of the attachment as though it were a standard text message.

> **NOTE:** Attachment encoding is necessary because many characters in a binary file (a Word for Windows document, an Excel spreadsheet, an executable, and so on) contain nonprintable characters, which are not transmittable in the body of a mail message or which may be seen as control characters. By converting the attachments to ASCII, the attachments can be sent as a standard e-mail message, which is decoded by the recipient's e-mail reader client application.

Listing 11-12   *UUENCODE* Method

```
int CSmtpCtrl::UUENCODE(CString attachmentfile)
{


        int       i, cval[4];
        char      readbytes;
        char      tempbuffer[50];
        char      encval[2];
        HFILE      infile;
```

```
        CString attachmentcontent;

  · m_totalEncodedBytes = 0;

        infile = _lopen(attachmentfile, OF_READ);
        if(infile == HFILE_ERROR) return 0;

        do
        {
                attachmentcontent.Empty();
                memset(tempbuffer, 0, sizeof(tempbuffer));
                readbytes = _lread(infile, tempbuffer, 45);
                encval[0] = ((readbytes & 077) + ' ');
                attachmentcontent += CString(encval, 1);

                for(i = 0;i<readbytes;i += 3)
                {
                        cval[0] = (tempbuffer[i+0] >> 2);
                        cval[1] = (tempbuffer[i+0] << 4) & 060 ¦ (tempbuffer[i+1] >> 4)
➥& 017;
                        cval[2] = (tempbuffer[i+1] << 2) & 074 ¦ (tempbuffer[i+2] >> 6)
➥& 03;
                        cval[3] = (tempbuffer[i+2] & 077);

                        encval[0] = ((cval[0] & 077) + ' ');
                        attachmentcontent += CString(encval, 1);
                        encval[0] = ((cval[1] & 077) + ' ');
                        attachmentcontent += CString(encval, 1);
                        encval[0] = ((cval[2] & 077) + ' ');
                        attachmentcontent += CString(encval, 1);
                        encval[0] = ((cval[3] & 077) + ' ');
                        attachmentcontent += CString(encval, 1);
                }
```

continues

Listing 11-12   Continued

```
                SendData(attachmentcontent);
                m_totalEncodedBytes += readbytes;
        }while(readbytes == 45);
        _lclose(infile);
        return(1);

}
```

Upon completion of the entire operation of sending the header, body, and any attachments, the SMTP module closes the connection with a call to the `CloseRemote` method. This method (see Listing 11-13) sends the termination character sequence to the remote SMTP server to notify it that the client has completed sending the mail message body. The procedure then sends a QUIT command to close the connection, clear all allocated resources, and inform the server to begin relaying the mail message to the destination user or users.

Listing 11-13   *CloseRemote* Method

```
int CSmtpCtrl::CloseRemote()
{
        CString         msgbuffer;

        //Send final <CRLF.CRLF>
        msgbuffer = "\xD\xA.\xD\xA";

        if(!SendRemote(msgbuffer)) return 0;
        if(!RecvRemote(msgbuffer)) return 0;
        if(!CheckMsg(msgbuffer))
        {
                m_errorNumber = 215;
                return 0;
        }

        //Send QUIT to end conversation
        msgbuffer = "QUIT\xD\xA";
```

```
if(!SendRemote(msgbuffer)) return 0;

if(!RecvRemote(msgbuffer)) return 0;

if(!CheckMsg(msgbuffer))

{

        m_errorNumber = 216;

        return 0;

}


closesocket(skt);

return 1;

}
```

Notifying the Container of Completion

The final lines of code of the TSendMail function (see Listing 11-14) allow the module to fire an event to notify the container that the operation has completed. This operation allows for a clean completion and exit of the thread procedure with the execution of the event based on the message sent by the call to SendMessage(WM_TIMER, 1, 0). It is a good idea, when handling threads, to provide a message-oriented means of event notification due to the calling stack.

> **WARNING:** If a thread exits when it calls a procedure, the called procedure returns to nothing, therefore causing (in most cases) some hideous crash. Messages allow threads to execute procedures cleanly without having the called procedure return to the calling thread procedure.

Listing 11-14 Thread Completion

```
if (retval)
        thisObject->m_errorNumber = 0;


//Close sockets
thisObject->m_currentState = CLOSING_CONNECTION;
```

continues

Listing 11-14   Continued

```
        thisObject->CloseRemote();
        thisObject->m_currentState = WAITING_FOR_ACTION;
        thisObject->m_bSendMailEvent = TRUE;
        thisObject->SendMessage(WM_TIMER, 1, 0);


        return(retval);
```

To catch the message sent by the completion of the thread, we are using the Timer event procedure (see Listing 11-15). In this procedure, we look at the flags set by the thread when it ended. If the flag is set to TRUE, the appropriate event procedure is fired, with arguments to notify the container of the resulting completion state of the associated operation.

Listing 11-15   *Timer* Event Procedure

```
void CSmtpCtrl::OnTimer(UINT nIDEvent)
{
        if(m_bSendMailEvent == TRUE)
        {
                m_bSendMailEvent = FALSE;
                FireEndSendMail(m_errorNumber);
        }


        COleControl::OnTimer(nIDEvent);
}
```

POP Module

The POP module consists of several properties and seven methods. The properties of this module are assigned values that allow for logging on to a remote POP3 server to retrieve e-mail from a mailbox. As you see in Listing 11-16, each of the properties and methods of the SMTP module provides a means of storing the necessary values for retrieving e-mail from a mailbox.

Listing 11-16 Properties and Methods of the POP Module

```
BEGIN_DISPATCH_MAP(CPopCtrl, COleControl)
        //{{AFX_DISPATCH_MAP(CPopCtrl)
        DISP_PROPERTY_NOTIFY(CPopCtrl, "UserName", m_userName, OnUserNameChanged, VT_BSTR)
        DISP_PROPERTY_NOTIFY(CPopCtrl, "RetryCount", m_retryCount, OnRetryCountChanged,
➡VT_I2)
        DISP_PROPERTY_NOTIFY(CPopCtrl, "ErrorNumber", m_errorNumber, OnErrorNumberChanged,
➡VT_I2)
        DISP_PROPERTY_NOTIFY(CPopCtrl, "TotalReceiveBytes", m_totalReceiveBytes,
                OnTotalReceiveBytesChanged, VT_I4)
        DISP_PROPERTY_NOTIFY(CPopCtrl, "TotalDecodedBytes", m_totalDecodedBytes,
                OnTotalDecodedBytesChanged, VT_I4)
        DISP_PROPERTY_NOTIFY(CPopCtrl, "HeaderLineCount", m_headerLineCount,
                OnHeaderLineCountChanged, VT_I2)
        DISP_PROPERTY_NOTIFY(CPopCtrl, "CurrentState", m_currentState,
➡OnCurrentStateChanged,
                VT_I2)
        DISP_PROPERTY_NOTIFY(CPopCtrl, "Action", m_action, OnActionChanged, VT_I2)
        DISP_PROPERTY_NOTIFY(CPopCtrl, "UserPassword", m_userPassword,
➡OnUserPasswordChanged,
                VT_BSTR)
        DISP_PROPERTY_NOTIFY(CPopCtrl, "HostAddress", m_hostAddress, OnHostAddressChanged,
                VT_BSTR)
        DISP_PROPERTY_NOTIFY(CPopCtrl, "MessageNumber", m_messageNumber,
➡OnMessageNumberChanged,
                VT_I2)
        DISP_PROPERTY_EX(CPopCtrl, "Version", GetVersion, SetVersion, VT_BSTR)
        DISP_FUNCTION(CPopCtrl, "GetMail", GetMail, VT_BSTR, VTS_I2)
        DISP_FUNCTION(CPopCtrl, "Delete-mail", Delete-mail, VT_BOOL, VTS_I2)
        DISP_FUNCTION(CPopCtrl, "ListMail", ListMail, VT_BSTR, VTS_NONE)
        DISP_FUNCTION(CPopCtrl, "GetUIDL", GetUIDL, VT_BSTR, VTS_NONE)
        DISP_FUNCTION(CPopCtrl, "GetStatus", GetStatus, VT_BSTR, VTS_NONE)
        DISP_FUNCTION(CPopCtrl, "Logon", Logon, VT_BOOL, VTS_BSTR VTS_BSTR)
```

continues

Listing 11-16   Continued

```
      DISP_FUNCTION(CPopCtrl, "Logoff", Logoff, VT_BOOL, VTS_NONE)
      //}}AFX_DISPATCH_MAP
      DISP_FUNCTION_ID(CPopCtrl, "AboutBox", DISPID_ABOUTBOX, AboutBox, VT_EMPTY,
➡VTS_NONE)
END_DISPATCH_MAP()
```

The different operations of the POP module are initialized by the Action property of the module. When values are assigned to the property, the OnAction property procedure is executed, allowing the different threads of the module to become active (see Listing 11-17). In each case, when a value is assigned to the Action property of the POP module, the property procedure checks to see whether the associated thread is already active. If the thread is already active, an error is returned by a call to the respective event procedure, where the container receives value of any information and errors passed as the arguments. If the thread is not already active, the procedure attempts to start the respective procedure as a thread to perform the desired operation.

Listing 11-17   *Action* Property Procedure

```
void CPopCtrl::OnActionChanged()
{
      // TODO: Add notification handler code
      DWORD                   ThreadId;
      DWORD                   ThreadExitCode;
      CString                 cTempStr;


      switch (m_action)
      {
      case GET_MAIL :
            GetExitCodeThread(m_hGetMailThreadHandle,&ThreadExitCode);
            if(ThreadExitCode!=STILL_ACTIVE)
            {
```

```
                    m_hGetMailThreadHandle =
➥CreateThread(NULL,0,TGetMail,this,0,&ThreadId);
            }
            else
            {
                    m_errorNumber=11000;
                    cTempStr.Empty();
                    FireEndGetMail(m_messageNumber, cTempStr, m_errorNumber);
            }
            break;


    case DELETE_MAIL :
            GetExitCodeThread(m_hDelMailThreadHandle,&ThreadExitCode);
            if(ThreadExitCode!=STILL_ACTIVE)
            {
                    m_hDelMailThreadHandle =
➥CreateThread(NULL,0,TDelMail,this,0,&ThreadId);
            }
            else
            {
                    m_errorNumber=11000;
                    FireEndDelete-mail(m_messageNumber, m_errorNumber);
            }
            break;


    case LOGON :
            m_bLogonState=LOGON;
            GetExitCodeThread(m_hLogonThreadHandle,&ThreadExitCode);
            if(ThreadExitCode!=STILL_ACTIVE)
            {
                    m_hLogonThreadHandle =
➥CreateThread(NULL,0,TLogon,this,0,&ThreadId);
            }
```

continues

Listing 11-17 Continued

```
            else
            {
                    m_errorNumber=11000;
                    FireEndLogon(m_errorNumber);
            }
            break;

    case LOGOFF:
            m_bLogonState=LOGOFF;
            GetExitCodeThread(m_hLogonThreadHandle,&ThreadExitCode);
            if(ThreadExitCode!=STILL_ACTIVE)
            {
                    m_hLogonThreadHandle =
➥CreateThread(NULL,0,TLogon,this,0,&ThreadId);
            }
            else
            {
                    m_errorNumber=11000;
                    FireEndLogoff(m_errorNumber);
            }
            break;

    case LIST_MAIL:
            m_bStatusState=LIST_MAIL;
            GetExitCodeThread(m_hMailStatusThreadHandle,&ThreadExitCode);
            if(ThreadExitCode!=STILL_ACTIVE)
            {
                    m_hMailStatusThreadHandle =
                            CreateThread(NULL,0,TMailStatus,this,0,&ThreadId);
            }
            else
            {
                    m_errorNumber=11000;
```

```
                    cTempStr.Empty();

                    FireEndGetList(cTempStr, m_errorNumber);

            }

            break;


    case MAIL_STATUS :

            m_bStatusState=MAIL_STATUS;

            GetExitCodeThread(m_hMailStatusThreadHandle,&ThreadExitCode);

            if(ThreadExitCode!=STILL_ACTIVE)

            {

                    m_hMailStatusThreadHandle =

                            CreateThread(NULL,0,TMailStatus,this,0,&ThreadId);

            }

            else

            {

                    m_errorNumber=11000;

                    cTempStr.Empty();

                    FireEndGetStatus(cTempStr, m_errorNumber);

            }

            break;


    case GET_UIDL:

            m_bStatusState=GET_UIDL;

            GetExitCodeThread(m_hMailStatusThreadHandle,&ThreadExitCode);

            if(ThreadExitCode!=STILL_ACTIVE)

            {

                    m_hMailStatusThreadHandle =

                            CreateThread(NULL,0,TMailStatus,this,0,&ThreadId);

            }

            else

            {          .

                    m_errorNumber=11000;

                    cTempStr.Empty();
```

continues

Listing 11-17 Continued

```
                                FireEndGetUIDL(cTempStr, m_errorNumber);
                    }
                    break;


            case CANCEL_REQUEST:
                    GetExitCodeThread(m_hMailStatusThreadHandle,&ThreadExitCode);
                    if(ThreadExitCode==STILL_ACTIVE)
➥TerminateThread(m_hMailStatusThreadHandle,0);


                    GetExitCodeThread(m_hGetMailThreadHandle,&ThreadExitCode);
                    if(ThreadExitCode==STILL_ACTIVE)
➥TerminateThread(m_hGetMailThreadHandle,0);


                    GetExitCodeThread(m_hDelMailThreadHandle,&ThreadExitCode);
                    if(ThreadExitCode==STILL_ACTIVE)
➥TerminateThread(m_hDelMailThreadHandle,0);


                    GetExitCodeThread(m_hLogonThreadHandle,&ThreadExitCode);
                    if(ThreadExitCode==STILL_ACTIVE) TerminateThread(m_hLogonThreadHandle,0);
                    CloseRemote();


                    m_currentState=WAITING_FOR_ACTION;
                    m_errorNumber=12050;
                    m_bLogonState=LOGOFF;
                    FireEndLogoff(m_errorNumber);


                    break;
            }


            SetModifiedFlag();

}
```

Connecting to a POP Server

If a LOGON or LOGOFF value is assigned to the Action property of the TLogon thread function (see Listing 11-18) is executed to either log on to a remote POP server or log off and close the connection. The LOGON operation uses the m_userName and m_userPassword properties for authentication on the remote POP server specified in m_hostAddress. For each operation, the thread procedure waits for a response to determine whether the operation was successful. If it was, the procedure continues; otherwise, an error is generated.

Listing 11-18 *TLogon* **Thread Function**

```
DWORD WINAPI TLogon(LPVOID pParam)
{
        // TODO: Add your dispatch handler code here
        CString         s;
        CString         msgbuffer;
        CPopCtrl*       thisObject = (CPopCtrl*)pParam;
        int             retval = 1, localFlag;

        switch(thisObject->m_bLogonState)
        {
            case LOGON:
            {
                    localFlag=LOGON;

                    thisObject->m_errorNumber = 0;

                    thisObject->m_currentState=CONNECTING;
                    if(!thisObject->OpenSocket()) END_THREAD(0);
                    if(!thisObject->ConnectRemote(thisObject->m_hostAddress))
    ➡END_THREAD(0);

                    thisObject->m_currentState=LOGGING_ON;
                    msgbuffer = "USER " + thisObject->m_userName + "\xD\xA";
```

continues

Listing 11-18 Continued

```
                    if(!thisObject->SendRemote(msgbuffer,0)) END_THREAD(0);
                    if(!thisObject->RecvRemote(msgbuffer,2000)) END_THREAD(0);
                    if(msgbuffer.Left(3)!="+OK") END_THREAD_WITH_ERROR(223);

                    msgbuffer = "PASS " + thisObject->m_userPassword + "\xD\xA";
                    if(!thisObject->SendRemote(msgbuffer,0)) END_THREAD(0);
                    if(!thisObject->RecvRemote(msgbuffer,2000)) END_THREAD(0);
                    if(msgbuffer.Left(3)!="+OK") END_THREAD_WITH_ERROR(224);

                    thisObject->m_strSystemString =
➥msgbuffer.Mid(4,msgbuffer.GetLength());
                       break;
            }

            case LOGOFF:
            {
                    thisObject->m_currentState=CLOSING_CONNECTION;
                    localFlag=LOGOFF;
                    thisObject->m_strSystemString.Empty();
                    if(!thisObject->CloseRemote()) END_THREAD(0);
                    break;
            }

            default :
            {
                    thisObject->m_strSystemString.Empty();
                    break;
            }
        }

        retval=1;

    byebye:
```

```
        if (retval)
        {
                thisObject->m_errorNumber = 0;
        }
        else
        {
                thisObject->m_strSystemString.Empty();
        }


        thisObject->m_bLogonState=localFlag;
        if (localFlag == LOGON)
                thisObject->m_bLogonEvent=TRUE;
        else
                thisObject->m_bLogoffEvent=TRUE;
        thisObject->m_currentState=WAITING_FOR_ACTION;
        thisObject->SendMessage(WM_TIMER,1,0);


        return(retval);
}
```

If an error is generated, the `END_THREAD(x)` or `END_THREAD_WITH_ERROR(x)` macro is called. Both of these macros merely jump to the end of the function to perform an orderly cleanup and to return the error information to the container through an event procedure, using the `SendMessage(WM_TIMER,1,0)` function.

Logging off the POP server is accomplished with the `CloseRemote` procedure. This procedure, like that in the SMTP module, simply sends a `QUIT` command to the remote POP server and closes the connection.

CAUTION: If the POP module is logged on to a remote POP server and the connection abnormally closes, the mailbox will be locked. If an attempt to reconnect is made after an abnormal closure of the connection occurs, an error is generated during each attempt until the mailbox is unlocked. You can wait until the mailbox lock times out, or you can e-mail the system administrator and ask him or her to unlock the mailbox locally.

Retrieving E-Mail

If the value of GET_MAIL is assigned to the Action property, the module attempts to retrieve e-mail from the remote POP server. To perform the actual operation, the TGetMail thread procedure is used. As shown in Listing 11-19, the procedure simply sends a command, based on the m_headerLineCount property, to retrieve a particular e-mail from the remote POP server. The mail number, specified in the m_messageNumber property, identifies the particular e-mail that the client wants to retrieve from his or her mailbox. Using the TOP command extracts m_headerLineCount lines of the message body from the specified message, whereas RETR command retrieves the entire message header and body.

Listing 11-19   *TGetMail* **Thread Function**

```
DWORD WINAPI TGetMail(LPVOID pParam)
{
        // TODO: Add your dispatch handler code here

        CString              s;
        CString              msgbuffer, Boundary;
        char                 tempstr[20];
        CPopCtrl*            thisObject = (CPopCtrl*)pParam;
        int                  retval = 1;

        thisObject->m_errorNumber = 0;

        if (thisObject->m_headerLineCount>0)
        {
                sprintf(tempstr,"%d %d",thisObject->m_messageNumber,
                        thisObject->m_headerLineCount);
                msgbuffer = "TOP ";
                msgbuffer += tempstr;
                msgbuffer += "\xD\xA";
        }
        else
        {
```

```
            sprintf(tempstr,"%d",thisObject->m_messageNumber);
            msgbuffer = "RETR ";
            msgbuffer += tempstr;
            msgbuffer += "\xD\xA";
    }


    thisObject->m_currentState=SENDING_REQUEST;
    if(!thisObject->SendRemote(msgbuffer,0)) END_THREAD(0);
    thisObject->m_currentState=RETRIEVING_MAIL;
    if(!thisObject->RecvRemote(msgbuffer,5000)) END_THREAD(0);


    if(msgbuffer.Left(3)!="+OK") END_THREAD_WITH_ERROR(227);


    thisObject->m_strMailString = msgbuffer.Mid(4,msgbuffer.GetLength());


    //If attachments then parse. UUENCODE and BASE64 only.
    if(thisObject->GetAttachmentInfo(thisObject->m_strMailString , Boundary))
    {
            thisObject->m_currentState=DECODING_ATTACHMENT;
            if(!thisObject->HandleAttachment(thisObject->m_strMailString, Boundary,
                    thisObject->m_strMailString)) END_THREAD(0);
    }


    retval=1;


byebye:


    if (retval)
    {
            thisObject->m_errorNumber = 0;
    }
    else
    {
```

continues

Listing 11-19 Continued

```
        thisObject->m_strMailString.Empty();
    }


    thisObject->m_bGetMailEvent=TRUE;
    thisObject->m_currentState=WAITING_FOR_ACTION;
    thisObject->SendMessage(WM_TIMER,1,0);


    return(retval);
}
```

The thread procedure also handles the decoding of attachments for either Base64 or uuencoded MIME encoded documents. This type of decoding operation conforms to the MIME standards to provide a compatible mechanism for exchanging e-mail attachments with different e-mail packages used by remote users. Regardless of the type of encoding used for a given attachment, the procedure calls the HandleAttachment procedure (see Listing 11-20), which decodes the attachment and writes it to a file on the local machine.

As shown in Listing 11-20, the function determines the type of encoding that was used on the attachment. The attachment is then passed through the appropriate parsing routine within the function to turn the textual representation of the attachment into a file of the attachment's original form.

Listing 11-20 *HandleAttachment* Function

```
int CPopCtrl::HandleAttachment(CString buffer, CString boundary, CString& msgbuff)
{
    CString         MainBuffer, ParseBuffer;
    CString         AsciiBoundary, MainBoundary, UUEBuffer, B64Buffer;
    CString         AttachmentInfo1, AttachmentInfo2;
    CString         filename;
    int             beginoffset,endoffset, OpValue=0;

    MainBoundary = "—"+boundary;
```

```
AsciiBoundary = "Content-Type: text/plain; charset=\"us-ascii\"";

AttachmentInfo1 = "Content-Transfer-Encoding: x-uuencode";
AttachmentInfo2 = "Content-Transfer-Encoding: base64";

MainBuffer=buffer;
msgbuff.Empty();

//Extract the header
if((endoffset=MainBuffer.Find(LPCTSTR(MainBoundary)))!=-1)
{
        msgbuff+=MainBuffer.Mid(0,endoffset);
        MainBuffer=MainBuffer.Mid(endoffset,MainBuffer.GetLength()-endoffset);
}
else
{
        msgbuff=buffer;
        m_errorNumber=1100;
        return(0);
}

//Loop and extract all
while((beginoffset=MainBuffer.Find(LPCTSTR(MainBoundary)))!=-1)
{
        MainBuffer=MainBuffer.Mid(beginoffset+MainBoundary.GetLength()+1,
                MainBuffer.GetLength()-(beginoffset+MainBoundary.GetLength()+1));

        //check for closing boundary
        if((endoffset=MainBuffer.Find(LPCTSTR(MainBoundary)))==-1)
        {
                //end of mail message
                if((endoffset=MainBuffer.Find((LPCTSTR)"."))!=-1)
                {
```

continues

Listing 11-20 Continued

```
                                return(1);
                }
                else
                {
                        m_errorNumber=1100;
                        return(0);
                }
        }


ParseBuffer=MainBuffer.Mid(0,endoffset);

MainBuffer=MainBuffer.Mid(endoffset, MainBuffer.GetLength()-endoffset);

//us-ascii
if((beginoffset=ParseBuffer.Find(LPCTSTR(AsciiBoundary)))!=-1)
{
        msgbuff+=ParseBuffer.Mid(AsciiBoundary.GetLength()+1,
                ParseBuffer.GetLength()-AsciiBoundary.GetLength());
}
else
{
        //No valid attachments
        OpValue = 3;
        //UUENCODE
        if((beginoffset=ParseBuffer.Find(LPCTSTR(AttachmentInfo1)))!=-1)
                OpValue = 1;
        //BASE64
        if((beginoffset=ParseBuffer.Find(LPCTSTR(AttachmentInfo2)))!=-1)
                OpValue = 2;

        switch(OpValue)
        {
                case 1 :        //UUENCODED Attachment
```

```
                            {
                                    //Get filename
                                    filename.Empty();
                                    if((beginoffset=ParseBuffer.Find((LPCTSTR)"file
►name="))!=-1)

                                    {
                                            beginoffset+=10;
                                            while(ParseBuffer.GetAt(beginoffset)!='"')
                                            {
                                                    filename+=
►ParseBuffer.GetAt(beginoffset);

                                                    beginoffset++;
                                            }
                                    }

                                    //locate begin and end

if((beginoffset=ParseBuffer.Find((LPCTSTR)"begin"))!=-1)
                                    {

if((endoffset=ParseBuffer.Find((LPCTSTR)"end"))!=-1)
                                            {
                                                    UUEBuffer=
►ParseBuffer.Mid(beginoffset,

                                                            (endoffset-beginoffset)+3);
                                            }
                                            else
                                                    m_errorNumber=1100;
                                    }
                                    else
                                            m_errorNumber=1100;

                                    if(UUEDECODE(UUEBuffer, filename))
```

continues

Listing 11-20   Continued

```
                                    {
                                            msgbuff+="\xD\xAAttachment Saved
➥in "+filename+

                                                " \xD\xA";
                                    }
                                    else
                                    {
                                            msgbuff+="\xD\xAUnable to Save Attachment
➥in "+

                                                filename+" \xD\xA";
                                            m_errorNumber=1100;
                                    }
                                    break;
                            }


                    case 2:        //MIME Attachment
                            {
                            //Get filename
                            filename.Empty();
                            if((beginoffset=
➥ParseBuffer.Find((LPCTSTR)"filename="))!=-1)
                                    {
                                            beginoffset+=10;
                                            while(ParseBuffer.GetAt(beginoffset)!='"')
                                            {
                                                    filename+=
➥ParseBuffer.GetAt(beginoffset);

                                                    beginoffset++;
                                            }

B64Buffer=ParseBuffer.Mid(beginoffset+1,(endoffset-

                                                (beginoffset+1)));
                                    }
```

```
                              else
                              {
                                      m_errorNumber=1100;
                              }

                              if(BASE64(B64Buffer, filename))
                              {
                                      msgbuff+="\xD\xAAttachment Saved in
➥"+filename+

                                      " \xD\xA";
                              }
                              else
                              {
                                      msgbuff+="\xD\xAUnable to Save Attachment
➥in "+

                                              filename+" \xD\xA";
                                      m_errorNumber=1100;
                              }
                              break;
                      }

                  default:        //No valid attachment
                      {
                              //Get filename
                              filename.Empty();
                              if((beginoffset=
➥ParseBuffer.Find((LPCTSTR)"filename="))!=-1)
                              {
                                      beginoffset+=10;
                                      while(ParseBuffer.GetAt(beginoffset)!='"')
                                      {
                                              filename+=
➥ParseBuffer.GetAt(beginoffset);
```

continues

Listing 11-20   Continued

```
                                                beginoffset++;
                                        }
                                }

                                msgbuff+="\xD\xAUnable to Extract Attachment
➥"+filename+
                                        " \xD\xA";
                                break;
                            }
                        }
                    }
                }
        return(1);
}
```

Deleting E-Mail

Once mail is retrieved, the client POP application can delete the e-mail from the server. This operation is useful in that the POP server can clean the mailbox of old or read e-mail immediately upon receipt of the e-mail by the POP client. This operation is accomplished by the assignment of DELETE_MAIL to the Action property and the associated execution of the TDelMail thread procedure (see Listing 11-21). This procedure uses the m_messageNumber property to send the message number to delete with the DELE command. Upon completion of the operation, an error or success value is returned to the container through the associated event procedure.

Listing 11-21   *TDelMail* Thread Function

```
DWORD WINAPI TDelMail(LPVOID pParam)
{
        // TODO: Add your dispatch handler code here
```

```
CString                     msgbuffer;
char                          tempstr[20];
CPopCtrl*              thisObject = (CPopCtrl*)pParam;
int                         retval = 1;

thisObject->m_errorNumber = 0;

sprintf(tempstr,"%d",thisObject->m_messageNumber);

msgbuffer = "DELE ";
msgbuffer += tempstr;
msgbuffer += "\xD\xA";

thisObject->m_currentState=SENDING_REQUEST;
if(!thisObject->SendRemote(msgbuffer,0)) END_THREAD(0);
thisObject->m_currentState=RETRIEVING_DATA;
if(!thisObject->RecvRemote(msgbuffer,1500)) END_THREAD(0);
if(msgbuffer.Left(3)!="+OK") END_THREAD_WITH_ERROR(226);

retval=1;

byebye:

if (retval)
{
        thisObject->m_errorNumber = 0;
}

thisObject->m_currentState=WAITING_FOR_ACTION;
thisObject->m_bDelMailEvent=TRUE;
thisObject->SendMessage(WM_TIMER,1,0);

return(retval);
}
```

Sending and Receiving Messages

To send and receive messages, the POP module uses the same functions as the SMTP module for communications: RecvRemote and SendRemote. The only difference is in the way that the information is sent and received, because of the handling of attachments, timeouts, and multiple-line messages coming in from the POP server. The RecvRemote and SendRemote functions (see Listing 11-22) allow the POP module to receive messages, detect the termination character sequence of an e-mail message and multiple-line messages, perform timeout recovery operations, and perform retries based on the m_retryCount property as necessary.

One argument to note for both functions is the TimeOut argument. This argument allows a millisecond timeout value to be passed to determine when the connection or command/response exchange has timed out. This argument is useful for certain operations that take extended amounts of time, so that the module can determine when to stop waiting for a response. This timeout value works in conjunction with the m_retryCount argument to provide a means of looping several times in case of continuous timeouts on, for example, a busy server.

Listing 11-22 *RecvRemote* and *SendRemote* Functions

```
int CPopCtrl::RecvRemote(CString& buffer, int TimeOut)
{
        int            NumOfChars, valsize, loopcount=0;
        char           inbuff[1500];

        buffer.Empty();
        m_totalReceiveBytes=0;
        if(TimeOut==0)
                valsize=0;
        else
                valsize=sizeof(TimeOut);

        setsockopt(skt,SOL_SOCKET,SO_RCVTIMEO,(const char *)&TimeOut,valsize);

        if(TimeOut==0)
```

```
        {
                memset(inbuff,0,sizeof(inbuff));

                do
                {
                        NumOfChars = recv(skt, inbuff, sizeof(inbuff), 0);

                        switch(NumOfChars)
                        {
                                case -1         :       m_errorNumber = WSAGetLastError()
➥- WSABASEERR;
                                                        if(m_errorNumber==60 &&
                                                        (buffer.Mid(buffer.GetLength()-3,3)==
➥".\xD\xA"))
                                                        {
                                                                m_errorNumber=0;
                                                                return 1;
                                                        }
                                                        if(m_errorNumber==60 && (loopcount <
➥m_retryCount))
                                                        {
                                                                loopcount++;
                                                                continue;
                                                        }
                                                        return 0;
                                case 0          :       return 1;
                                default         :       buffer =
➥CString(inbuff,NumOfChars);
                                                        m_totalReceiveBytes=buffer.GetLength();
                                                        return 1;
                        }
                }while(loopcount<m_retryCount);
        }
```

continues

Listing 11-22   Continued

```
     else
     {
          do{
               memset(inbuff,0,sizeof(inbuff));
               NumOfChars = recv(skt, inbuff, sizeof(inbuff), 0);

               switch(NumOfChars)
               {
                    case -1     :          m_errorNumber = WSAGetLastError()
➥- WSABASEERR;

                                          if(m_errorNumber==60 &&
                                          (buffer.Mid(buffer.GetLength()-3,3)
➥==".\xD\xA"))

                                          {
                                               m_errorNumber=0;
                                               return 1;
                                          }

                                          if (m_errorNumber==4) continue;

                                          if(m_errorNumber==60 && (loopcount <
➥m_retryCount))

                                          {
                                               loopcount++;
                                               continue;
                                          }

                                          if(m_errorNumber==60 || m_errorNumber==0 ||
                                               m_errorNumber==-10000)
                                          {
                                               m_errorNumber=0;
                                               return 1;
                                          }
```

```
                                else
                                        return 0;

                        case 0        :        return(1);

                        default       :        buffer +=
➥CString(inbuff,NumOfChars);
                                        m_totalReceiveBytes=buffer.GetLength();
                                        break;
                }
        }while(loopcount < m_retryCount);
    }


    return 1;
}



int CPopCtrl::SendRemote(CString buffer, int TimeOut)
{
        setsockopt(skt,SOL_SOCKET,SO_SNDTIMEO,(const char *)&TimeOut,sizeof(TimeOut));
        if (send(skt, buffer.GetBuffer(buffer.GetLength()), buffer.GetLength(), 0)<0)
        {
                m_errorNumber = WSAGetLastError() - WSABASEERR;
                if(m_errorNumber==60 || m_errorNumber==0 || m_errorNumber==-10000)
                {
                        m_errorNumber=0;
                        return 1;
                }
                else
                        return 0;
        }
        return 1;
}
```

Retrieving Status Information

Status information can be retrieved from the remote POP server by assigning one of several values to the Action property. Available values for different operations include LIST_MAIL, MAIL_STATUS, and GET_UIDL. The TMailStatus thread procedure (see Listing 11-23) provides the mechanisms to make requests from a remote POP server so as to extract the status of the mailbox on the POP server. For each of the respective commands, the POP module simply formats the command, sends it to the remote POP server, and then retrieves the response. This response usually contains the status information but may also contain error information if the POP server encounters an error during the request.

Listing 11-23 *TMailStatus* **Thread Function**

```
DWORD WINAPI TMailStatus(LPVOID pParam)
{
        // TODO: Add your dispatch handler code here
        CString                s;
        CString                msgbuffer;
        CPopCtrl*              thisObject = (CPopCtrl*)pParam;
        int                    retval = 1, localFlag;

        switch(thisObject->m_bStatusState)
        {
                case LIST_MAIL:
                {
                        localFlag=LIST_MAIL;

                        thisObject->m_errorNumber = 0;

                        msgbuffer = "LIST\xD\xA";

                        thisObject->m_currentState=SENDING_REQUEST;
                        if(!thisObject->SendRemote(msgbuffer,0)) END_THREAD(0);
                        thisObject->m_currentState=RETRIEVING_DATA;
                        if(!thisObject->RecvRemote(msgbuffer,1500)) END_THREAD(0);
```

```
                    if(msgbuffer.Left(3)!="+OK") END_THREAD_WITH_ERROR(222);

                    thisObject->m_strStatusString=
msgbuffer.Mid(4,msgbuffer.GetLength());

                    break;
            }

            case MAIL_STATUS:
            {
                    localFlag=MAIL_STATUS;

                    thisObject->m_errorNumber = 0;

                    msgbuffer = "STAT\xD\xA";

                    thisObject->m_currentState=SENDING_REQUEST;
                    if(!thisObject->SendRemote(msgbuffer,0)) END_THREAD(0);
                    thisObject->m_currentState=RETRIEVING_DATA;
                    if(!thisObject->RecvRemote(msgbuffer,1500)) END_THREAD(0);
                    if(msgbuffer.Left(3)!="+OK") END_THREAD_WITH_ERROR(221);

                    thisObject->m_strStatusString =
msgbuffer.Mid(4,msgbuffer.GetLength());

                    break;
            }

            case GET_UIDL:
            {
                    localFlag=GET_UIDL;

                    thisObject->m_errorNumber = 0;
```

continues

Listing 11-23 Continued

```
                        msgbuffer = "UIDL\xD\xA";

                        thisObject->m_currentState=SENDING_REQUEST;
                        if(!thisObject->SendRemote(msgbuffer,0)) END_THREAD(0);
                        thisObject->m_currentState=RETRIEVING_DATA;
                        if(!thisObject->RecvRemote(msgbuffer,1500)) END_THREAD(0);
                        if(msgbuffer.Left(3)!="+OK") END_THREAD_WITH_ERROR(229);

                        thisObject->m_strStatusString =
➥msgbuffer.Mid(4,msgbuffer.GetLength());

                        break;
                }

                default:
                {
                        thisObject->m_strStatusString.Empty();
                        thisObject->m_errorNumber=0;
                        break;
                }
        }

        retval = 1;


byebye:

        if (retval)
        {
                thisObject->m_errorNumber = 0;
        }
        else
```

```
        {
                thisObject->m_strStatusString.Empty();

        }

        thisObject->m_currentState=WAITING_FOR_ACTION;
        thisObject->m_bStatusState=localFlag;

        switch(thisObject->m_bStatusState)
        {
                case LIST_MAIL        :
                        thisObject->m_bListStatusState=TRUE;
                        break;
                case MAIL_STATUS      :
                        thisObject->m_bStatusState=TRUE;
                        break;
                case GET_UIDL         :
                        thisObject->m_bUIDLStatusState=TRUE;
                        break;
        }

        thisObject->SendMessage(WM_TIMER,1,0);

        return(retval);
}
```

Completion Notification

As with the SMTP module, for each of the thread functions discussed, a message is sent via SendMessage(*WM_TIMER,1,0*) to inform the module that the thread has completed, and an event should be fired to notify the container of the operation's completion status. In Listing 11-24, each of the threads has a corresponding block of code in the OnTimer procedure. Based on the completed thread operation, a specific block of code is executed to fire the event procedure to inform the container application of the operation's status.

Listing 11-24 *Timer* **Event Procedure**

```
void CPopCtrl::OnTimer(UINT nIDEvent)
{
        // TODO: Add your message handler code here and/or call default
        if(m_bListStatusState==TRUE)
        {
                m_bListStatusState=FALSE;
                FireEndGetList(m_strStatusString, m_errorNumber);
        }


        if(m_bStatusState==TRUE)
        {
                m_bStatusState=FALSE;
                FireEndGetStatus(m_strStatusString, m_errorNumber);
        }


        if(m_bUIDLStatusState==TRUE)
        {
                m_bUIDLStatusState=FALSE;
                FireEndGetUIDL(m_strStatusString, m_errorNumber);
        }


        if(m_bGetMailEvent==TRUE)
        {
                m_bGetMailEvent=FALSE;
                FireEndGetMail(m_messageNumber, m_strMailString, m_errorNumber);
        }


        if(m_bDelMailEvent==TRUE)
        {
                m_bDelMailEvent=FALSE;
                FireEndDelete-mail(m_messageNumber, m_errorNumber);
        }
```

```
        if(m_bLogonEvent==TRUE)
        {
                m_bLogonEvent=FALSE;
                FireEndLogon(m_errorNumber);
        }

        if(m_bLogoffEvent==TRUE)
        {
                m_bLogoffEvent=FALSE;
                FireEndLogoff(m_errorNumber);
        }

        COleControl::OnTimer(nIDEvent);
}
```

Testing the Mail Client

Now that you have a basic understanding of the SMTP and POP protocols, as well as their implementation, let's test and implement the custom control in Visual Basic 4.0. As shown in Figure 11-9, the VB Mail Thing allows you to send and receive e-mail by using the MAIL custom control's SMTP and POP modules.

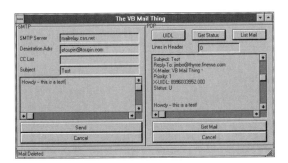

FIGURE 11-9

The VB Mail Thing uses the MAIL control to send and receive e-mail on the Internet.

On the left side of the window is the SMTP portion of the application, which allows you to submit e-mail to an SMTP server for relaying across the Internet. The POP portion, on the right side of the window, allows you to issue commands to the POP server to retrieve status information and e-mail.

Submitting E-Mail with the VB Mail Thing

As shown in Listing 11-25, using the SMTP module of the MAIL control involves only three steps. The first step resolves the address for the SMTP server's name; the next step sends the e-mail to the resolved address. The final step is merely a message being generated to inform the user that the operation is complete.

Listing 11-25   SMTP Operations in VB

```
Private Sub Command1_Click()
  GetAdrs1.HostName = Text6.Text
End Sub


Private Sub GetAdrs1_EndGetHostAddress(ByVal IPAddress As String, ByVal ErrorNum As
➥Integer)
  If ErrorNum <> 0 Then
    StatusBar1.SimpleText = "Error Retrieve SMTP Server Address : " + Str(ErrorNumber)
    Exit Sub
  End If

  SMTP1.OriginatingAddress = "jimbo@jackson.com"
  SMTP1.OriginatingName = "Jimbo Jackson"
  SMTP1.HostAddress = IPAddress
  SMTP1.MailSubject = Text4.Text
  SMTP1.DestinationUserList = Text2.Text
  SMTP1.MailBody = Text1.Text
  SMTP1.DomainName = "TOUPIN"
  SMTP1.CCUserList = Text3.Text
  SMTP1.MailAttachment = InputBox("Attachment")
```

```
   SMTP1.MailApplication = "VB Mail Thing"
   SMTP1.MailPriority = HIGHEST_PRIORITY
   SMTP1.Action = SEND_MAIL
End Sub


Private Sub SMTP1_EndSendMail(ByVal ErrorNum As Integer)
   If ErrorNum <> 0 Then
      StatusBar1.SimpleText = "Error Sending Mail : " + Str(ErrorNum)
   Else
      StatusBar1.SimpleText = "Mail Sent!"
   End If


End Sub
```

The address resolution is handled by an external control called GetHost. This control, like the MAIL control, consists of two modules: GetHost and GetAdrs. In this application, we want to locate the address for a given name (mailrelay.csn.net). The control takes that name, submits a query to the client host's DNS servers, and waits for the IP address to be returned. Upon completion, the GetAdrs1_EndGetHostAddress event procedure is called, passing the IP address that will be used with the SMTP module to submit the e-mail.

When the e-mail is submitted, each of the properties of the SMTP module is filled in with the appropriate value. These values are used either for connecting to the SMTP server or for filling in the header of the outbound e-mail message. Once all the information is filled in appropriately, the SEND_MAIL value is assigned to the Action property to submit the e-mail to the SMTP server. Upon completion, the SMTP1_EndSendMail event procedure is called with an error value regarding either a successful transmission or an error.

Receiving E-Mail with the VB Mail Thing

Retrieving e-mail is a bit more complicated than sending e-mail due to the fact that logons have to be consistent. Each time that an operation is desired, a logon operation must be executed, followed by the command, and concluded with a logoff.

> **CAUTION:** If a logoff is not executed, the associated mailbox on the POP server will be locked, and no additional attempts at logons will be allowed until the mailbox unlocks.

Listing 11-26 contains all the operations required to initiate e-mail retrieval with the POP module. The operations are event procedures for buttons on the user interface. The first operation within each procedure resolves the address for the POP server—the same operation as with the SMTP module. The procedure also sets a particular flag associated with the desired operation.

Listing 11-26   Initiating E-Mail Retrieval

```
Private Sub Command2_Click()
  GetAdrs2.HostName = uhostname
  gStatus = FLAG_GET_STATUS
End Sub


Private Sub Command3_Click()
  GetAdrs2.HostName = uhostname
  gStatus = FLAG_LIST_MAIL
End Sub


Private Sub Command4_Click()
  GetAdrs2.HostName = uhostname
  gStatus = FLAG_GET_MAIL
End Sub


Private Sub Command5_Click()
  StatusBar1.SimpleText = "Cancelling Get Mail Operation"
  POP1.Action = CANCEL_REQUEST
End Sub
```

```
Private Sub Command6_Click()
  GetAdrs2.HostName = uhostname
  gStatus = FLAG_GET_UIDL
End Sub
```

Upon completion of the address resolution operation, shown in Listing 11-27, we attempt to log on to the remote POP server. During the operation, appropriate values are assigned to the POP module's properties. The logon operation is initiated with the assignment of LOG_ON to the POP module's Action property.

Listing 11-27   Completion of Address Resolution

```
Private Sub GetAdrs2_EndGetHostAddress(ByVal IPAddress As String, ByVal ErrorNum As
➡Integer)
  If ErrorNum <> 0 Then
    StatusBar1.SimpleText = "Error Retrieve POP Server Address : " + Str(ErrorNumber)
    Exit Sub
  End If


  StatusBar1.SimpleText = "Logging On to POP Server"
  POP1.UserName = uname
  POP1.UserPassword = upassword
  POP1.HostAddress = IPAddress
  POP1.Action = LOG_ON
End Sub
```

As shown in Listing 11-28, once the POP module has logged on to the remote POP server, the EndLogon event procedure is initiated. The flag assigned with the action of the button controls from Listing 11-26 is used to determine which operation to execute within the procedure. Once determined, the appropriate value is assigned to the POP module's Action property to log the client off the POP server.

Listing 11-28   Completion of *LOG_ON* Action

```
Private Sub POP1_EndLogon(ByVal ErrorNumber As Integer)
    If ErrorNumber <> 0 Then
        StatusBar1.SimpleText = "Error Logging On : " + Str(ErrorNumber)
        POP1.Action = LOG_OFF
            Exit Sub
    End If


    If gStatus = FLAG_GET_STATUS Then
        StatusBar1.SimpleText = "Checking Mail Status"
        POP1.Action = MAIL_STATUS
    End If


    If gStatus = FLAG_GET_UIDL Then
        StatusBar1.SimpleText = "Checking UIDL Information"
        POP1.Action = GET_UIDL
    End If


    If gStatus = FLAG_LIST_MAIL Then
        StatusBar1.SimpleText = "Retrieving List of Mail"
        POP1.Action = LIST_MAIL
    End If


    If gStatus = FLAG_GET_MAIL Then
        StatusBar1.SimpleText = "Retrieving Mail"
        Timer2.Enabled = True
        POP1.HeaderLineCount = Val(Text7.Text)
        POP1.MessageNumber = 1
        POP1.Action = GET_MAIL
    End If
End Sub
```

The operation to retrieve e-mail (see Listing 11-29) contains two steps: retrieving an e-mail message from the POP server and deleting that e-mail. This sequence is left entirely up to the developer. It is usually a good idea, however, to clean out the mailbox once the e-mail has been downloaded locally. Notice that once the POP1_EndGetMail event procedure is fired to note the completion of e-mail retrieval, DELETE_MAIL is assigned to the Action property. The POP module sends the DELE command to the server and, once the command is completed, fires the POP1_EndDelete-mail event procedure. Once the sequence of operations is completed, the application issues a LOG_OFF to log off the remote POP server.

Listing 11-29   Retrieving Mail

```
Private Sub POP1_EndGetMail(ByVal MailNumber As Integer, ByVal Message As String, ByVal
➥ErrorNum As Integer)
  If ErrorNum <> 0 Then
    StatusBar1.SimpleText = "Error Retrieving Mail : " + Str(ErrorNumber)
  Else
    StatusBar1.SimpleText = "Mail Retrieved"
  End If


  Text5.Text = Message
  Timer2.Enabled = False
  POP1.MessageNumber = 1
  POP1.Action = DELETE_MAIL


End Sub


Private Sub POP1_EndDelete-mail(ByVal MailNum As Integer, ByVal ErrorNumber As Integer)
  If ErrorNumber <> 0 Then
    StatusBar1.SimpleText = "Error Deleting Mail : " + Str(ErrorNumber)
  Else
    StatusBar1.SimpleText = "Mail Deleted"
  End If


  POP1.Action = LOG_OFF


End Sub
```

The status-information-retrieval operation concludes with the execution of the event procedures shown in Listing 11-30. Each of the procedures shown in the listing provides a means of presenting the retrieved status information to the user of the application, followed by executing a LOG_OFF operation to free used resources, unlocking the mailbox, and closing the link to the POP server.

Listing 11-30   Status Information

```
Private Sub POP1_EndGetList(ByVal Information As String, ByVal ErrorNumber As Integer)
    If ErrorNumber <> 0 Then
        StatusBar1.SimpleText = "Error Retrieving Status Information : " + Str(ErrorNumber)
    Else
        StatusBar1.SimpleText = "Status Retrieved"
    End If


    Text5.Text = Information


    POP1.Action = LOG_OFF



End Sub


Private Sub POP1_EndGetStatus(ByVal Information As String, ByVal ErrorNumber As Integer)
    If ErrorNumber <> 0 Then
        StatusBar1.SimpleText = "Error Retrieving Status Information : " + Str(ErrorNum)
    Else
        StatusBar1.SimpleText = "Status Retrieved"
    End If


    Text5.Text = Information


    POP1.Action = LOG_OFF


End Sub
```

```
Private Sub POP1_EndGetUIDL(ByVal Information As String, ByVal ErrorNumber As Integer)
        If ErrorNumber <> 0 Then
            StatusBar1.SimpleText = "Error Retrieving Status Information : " +
➥Str(ErrorNum)
        Else
                    StatusBar1.SimpleText = "Status Retrieved"
        End If


        Text5.Text = Information
        POP1.Action = LOG_OFF
End Sub


Private Sub POP1_EndLogoff(ByVal ErrorNumber As Integer)
    If ErrorNumber <> 0 Then
        StatusBar1.SimpleText = "Error Logging Off : " + Str(ErrorNumber)
        Exit Sub
    End If
End Sub
```

Nifty Things to Do with Mail

With Internet e-mail, you can communicate with anyone anywhere. The OCX discussed in this chapter, however, allows you to develop some little applications above and beyond the standard e-mail client. For example, the OCX can be used to develop the popular autoresponder, which can provide automated feedback to users based on keywords that they place in the Subject line of their e-mail.

In an autoresponder, an application can simply monitor for incoming e-mail. Once e-mail is received, the application parses the subject and sends a file containing the desired literature or applications back to the requesting party. This type of operation is very simple with the MAIL control and is very popular for marketing on the Internet.

Another useful application is a mass e-mailer. In many cases, such as for large telecommuting and contracting firms, a mass e-mailer is wonderful for distributing documents and memos. Software companies can also use such an application to distribute software across the Internet to their clients for upgrades and trials.

CAUTION: Be careful if you develop a spam-oriented application. Being spammed is similar to receiving unsolicited postal mail from vendors. Make sure that you target only those individuals who are interested in receiving such mail. Also, be aware that such operations use large amounts of bandwidth.

Chapter Summary

As you learned in this chapter, e-mail is an essential part of the Internet community. Using the SMTP and POP protocols to manage e-mail, you can now develop incredible applications and tools to help yourself and other Internet and intranet users around the globe—literally! With the information you learned in this chapter, you can create mass e-mailers, integrated office applications, and autoresponders to bring the enormity of the Internet down to the desktop of the individual.

Chapter | 12

Plug-in FTP

by Jose Mojica

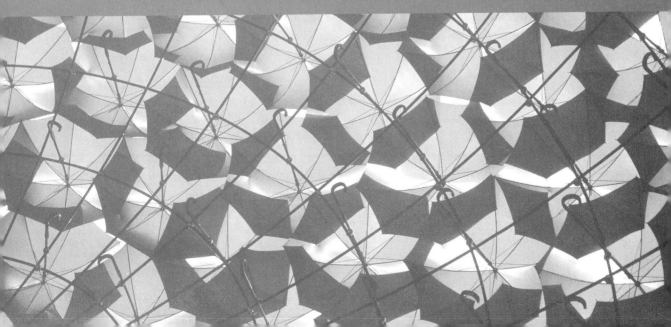

If you have ever used a browser to surf the Internet, chances are you have noticed that sometimes, you click a link to a file, and something like `ftp://ftp.site.com` appears in your URL box. *FTP* (File Transfer Protocol) is another member of the family of protocols, TCP/IP. The idea behind TCP/IP is communication among computers. Because these computers can be of many types, storing files in many different formats, a common protocol needed to be developed to transfer files between the computers. Thus, FTP was born.

Even before the Web was created, it was possible to connect to another computer in the Internet and transfer a file from a server to a client or vice versa by using FTP. After the Web emerged, FTP was incorporated into the Web browsers. Many of these browsers treat an FTP server as another Web page, giving you the ability to navigate files in the same way that you navigate Web pages.

In this chapter, you learn to create several OCXs that allow you to display a list of files in a remote server and transfer files from and to the server. This chapter also covers techniques for subclassing Windows common controls.

The Real Problem

Douglas Adams, the author of *The Hitchhiker's Guide to the Galaxy*, once said that the problem with time travel is not that you could go back in time and marry your mother, thereby becoming your own father. He asserted that that complication is nothing a well-adjusted family couldn't work out. Adams saw the real problem with time travel as being one of grammar. You can never find the right verb for trying to describe something in the past, that you are currently doing, that is going to take effect in the future.

In the same way, the real problem with FTP is not that you have to establish a connection to an FTP server and monitor the transfer of a file. Those tasks have been greatly simplified by Microsoft, as you will see later in this chapter. The problem that remains is one of grammar. For example, you may be tempted to say something like "I FTPed that file to my computer" or "My computer was busy all night FTPing a file." You would be incorrect, because as indicated earlier, *FTP* stands for *File Transfer Protocol*. Just as you couldn't say, "I File Transfer Protocoled that file to my computer," you shouldn't say, "I FTPed that file to my computer." Saying "I FTed that file to my computer" would be more correct.

FTP Programs

Before getting into the creation of the controls, let's talk a little about FTP. Several programs allow you to use FTP to transfer files between computers.

FTP.EXE for Windows 95

Windows 95 comes with a text-based program conveniently named FTP.EXE. To run it from the command prompt, type **ftp** and the name of the FTP server. A popular FTP server is ftp.microsoft.com. The command in that case would be **ftp ftp.microsoft.com**.

FTP servers normally ask for a user login and a password. Normally, this password is assigned to you by the system administrator of the server. Most of the time, however, there is also what is called an anonymous login. An *anonymous login* provides public access to directories chosen by the system administrator. To connect, a user would enter the word **anonymous** as the login and the word **guest** as the password. Sometimes, servers require you to enter a valid e-mail address for the password.

Once connected, the user can use UNIX-like commands to browse through the file structure. cd pub, for example, changes the current directory to the pub directory, and the command ls is used to get a listing of the files in the directory.

After you locate the file that you want to obtain, you should set the transfer mode. The possible transfer modes are ASCII and binary. Switch to binary mode by entering the word **bin**. Then use the get command to begin transferring the file. To specify the destination of the file, use the lcd (stands for *local directory*) command.

Table 12-1 shows a list of several commands in the Windows 95 version of FTP.EXE.

For a more extensive list, run the program FTP.EXE without any parameters. You will find yourself at an ftp> prompt. There, you can enter **help** to get a list of commands. Then you can enter **help [command]** to get help on the particular command.

WS FTP

A very popular program for transferring files is WS_FTP, a freeware Windows program designed to transfer files. Figure 12-1 shows a screen shot of this program.

Table 12-1   **Commands for Windows 95 Version of FTP.EXE**

Command	Description
cd	Changes the current directory on the server
lcd	Changes the current directory on your local computer
ls	Lists the files in the current directory on the server
bin	Sets the transfer mode to binary
get	Transfers a file from the server to your local computer
put	Transfers a file from your local computer to the server
help	Gives a complete list of commands

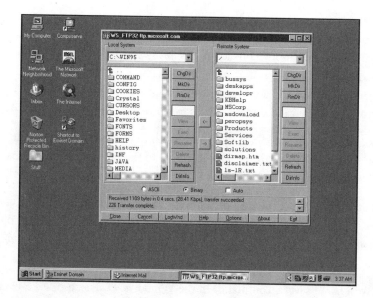

FIGURE 12-1

WS_FTP is freeware for Windows that allows you to use FTP to transfer files.

Basically, the program displays a list of the files in your local directory (left side of the window) and a list of the files in the remote system (right side of the window). The program allows you to highlight files and then click an arrow button (->) to begin transfer of the files. The program has a mode for automatically detecting whether the file is binary or ASCII. While transferring the files, WS_FTP displays a progress bar and then makes some type of noise when the transfer is complete.

Creating the Framework

Our controls will be based on the WS_FTP program. We are going to make three controls in one OCX file: a Connection control, a Directory control, and a File control.

The first control will be responsible for connecting to the FTP server. Once the Connection control has connected, it will fire an event called ConnectionChanged. Here, the programmer can write code to link the Connection control with the Directory control.

The Directory control is a list box that lists the directories of a certain location in the FTP server. The user will be allowed to change directories by double-clicking the name of the directory to which he or she wants to change. This action clears the previous list and displays a new list of directories. The action also triggers an event called DirectoryChanged. Here, the programmer can link the Directory control to our third control: the File control. This control lists all the files located in a particular directory.

Let's get started. By now, you should be quite familiar with running the OLE ControlWizard to make an OCX file. Go ahead and run the ControlWizard. I called my project FTPOCX. You will be asked how many controls you want to make. Change the number from 1 to 3. Leave all the other questions in that page set to the defaults. Then click the Next button.

It is a good idea to edit the names of your controls at this time, since the default names are not very useful in this case. I named my first control FTPConnect; it is invisible at run time. I named the second control FTPDir; it is visible at run time, and it subclasses a list control. I named the third control FTPFile; it is also visible at run time and subclasses the List control.

Table 12-2 shows a list of the controls to be created and their properties.

Table 12-2 Controls to Be Created

Control	Invisible?	Subclasses
FTPConnect	Yes	None
FTPDir	No	LISTBOX
FTPFile	No	LISTBOX

Modifying *FTPConnect*

Now that the skeleton source code is in place, we can begin adding muscle to it. Let's start by modifying the FTPConnect control.

Adding Properties, Methods, and Events

This control is going to need one method for connecting and another one for disconnecting. It should also have an event that gets triggered whenever the connection status changes. In addition, it is useful to have a method called IsConnected to inform the programmer of the connection status. Also, we need to have a property to store the name of the site we are connecting to, a property to store the login, and a property to store the password.

Go ahead and add these elements to your control; by now, you should be an expert at using the ClassWizard. Table 12-3 shows the properties, methods, and events that need to be added at this point.

Table 12-3   Properties, Methods, and Events for Connection Control

Name	Type	Returns	Parameters
Connect	Method	void	none
Disconnect	Method	void	none
ConnectionChanged	Event	void	none
IsConnected	Method	BOOL	none
URL	Property	none	CString
Login	Property	none	CString.
Password	Property	none	CString

MFC Classes for FTP

I have always found that there are mainly two kinds of programmers: those who love Microsoft, and those who hate Microsoft. Well, I'm going to give you two reasons to love Microsoft: CInternetSession and CFtpConnection.

In previous chapters, you might have seen what it takes to connect to a server by using the Windows sockets library. Connecting involves finding out the port that supports the particular protocol, finding a particular site on the Internet, and setting up asynchronous routines to monitor the receiving of information from the server. It would be the same thing with FTP, except for the fact that in version 4.2 of Visual C++, Microsoft introduced several classes that greatly simplify FTP transactions as well as Gopher transactions, as you will see in the next chapter. The CInternetConnection class allows the programmer to establish a connection to the Internet. It is capable of managing many connections simultaneously and asynchronously.

There are three other classes for connecting to FTP sites, Gopher sites, and HTTP sites. The one that we are interested in is CFtpConnection.

Adding Member Variables

With that said, let's go to the include file for our control and add the member variables. We are also going to need a variable to keep track of the connection status. The following code shows the declarations of the variables that keep track of the connection status:

```
CInternetSession *m_pInetSession;
CFtpConnection *m_pFtpConnection;
BOOL m_bIsConnected;
```

Connecting and Disconnecting

Before you do anything else, remember to initialize the pointer in the constructor function of the control and then to release it in the destructor, as illustrated in the following code:

```
CFTPConnectCtrl::CFTPConnectCtrl()
{
        InitializeIIDs(&IID_DFTPConnect, &IID_DFTPConnectEvents);

        m_bIsConnected=FALSE;
        m_pInetSession=NULL;
        m_pFtpConnection=NULL;
}
```

The following code serves as a safeguard in case the programmer forgot to issue the Disconnect method. Notice that to disconnect from the FTP server and to terminate the connection to the Internet, all we need to do is deallocate the variable.

```
CFTPConnectCtrl::~CFTPConnectCtrl()
{
        if (m_pFtpConnection != NULL)
        {
                delete m_pFtpConnection;
                m_pFtpConnection = NULL;
        }

        if (m_pInetSession != NULL)
        {
                delete m_pInetSession;
                m_pInetSession = NULL;
        }
}
```

Listing 12-1 shows the code to connect to the Internet and to the FTP server.

Listing 12-1   Connecting to the FTP Server

```
void CFTPConnectCtrl::Connect()
{
        m_bIsConnected = FALSE;

        //...close previous FTP connection if there is any
        if (m_pFtpConnection != NULL)
        {
                delete m_pFtpConnection;
                m_pFtpConnection = NULL;
        }

        //...close previous Internet session if there is any
```

```
if (m_pInetSession != NULL)
{
        delete m_pInetSession;
        m_pInetSession = NULL;
}

m_pInetSession = new CInternetSession(NULL, PRE_CONFIG_INTERNET_ACCESS);

if (m_pInetSession == NULL)
        return;

CString sServerName;
CString sObject;
INTERNET_PORT nPort;
DWORD dwServiceType;

if (!AfxParseURL(m_URL, dwServiceType, sServerName, sObject, nPort))
{
        // try adding the "ftp://" protocol
        CString sFtpURL = _T("ftp://");
        sFtpURL += m_URL;

        if (!AfxParseURL(sFtpURL, dwServiceType, sServerName, sObject, nPort))
        {
                return;
        }
}

// ...now open an FTP connection to the server
if ((dwServiceType == INTERNET_SERVICE_FTP) && !sServerName.IsEmpty())
{
        try
        {
```

continues

Listing 12-1   **Continued**

```
                    m_pFtpConnection = m_pInetSession-
➡>GetFtpConnection(sServerName,m_Login,m_Password);
            }
            catch (CInternetException* pEx)
            {
                    pEx->Delete();
                    m_pFtpConnection = NULL;
                    return;
            }
        }
        else
        {
            return;
        }


        if (m_pFtpConnection != NULL)
        {
                m_bIsConnected = TRUE;
                FireConnectionChanged();
        }


}
```

First, we make sure that we close any old connections. We do this in case a programmer calls the Connect method twice without calling the Disconnect method first. Second, we create an instance to the CInternetSession class:

```
m_pInetSession = new CInternetSession();
```

The constructor takes several parameters. For our code example, we can use the defaults. For more information on this constructor, look at the Visual C++ Books Online help file included with Visual C++.

Following is the next statement of importance:

```
AfxParseURL(m_URL, dwServiceType, sServerName, sObject, nPort)
```

This function has three purposes. Primarily, it verifies that the server exists. Secondarily, it tells us whether the specified server is in fact an FTP server by sending the value `AFX_INET_SERVICE_FTP` in the variable `dwServiceType`. The third purpose is to separate the server name specified by the programmer in the property `ServerName` into more significant pieces.

URL stands for *Universal Resource Locator*. In plain English, it means an Internet address. The typical Internet address consists of a service type, a server name, and an object address. Following is an example of a URL:

```
http://www.microsoft.com/index.htm
```

In this case, the server type is `http`, the server name is `microsoft.com`, and the object that we want to obtain is `index.htm`. If the call to `AfxParseURL` is successful, the return value will be nonzero.

The other piece of information that we'll need later is the server name from the URL. Notice also in the preceding code that if the call to `AfxParseURL` is unsuccessful, we try inserting `ftp://` (in case the programmer did not specify a complete URL), and we try the `AfxParseURL` command again.

Next, we check to see that the service requested is in fact FTP, and we start the connection to the FTP server. The command responsible for establishing the connection is:

```
m_pFtpConnection = m_pInetSession->GetFtpConnection(sServerName,m_Login,m_Password);
```

This command creates an instance to the class `CFtpConnection`. Although the function takes other parameters, the ones that we are concerned with in this piece of code are the server name returned from the function `AfxParseURL`, the user name, and the password. For more information on this function, see the Visual C++ Books Online help included with Visual C++ 4.2. The documentation for this command says that if the values `m_UserName` and `m_Password` are blank, the function will attempt an anonymous connection.

Last but not least, we set the value of the member variable `m_bIsConnected` to `True`. This value, used by the `IsConnected` method, stores the status of the connection. Each time a connection is attempted, the value of this variable is set to `False`. If any errors occur along the way, we exit the `Connect` method immediately. After the value of the `m_bIsConnected` variable is set to `True`, we fire the `ConnectionChange` event.

Houston, we have touchdown. We have connected to the FTP server, and all that remains to do is write the code for the Disconnect method.

The code for the Disconnect method is similar to the code for the destructor, with the addition of the call to the FireConnectionChange function. The code is:

```
void CFTPConnectCtrl::Disconnect()
{
        if (m_pFtpConnection != NULL)
        {
                delete m_pFtpConnection;
                m_pFtpConnection = NULL;
        }

        if (m_pInetSession != NULL)
        {
                delete m_pInetSession;
                m_pInetSession = NULL;
        }

        m_bIsConnected=FALSE;
        FireConnectionChanged();
}
```

You could compile now, but you would be very upset with me afterward. You need to add the following entry to stdafx.h: #include <afxinet.h>. This entry includes the new Internet class definitions; without it, you would have had many errors.

OK, go ahead and click that Compile button, and test your progress thus far. Reward yourself with a snack, stretch those legs, and take a deep breath before you jump into the next control.

Modifying the Directory Control

Before we start modifying the Directory control, we need to have a way to bind it to the first control. You see, we have one control that has made a connection to an FTP server via the CFtpConnection class. Now we need to pass this information to the Directory control so that it will know where to read the directory. The ability to transfer the information from one control to the other prevents the redundancy of having to create a separate connection for each control.

To do this, we need to modify the connect control by adding a GetConnection method. This GetConnection method returns the memory address of the CFtpConnection object we have created.

There is a nice, convenient way to pass pointers from one control to the other. In fact, you can use this trick with languages that do not use pointers inherently, such as Visual Basic 4.0. To do this, make the return value of your method of type OLE_HANDLE. Also, on the receiving side, set the incoming parameter for the method to type OLE_HANDLE. Then simply typecast the incoming parameter to the expected type—in this case, a pointer to the class CFtpConnect.

I'm sure I do not have to tell you at this point that you need to use the ClassWizard. Go ahead—do that Ctrl+W thing, and add the GetConnection method. The details follow:

Name	Type	Returns	Parameters
GetConnection	Method	OLE_HANDLE	none

The code for this method looks like this:

```
OLE_HANDLE CFTPConnectCtrl::GetConnection()
{
        return (OLE_HANDLE)m_pFtpConnection;
}
```

Adding Member Variables

On the receiving side, we have a member variable that stores a pointer to CFtpConnection and a SetConnection method to set the value of this variable. The code looks like this:

```
void CFTPDirCtrl::SetConnection(OLE_HANDLE pFtpConnection)
{
        m_pFtpConnection = (CFtpConnection *)pFtpConnection;
```

That's not all the code for that method, but I can't give it all away yet. Be patient.

Adding Properties and Methods

We need to add a few properties and methods to the Dir control. We need a method for setting the connection handle that we obtained from the GetConnection method. We also need a property to indicate the current directory in the FTP server that we are looking at. This property should not only inform the programmer of the current directory, but also change the current directory when set explicitly in code. We also need a method to refresh the list of directories and a method to clear the list. It would also be useful to add a method called IsConnected. We are going to need an event to inform the programmer of changes to the current directory as well.

Table 12-4 summarizes all the properties, methods, and events that we have added.

Table 12-4   Properties, Methods, and Events for Directory Control

Name	Type	Returns	Parameters
SetConnectionHandle	Method	void	OLE_HANDLE
CurrentDir	Property	none	CString
Refresh	Method	void	none (do not add the Stock property version)
Clear	Method	void	none
IsConnected	Method	BOOL	none

Subclassing a Windows Control

This control subclasses the standard Windows list-box control. If you have attempted to create a control by subclassing a standard Windows control, you know by now that just because the ProjectWizard has a nice little option for subclassing a Windows control does not mean that you are going to be done when you click that Create button. A great deal of work is involved in making that control look like the standard Windows control. You also might want to allow users to set font and colors.

It also takes a little bit of work to make the control act like the standard Windows control. For a list-box control, for example, many languages, including MFC, have high-level commands that facilitate the addition and removal of items to/from the list box. (MFC is not really a language, but then again, how do you define a computer language except as a set of instructions?) Unfortunately, you cannot use the high-level commands when you are subclassing a control; that's why they pay you the big bucks. There is no ready-made code to facilitate the addition and removal of items to/from the list box. You must write code yourself to add items to the list box and to remove them.

I will not go into details about to how to change the look and feel of the list box. For help with that, I recommend looking into the xlist example located in the MSDEV\SAMPLES\MFC\CONTROLS directory of your Visual C++ 4.2 CD-ROM. The example shows you all that is necessary for subclassing a list-box control.

I will discuss how to manipulate the data in the control, however. One thing that makes it easier for us is that the programmer using our control cannot modify the items in the list box directly. The purpose of our list box is to list the contents of a directory in a remote server, and this is not something that should be modified by the programmer.

With all that said, let's take care of the subclassing aspect of our control first.

Adding Items to and Removing Items from the List Box

You need several functions for manipulating the data. The first is the AddItem function, which follows:

```
void CFTPDirCtrl::AddItem(CString sItem)

{

        SendMessage(LB_ADDSTRING, 0, (long)(LPCTSTR)sItem);

        InvalidateControl();

}
```
followed by RemoveItem

```
void CFTPDirCtrl::RemoveItem(int nIndex)

{

        SendMessage(LB_DELETESTRING, nIndex, 0L);

        InvalidateControl();

}
```

The AddItem function simply takes a CString as a parameter and adds the string to the list box by sending our control a LB_ADDSTRING message. The second parameter must be zero, and the third parameter is a long representation of the memory address that contains the string we are going to add to the list. Notice that after the item has been added, we inform the control that it should repaint itself.

Incidentally, something I did not implement that will certainly optimize your code is to rewrite it so that the AddItem function does not repaint the list box until all the items have been added. The list-box control keeps track of all the items in the list by assigning index numbers to them. To remove an item, simply send your control the message LB_DELETESTRING, and send the index number as the second parameter.

Clearing the List Box

We need to add a Clear function to delete all the entries in the list. The one nice thing about subclassing a Windows control is that we do not have to worry about storing the entries; Windows does that automatically. Following is the code for the Clear function:

```
void CFTPDirCtrl::Clear()
{
        // Remove all text from listbox
        SendMessage(LB_RESETCONTENT, 0, 0L);

        InvalidateControl();
}
```

To find out more about the messages that a list-box control accepts, search the Visual C++ Books Online documentation under Listbox Messages.

Reading the Server Directory

Now that we have written methods to manipulate the data, we can get into FTP code. Certainly, the heart of this control is the function that reads a directory from the FTP server, as shown in Listing 12-2.

Listing 12-2   Reading a Directory from the FTP Server

```
\void CFTPDirCtrl::ReadDirectory()
{
        CWaitCursor cursor;         // this will automatically display a wait cursor

        CString sDir="";
        m_pFtpConnection->GetCurrentDirectory(sDir);
        CString strSearchDir = sDir + _T("/*");

        BOOL bContinue = m_pFtpFileFind->FindFile(strSearchDir);
        if (!bContinue)
        {
                // the directory is empty; just close up and return.
                m_pFtpFileFind->Close();
                return;
        }
        else
                AddItem ("..");

        while (bContinue)
        {
                // FindNextFile must be called before info can be gleaned from ftpFind
                bContinue = m_pFtpFileFind->FindNextFile();
                CString strFileName = m_pFtpFileFind->GetFileName();

                if (m_pFtpFileFind->IsDirectory())
                {
                        AddItem(strFileName);
                }
        }

        m_pFtpFileFind->Close();
}
```

The following lines get the current directory and append the string /*:

```
m_pFtpConnection->GetCurrentDirectory(sDir);
CString strSearchDir = sDir + _T("/*");
```

This is what is called the search path. The idea is to get a listing of all the files in the current directory—much like the way that we get a directory of all the files in DOS with the command dir *.*. The Internet was primarily composed of machines running the UNIX operating system, and although things are changing now with the emergence of Internet Server software written for Windows NT and even Windows 95, many of the commands use UNIX syntax. In UNIX, directories use the front slash (/) rather than the back slash (\) that is used in DOS.

The following line uses the FindFile method to search for a particular file in the FTP server:

```
BOOL bContinue = m_pFtpFileFind->FindFile(strSearchDir);
```

This method is a member of the class CFtpFileFind, which is another of Microsoft's creations. Even though I do not want to give the impression that Microsoft is the greatest, I feel obliged to thank the company for this one, which makes searching for a file easy. The function nicely returns 0 if the directory is empty or 1 if the directory contains at least one item. If there are no items, we simply exit the function. If there are items, the first thing we do is add the string .. to the list. The reason we do that is to provide a way to navigate backward. This device allows you to go from a subdirectory back to the parent directory. All that remains to do is read the directory sequentially until there are no other files to read, as shown in the following code:

```
while (bContinue)
{
        // FindNextFile must be called before info can be gleaned from ftpFind
        bContinue = m_pFtpFileFind->FindNextFile();
        CString strFileName = m_pFtpFileFind->GetFileName();

        if (m_pFtpFileFind->IsDirectory())
        {
                AddItem(strFileName);
        }
}
```

The class CFtpFileFind provides a FindNextFile method to navigate through a directory. If you are not asleep now, you may be wondering whether this is going to give us not only the directories, but also the files. The answer is yes. But again, a nice method called IsDirectory returns TRUE for an entry in the server that is a directory. The GetFileName method returns the name of the directory, and this is what we pass over to our AddItem method.

The read directory function, therefore, loads the list box with a list of possible subdirectories. Before doing this, we call the Clear method to get rid of old information.

Now that all the directories are in the list box, it would be nice to allow the user to navigate through them by double-clicking an entry in the list box. To do this, we need to handle the dblclick event for the list box. Because we are subclassing a standard Windows list-box control, Windows sends our control a notification message each time a user double-clicks an entry in the list box. To handle this message, we add the following code:

```
LRESULT CFTPDirCtrl::OnOcmCommand(WPARAM wParam, LPARAM lParam)
{
#ifdef _WIN32
        WORD wNotifyCode = HIWORD(wParam);
#else
        WORD wNotifyCode = HIWORD(lParam);
#endif


        switch (wNotifyCode)
        {
        case LBN_DBLCLK:
                CString sDir="";
                char sSelection[255];

                m_pFtpConnection->GetCurrentDirectory(sDir);

                int idListBox = SendMessage(LB_GETCURSEL,0,0L);
                SendMessage(LB_GETTEXT,idListBox,(long)sSelection);

                if (sDir.Right(1) != "/")
                        sDir = sDir + "/";
```

```
                    CString sNewDir = sDir + CString(sSelection);

                    SetCurrentDir(sNewDir);

            break;
            }

            return 0;
    }
```

Normally, Windows sends a WM_COMMAND message, and the wParam contains information indicating what command message was sent. In the case of an OLE custom control, messages are sent to the container of the control first. The container in turn reflects the message to the control. These reflected messages are referred to as OCM messages, and to handle them, we add an OcmCommand message handler. Also, we need to add an entry to our message map so that OCM messages will trigger the event handler. The following code shows you how to add the entry:

```
BEGIN_MESSAGE_MAP(CFTPDirCtrl, COleControl)
        //{{AFX_MSG_MAP(CFTPDirCtrl)
        // NOTE - ClassWizard will add and remove message map entries
        // DO NOT EDIT what you see in these blocks of generated code !
        //}}AFX_MSG_MAP
        ON_MESSAGE(OCM_COMMAND, OnOcmCommand)
        ON_OLEVERB(AFX_IDS_VERB_PROPERTIES, OnProperties)
END_MESSAGE_MAP()
```

We are pretty much done. To make magic, however, we just need to complete our SetConnection method. The completed function looks like this:

```
void CFTPDirCtrl::SetConnection(OLE_HANDLE pFtpConnection)
{
        m_pFtpConnection = (CFtpConnection *)pFtpConnection;

        if (m_pFtpConnection != NULL)
        {
```

```
if (m_pFtpFileFind != NULL)
{
        delete m_pFtpFileFind;
        m_pFtpFileFind = NULL;
}

m_pFtpFileFind = new CFtpFileFind(m_pFtpConnection);
SetCurrentDir("/");
}
else

Clear();
}
```

In summary, the Connect control uses a URL to connect to an FTP server. Once it is connected, it triggers the ConnectionChanged event. In the ConnectionChanged event, the programmer can write code to set the connection handle of the FTP directory control, obtaining it by issuing the GetConnection method from the Connection control. Setting the connection handle of the FTP directory control sets the directory to the root directory and calls ReadDirectory, which finds all the subdirectories and displays them in the list box. Furthermore, the user can navigate through the directories by double-clicking.

Break number 2 is here. Compile your program, and play a minute of Doom on your other machine while compilation is taking place. When you are rested, we'll create our last control, FTPFiles.

Modifying *FTPFiles*

This control is exactly the same as the Directory control in appearance. In the same way that we linked the Directory control to the Connection control, we need to be able to connect the files control to the Directory control. The idea is that every time the user switches directories in the Directory control, an event is fired: DirectoryChanged. There, the programmer can set the directory handle in the files control to be the directory handle of the Directory control. This keeps the list of files in sync with the current directory and makes it possible to view the entire contents of any directory by double-clicking the list box. Here is the code:

```
void CFTPFilesCtrl::SetDirectory(OLE_HANDLE pDirectory)
{
        m_pFtpFileFind = (CFtpFileFind *)pDirectory;

        if (m_pFtpFileFind != NULL)
                Refresh();
        else
                Clear();
}
```

This code is basically the same as before. Again, we are going to need an AddItem function, a RemoveItem function, and a ClearAll.

The heart of this function is the ReadDirectory function, shown in the following code:

```
void CFTPFilesCtrl::ReadDirectory()
{
        CWaitCursor cursor;         // this will automatically display a wait cursor

        BOOL bContinue=m_pFtpFileFind->FindFile("*.*");

        while (bContinue)
        {
                // FindNextFile must be called before info can be gleaned from ftpFind
                bContinue = m_pFtpFileFind->FindNextFile();
                CString strFileName = m_pFtpFileFind->GetFileName();

                if (!m_pFtpFileFind->IsDirectory())
                {
                        AddItem(strFileName);
                }
        }

}
```

The main difference between this version of the function and the one in the Directory control is the line

```
if (!m_pFtpFileFind->IsDirectory())
```

in which we list anything that is not a directory.

Other Methods

Now we have three controls that allow you to navigate quite easily through an FTP server. One control connects, another lists the directories, and another lists the files. To fully complete the controls, however, we need to add a few more methods—for example, methods to transfer files from one machine to another. Another thing that an FTP program allows you to do is create and remove directories on the server side.

Table 12-5 shows a list of other methods that should be added:

Table 12-5 Other Methods to Add for Completeness

Command	Description
RemoveDirectory	Removes the specified directory from the server
CreateDirectory	Creates a directory on the server
Rename	Renames a file on the server
Remove	Removes a file from the server
PutFile	Places a file on the server
GetFile	Gets a file from the connected server
OpenFile	Opens a file on the connected server

This list was obtained from the Visual C++ Books Online documentation, and you will be happy to know that all these commands are member functions of the CFtpConnection class. The best place to add the methods is the Connect control. A good reason for this is that the control maintains the connection to the FTP server by keeping an instance of the CFtpConnection class, which is exactly the class that contains the methods we need.

Nifty Things to Do with FTP

Now that you have finished your controls, it is time to think about some nifty things to do with them.

One thing that you can do is create a version of WS_FTP that has more of a Windows 95 or Windows NT 4.0 format. You can enhance it by adding a search function. The search function can start in the root directory and navigate recursively through all the subdirectories until the desired file is found.

If you think that is boring, how about the ultimate challenge? An OCX is nothing more than an OLE DLL. An OLE DLL is a wonderful thing to have in Windows 95. Windows 95 allows you to write what are called shell extensions. You may have seen a briefcase object in Windows 95. If you have seen the briefcase object, you know that when you use Explorer and navigate through a briefcase object, the Explorer file list changes considerably from the standard. Explorer has been extended to recognize the briefcase format and change the file view to accommodate the new object. Consider expanding your DLL to serve as an extension to Explorer.

Here's how it would work. When you enter Explorer, the directory tree would have an entry called FTP neighborhood. When the user double-clicks this directory, a dialog box comes up, asking the user for the URL of the FTP server that he or she would like to connect to. After connecting successfully, the program can display a list of files that are in the server. It would be extremely easy to transfer files from the server to the client machine simply by dragging the file from Explorer to the destination directory. This project is considerably larger than the first, but it can be done.

Chapter Summary

You have certainly accomplished a lot in this chapter. Let's summarize all that you have learned:

- You learned that FTP is a protocol that is part of TCP/IP.
- You learned that before version 4.2 of Visual C++, this functionality was available only through Windows sockets.
- You learned about the new classes that Microsoft has created to facilitate FTP communication: `CInternetSession`, `CFtpConnection`, and `CFtpFileFind`.

◆ You learned how to create an OCX with three controls and how to make them communicate with one another.

◆ You learned the basics of subclassing and how to create functions to encapsulate low-level functionality.

Chapter | 13

Plug-in Gopher

by Jose Mojica

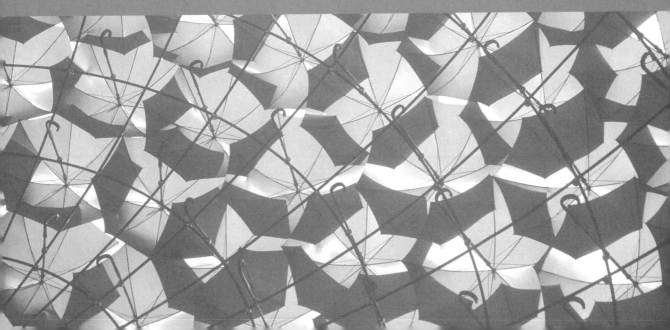

Once upon a time, long before the cyberspace era, the Web ancestors were forced to live underground, unable to display graphics or create fancy layouts. Back then, the thoughts of animated GIF files and sites with tables or frames were too advanced for them to even consider. The place was known as Gopherspace; the sites were known as Gophers.

This chapter talks about Gopher sites and about how to make a control that will let you browse Gopherspace. But before we get into the development of the tool, let's define Gopher.

Gopher Defined

Gopher is the name of a TCP/IP protocol. It is a set of commands developed by the University of Minnesota Microcomputer Center. FTP existed before Gopher, and although FTP was adequate for transferring information between computers, FTP file names were normally difficult to read and difficult to find. A protocol was needed to display menus in plain English and to provide links to other Gopher sites. Just as the Internet is sometimes referred to as cyberspace, the combination of Gopher severs is sometimes called Gopherspace.

As is true of all protocols, an RFC (Request for Comments) paper explains the protocol in detail. You can find the Gopher paper, which is RFC 1436, along with the others in InterNIC (`http://ds.internic.net/`). The exact address of this document is:

```
http://ds.internic.net/rfc/RFC 1436.txt
```

HGopher

As is true of FTP, which is described in Chapter 12, several freeware client programs that communicate with Gopher servers are available. A popular one is HGopher, which resembles a scaled-down Web browser.

HGopher can establish a connection to a Gopher site. In Gopher client programs, there exists the concept of a home site—the site that you always start with when you run the client program. Once the program connects to the Gopher server, it displays a list of documents available for retrieval. These documents can be plain text files, PostScript files, sound files, picture files, and so on. See Table 13-1 for the different types of files that you can find in a Gopher server.

Table 13-1   Gopher Document Types

File Type	Description
0	File
1	Directory
2	Phone-book server
4	BinHexed Macintosh file
5	DOS binary file
6	UNIX uuencoded file
7	Index-search server
8	Text-based Telnet session
9	Binary file
g	GIF file
I	Some kind of image file

The program also displays links to other directories within the same server, as well as links to other Gopher servers. Normally, you are unable to tell while browsing that you are in a different server, giving you the illusion of using one computer on which a world of information is available. Unlike Web browsers, Gopher client programs are unable to display the documents; they are forced to call on external viewers to show the contents of the document. Therefore, these programs generally ask you to specify the path to viewers for each kind of file that can be retrieved.

HGopher was made for Windows, so it has a set of predefined paths to different Windows accessories. It knows to use the Notepad to display text documents, for example.

Figure 13-1 shows the HGopher program.

Notice that the program displays different icons for the different types of documents it retrieves. HGopher sometimes displays two icons for a particular item.

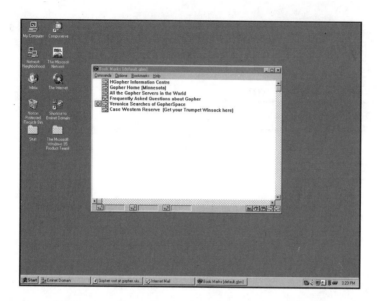

FIGURE 13-1

HGopher is a Gopher free-ware client program for Windows.

Gopher+

Now I am going to confuse you by telling you that HGopher is not a Gopher client program. It is more than that—it is capable of communicating with Gopher+ servers. Generally, programmers like to create a protocol and then, after some time has passed, enhance it and stick a plus sign next to the name. If the protocol is really cool, they can stick two plus signs next to the name. Thus far, no program has acquired three plus signs, but I'm sure that Microsoft will be the first to create one that does.

All joking aside, Gopher+ is an enhancement of Gopher that was created to solve several problems. One problem is that sometimes, two versions of the same document in a Gopher server can be retrieved. There might be a plain-text version and a PostScript version of the document, for example. Since Gopher programs rely on external viewers, it is useful to know that different versions are available. In this case, a PostScript viewer might not be available, so the program can allow the user to view the text version of the document.

The second problem that was solved with the enhancement was that Gopher did not return any information about the author of the document or when the document was first uploaded. Gopher+ returns this related information.

Internet Browsers

At this time, most Internet browsers allow you to specify a URL (an Internet address) to a Gopher site. This is by far the easiest way to navigate through Gopherspace, since most browsers have built-in viewers.

Creating the Gopher Control

Probably by now, you are eager to get started, so let's do it. I could bore you with details about using the Windows sockets library to connect to a Gopher server using a TCP/IP port or about how you need to send text commands asynchronously and parse the output according to the specifications in RFC 1436. And although your friends who use Visual C++ 4.0 might have to do all this, you—using Visual C++ 4.2—no longer have to care, because you now have CInternetSession, CGopherConnection, CGopherLocator, CGopherFile, and CGopherFileFind. In version 4.2, Microsoft introduced classes to make Internet processing easier. Among these are the classes mentioned earlier in this section, which make Gopher communication much easier.

Modifying FTPOCX.OCX

In Chapter 12, you created an OCX with three controls. One of these controls was invisible at run time and served as a connection control. The other two controls were derived from the standard Windows list-box control; they displayed directories and files. Gopher navigation is so similar to FTP navigation that it seems redundant to create a new set of controls. Rather than doing that, I'm going to show you how to enhance the OCX to handle Gopher connections as well.

We are going to enhance the controls in the following manner:

♦ First, we are going to allow the connection control to accept the address of a Gopher server. This control then will be capable of supporting two kinds of connections: an FTP connection and a Gopher connection. Although it is possible to maintain both types of connections simultaneously, it makes more sense to maintain only one kind at a time—that is, the connection will be either an FTP connection or a Gopher connection, but not both.

- Second, we will enhance the list-box controls in two ways. The first way is to enable them to list Gopher documents. The second way is founded in the fact that Gopher sites often have different types of documents, as you saw in Table 13-1 earlier in this chapter. For this reason, it is useful for us to display a bitmap next to each item. The bitmaps allow the user to identify the type of object being listed.

- Third, we will add an event to tell the programmer that the user has requested to view a document and that he or she needs to invoke a viewer for the object.

Creating a New Project

OK, let's get started. If you are like me, you hate having something named FTPOCX that also does Gopher support, so let's just create a new project and practice the art that is so essential for programmers to understand: how to copy and paste code. If you prefer to state it more elegantly, we will import the code that we need from the FTPOCX project.

Modifying the ODL File

At times, you want to change the name of the control. Doing that is not very difficult. The only thing that you need to do is edit the ODL file. ODL files contain the definition of all exposed methods and events, as well as display names for your control and property sheet. Therefore, to change the name of your control, simply locate the file with the extension .ODL in your project window, and open it. Near the top of the file, you will see an entry that looks like this:

```
[ uuid(3D30A8A0-F951-11CF-9827-00400519B8D3), version(1.0),
  helpstring("FTPOCX OLE Control module"), control ]
library FTPOCXLib
```

You can change the help string description. This description is what programming languages often use for display in the list of insertable objects. The only word of caution is that after you make the change, you need to reregister the object for the new description to take effect. Microsoft Visual C++ automatically reregisters the control after each compilation.

While we are looking at the .ODL file, it is worth mentioning that to make your OCXs into commercially distributable objects, you need to spend some time adding descriptions to each of the methods and adding links to an external help file. You do both of these things in the .ODL file as well. The following code shows the methods in the Connection control:

```
// Use extreme caution when editing this section.
//{{AFX_ODL_METHOD(CFTPConnectCtrl)
[id(4)] void Connect();
[id(5)] void Disconnect();
[id(6)] boolean IsConnected();
[id(7)] OLE_HANDLE ConnectionHandle();
//}}AFX_ODL_METHOD
```

To complete our OCX, we need to edit these entries (even though it says "Use extreme caution when editing this section" at the top). The result will be something like this:

```
    [id(4), helpstring("Connects to an FTP server"), helpcontext(100)] void
➥Connect();
```

This adds a description for the method, as well as a link to a page in a help file.

By now, you not only know how to run the OLE ControlWizard, but also probably know how to use the shortcut keys. So go ahead and press Ctrl+N for a new project, and select Project Workspace. Select OLE ControlWizard, and name your project. I named my project MiniBrowser.

Later, you might want to add support for HTTP; you can easily do this with the new Internet classes and make your set of controls fully capable of browsing the Web. For this task, however, you need another control to display HTML pages. Now click the Create button. Enter **3** for the number of controls, leave all the other questions with the default answers, and click Next. Let's change the names of the controls. To do this, click the Edit Names button. I named my controls Connect, Directory, and Document.

Table 13-2 summarizes the control properties. Notice that the Connect control is invisible at run time and that the Directory control and the Document control subclass the Windows list-box control.

Table 13-2   Control Properties

Name	Visible?	Subclasses
Connect	No	None
Directory	Yes	LISTBOX
Document	Yes	LISTBOX

Modifying the *Connect* Control

We begin by modifying the Connect control. Press Ctrl+V to bring up the ClassWizard, and add a method for connecting and one for disconnecting. This control is going to be able to connect to both an FTP server and a Gopher server. At times, the programmer might specify a URL that has neither the identifier ftp:// nor gopher:// in front. To make the control more efficient, we should have a property called DefaultToGopher. This means that if the control can't resolve a URL, it treats the site as a Gopher site, and if the connection fails, the control tries to connect as though the site were an FTP server.

Of course, we are going to need a URL property to specify the address of the server. The Login and Password properties from Chapter 12 are needed only for the FTP portion of the control and not for the Gopher portion. Also, let's not forget the ConnectionChange event that informs the programmer when the connection has been established.

Table 13-3 summarizes the properties and events that we have created for the control.

Table 13-3   *Connect* Control Properties and Events

Name	Type	Return	Parameters
Connect	Method	Void	None
Disconnect	Method	Void	None
GetConnectionHandle	Method	OLE_HANDLE	None
DefaultToFTP	Property	BOOL	None
Login	Property	CString	None
Password	Property	CString	None
URL	Property	CString	None

Connecting to Gopher

Now that we have the properties and events in place, let's do some coding. To establish a connection to a Gopher server, we first need to establish an Internet connection. We do this by using the CInternetSession class. Therefore, we are going to need member variables to contain a pointer to the CInternetSession class and a pointer to the CGopherSession class.

The FTP control that we created previously contains the following member variables:

```
CInternetSession *m_pInetSession;
CFtpConnection *m_pFtpConnection;
```

We need to add one more member variable to contain a connection to the Gopher server. The code now looks like this:

```
CInternetSession *m_pInetSession;
CFtpConnection *m_pFtpConnection;
CGopherConnection *m_pGopherConnection;
```

Before we forget, we should make sure that the pointers are set to NULL in our constructor and that any memory allocated is released in the destructor. The code for these two methods follows.

The constructor code is:

```
CConnectCtrl::CConnectCtrl()
{
    InitializeIIDs(&IID_DConnect, &IID_DConnectEvents);

    SetInitialSize(24, 22);

    m_pInetSession= NULL;
    m_pFtpConnection = NULL;
    m_pGopherConnection = NULL;
}
```

If you have never seen the line SetInitialSize from the preceding code segment until now, hold that thought; I'll come back to it when we discuss putting the final touches on our control.

The destructor code is:

```
CConnectCtrl::~CConnectCtrl()
{
        Disconnect();
}
```

The *Disconnect* Method

Notice that the destructor simply calls the Disconnect method, which checks to see whether the memory for our connection pointers has been deallocated. You may recall from previous chapters that to close the connections, all we have to do is destroy the instance to the connection classes. The MFC classes do the rest for us. If the memory has not been deallocated, the Disconnect method takes care of it, as shown in the following code:

```
        if (m_pGopherConnection != NULL)
        {
                delete m_pGopherConnection;
                m_pGopherConnection = NULL;
        }


        if (m_pFtpConnection != NULL)
        {
                delete m_pFtpConnection;
                m_pFtpConnection = NULL;
        }


        if (m_pInetSession != NULL)
        {
                delete m_pInetSession;
                m_pInetSession = NULL;
        }
```

In this code, notice that we close the Gopher and FTP connections before the Internet connection. This is not necessary, since the Internet class is supposed to close the other connections, but it is good practice, because even the programmers who work at Microsoft are human.

The *Connect* Method

Now we write the code for the Connect method, shown in Listing 13-1.

Listing 13-1   The *Connect* Method

```
void CConnectCtrl::Connect()
{
        m_bIsConnected = FALSE;

        //...close the previous Gopher connection if there is any
        Disconnect();

        m_pInetSession = new CInternetSession();

        if (m_pInetSession == NULL)
                return;

        CString sServerName;
        CString sObject;
        INTERNET_PORT nPort;
        DWORD dwServiceType;

        if (!AfxParseURL(m_URL, dwServiceType, sServerName, sObject, nPort))
        {
                // try adding the "ftp://" protocol
                CString sCompleteURL;
```

continues

Listing 13-1   Continued

```
                    if (m_DefaultToFTP == FALSE)
                            sCompleteURL = _T("Gopher://");
                else
                            sCompleteURL = _T("ftp://");


                sCompleteURL += m_URL;


                if (!AfxParseURL(sCompleteURL, dwServiceType, sServerName, sObject, nPort))
                {

                            if (m_DefaultToFTP == FALSE)
                                    sCompleteURL = _T("ftp://");
                            else
                                    sCompleteURL = _T("Gopher://");


                            sCompleteURL += m_URL;


                            if (!AfxParseURL(sCompleteURL, dwServiceType, sServerName, sObject,
➥nPort))

                            {
                                    return;
                            }
                }
        }

        // ...now open a Gopher or FTP connection to the server
        if (!sServerName.IsEmpty())
        {
                if (dwServiceType == INTERNET_SERVICE_GOPHER)
                {
                        try
                        {
```

```
                                m_pGopherConnection = m_pInetSession-
➥>GetGopherConnection(sServerName);
                    }
                    catch (CInternetException* pEx)
                    {
                            pEx->Delete();
                            m_pGopherConnection = NULL;
                            return;
                    }
            }
            else if (dwServiceType == INTERNET_SERVICE_FTP)
            {
                    try
                    {
                            m_pFtpConnection = m_pInetSession-
➥>GetFtpConnection(sServerName,m_Login,m_Password);
                    }
                    catch (CInternetException* pEx)
                    {
                            pEx->Delete();
                            m_pFtpConnection = NULL;
                            return;
                    }
            }
            else
                    return;
        }
        else
            return;

        if (m_pGopherConnection != NULL || m_pFtpConnection != NULL)
        {
            m_bIsConnected = TRUE;
```

continues

Listing 13-1   Continued

```
        FireConnectionChanged();
    }

}
```

The first thing that we do in the Connect method is close any previous connections that might exist. We do this by invoking the Disconnect method.

The next step is to create an Internet connection. To do this, we invoke the constructor for the CInternetSession class, as follows:

```
m_pInetSession = new CInternetSession();

if (m_pInetSession == NULL)
        return;
```

If the pointer returned is NULL, we exit the connect procedure immediately. Later, if you want to enhance the functionality of this control, you might choose to create an Error event and fire the event if the connection fails. The Visual C++ Books Online help explains the CInternetSession constructor in detail. For our code, we can just use the default values.

The next couple of lines in the procedure parse the URL specified in the URL property and attempt to classify the URL as an FTP or a Gopher connection. Notice that if the URL cannot be classified, we attempt to add ftp:// or gopher:// in front and then try again. We use the m_DefaultToFtp property to determine which one to use first. This is particularly useful if, for example, the programmer wants to use the control as a Gopher handler only. In this case, he or she would set the m_DefaultToFtp property to False, thereby wasting no time in attempting to use the URL as an FTP server address.

As far as the actual connection to the server is concerned, the portion of the code that we are mostly interested in for this chapter is this:

```
        if (dwServiceType == INTERNET_SERVICE_GOPHER)
        {
            try
            {
```

```
                          m_pGopherConnection = m_pInetSession-
⮕>GetGopherConnection(sServerName);
                }
                catch (CInternetException* pEx)
                {
                        pEx->Delete();
                        m_pGopherConnection = NULL;
                        return;
                }
        }
```

If the AfxParseURL function identifies the request as a Gopher type, we create a connection to the Gopher server. Notice that the GetGopherConnection function raises an exception if we are unable to connect; we need to write code to catch this exception. This is another place where you would fire an error event. For now, we simply exit the connect procedure.

The *GetConnectionHandle* Method

All that is left to do, as far as functionality is concerned, is write code for the GetConnectionHandle method. Chapter 12 discussed in detail how to bind the Connection control to the Directory control. We do this by supplying the Directory control with the address of the pointer to the connection class. The programmer retrieves this pointer by writing code in the ConnectionChanged event fired at the end of the Connect method. Then the programmer passes this pointer to the Directory control. Here is the code for the GetConnectionHandle method:

```
OLE_HANDLE CConnectCtrl::GetConnectionHandle()
{
        if (m_pFtpConnection != NULL)
                return (OLE_HANDLE) m_pFtpConnection;
        else
                return (OLE_HANDLE) m_pGopherConnection;
}
```

Finishing Touches

We have done a great deal so far, and this would be a good time to compile our project. Before you click that Compile button, do not forget to modify the stdafx.h file. You need to make sure that you include a definition file for the Internet classes. To do that, add the following line:

```
#include <afxinet.h>
```

I always forget to do this and end up very frustrated.

This is also a good time to talk a little more about how to make your control a commercially distributable control. Sometimes, there is almost as much work involved in figuring out how to put those final touches as there is in figuring out how to create the control. In our case, we have a control that is invisible at run time. Generally, invisible controls display an icon while the programmer is manipulating them during design time. Also, invisible controls generally cannot be resized. These two details are not handled automatically by the code in the OLE ControlWizard. To draw an icon at design time, place this code in the OnDraw method of your control:

```
void CConnectCtrl::OnDraw(
                    CDC* pdc, const CRect& rcBounds, const CRect& rcInvalid)
{
      CBitmap bitmap;
      BITMAP bmp;
      CPictureHolder picHolder;
      CRect rcSrcBounds;

      // Load clock bitmap
      bitmap.LoadBitmap(IDB_CONNECT);
      bitmap.GetObject(sizeof(BITMAP), &bmp);
      rcSrcBounds.right = bmp.bmWidth;
      rcSrcBounds.bottom = bmp.bmHeight;

      // Create picture and render
      picHolder.CreateFromBitmap((HBITMAP)bitmap.m_hObject, NULL, FALSE);
      picHolder.Render(pdc, rcBounds, rcSrcBounds);
```

```
        bitmap.DeleteObject();
}
```

This code basically creates a bitmap class containing the bitmap with the resource identifier IDB_CONNECT. This bitmap is created automatically by the OLE ControlWizard, but it contains only the word *OCX*; therefore, you need to modify it before distributing your control. Then copy the picture to the device context of your control. To make your control nonresizable at design time, just add the following code:

```
BOOL CConnectCtrl::OnSetExtent( LPSIZEL lpSizeL )
{
        return FALSE;
}
```

The OnSetExtent function is a virtual function derived from the COleControl parent class. It is triggered when the programmer requests to resize the control. Generally, it resizes the control and redraws it. We override the standard functionality and basically make it do nothing. This prevents the programmer from resizing the invisible control. It seems like a mean thing to do, but he or she will have to live with it. That's just the way invisible controls behave.

For the control to appear the right size to begin with, we use the SetInitialSize function shown in the constructor event.

OK, click that Compile button, and order a pizza before continuing with the next section.

Modifying the Directory Control

It is time to get started with the second control: the Directory control. If you read RFC 1436, you will discover that the suggested interface for a Gopher client program is an interface that resembles a file system, because the creators of the protocol used the file system as their design model. Therefore, a directory control fits in perfectly with any Gopher client program, but there are quite a few things to do before actually displaying a list of directories in your control. This is due mainly to the fact that the Gopher classes that came with Visual C++ 4.2 are not as easy to use as the FTP classes. For example, there is no easy way to navigate backward through directories. This means that we are going to have to keep track of everywhere we have been. Also, when you receive output from the server, it will come in the form of a locator string.

Understanding the Locator String

A *locator string* is a tab-delimited string that contains information about each item in the server. According to the specifications of the protocol, the first character in the locator string is a file-type identifier. Many kinds of files are available in a Gopher site. Table 13-4 shows the identifier for each file type.

Table 13-4   Gopher File Types and Identifiers

Identifier	File Type
GOPHER_TYPE_TEXT_FILE	ASCII text file
GOPHER_TYPE_DIRECTORY	Directory
GOPHER_TYPE_CSO	Phone-book server
GOPHER_TYPE_ERROR	Error condition
GOPHER_TYPE_MAC_BINHEX	BinHex Macintosh file
GOPHER_TYPE_DOS_ARCHIVE	DOS binary file
GOPHER_TYPE_UNIX_UUENCODED	UNIX uuencoded file
GOPHER_TYPE_INDEX_SERVER	Index server
GOPHER_TYPE_TELNET	Telnet server
GOPHER_TYPE_BINARY	Binary file
GOPHER_TYPE_REDUNDANT	Duplicated server
GOPHER_TYPE_TN3270	TN3270 server
GOPHER_TYPE_GIF	GIF file
GOPHER_TYPE_IMAGE	Image file
GOPHER_TYPE_BITMAP	Bitmap file
GOPHER_TYPE_MOVIE	Movie file
GOPHER_TYPE_SOUND	Sound file
GOPHER_TYPE_HTML	HTML document
GOPHER_TYPE_PDF	.PDF file
GOPHER_TYPE_CALENDAR	Calendar file
GOPHER_TYPE_INLINE	Inline file
GOPHER_TYPE_UNKNOWN	Unknown file
GOPHER_TYPE_ASK	Ask+ item
GOPHER_TYPE_GOPHER_PLUS	Gopher+ item

The identifier that we are interested in for this control is the directory identifier. The character that denotes a directory entry is the number 1. Immediately after the file-type identifier is a description of the object. The description is separated from the rest of the locator string by a tab symbol (escape sequence \t).

The next piece of information in the locator string is what is called the selector. *Selector* is a fancy word for *path*. It denotes the directory path in the server for the particular object. For items that are in another server, this may be another Gopher address. The rest of the information in the locator is not really important for us. But now you are curious, so I will tell you anyway.

There are two other pieces of information in the locator string: the server address (such as gopher.uiuc.edu) and the TCP/IP port that was used to open the connection. I told you that they are not very important; they are important only for low-level communication using the Windows sockets library. It is important to know how to interpret the locator string because we need to retrieve the description of the object so that we can display it in the list box. That's all. The rest of the information is manipulated through high-level functions in the Gopher classes.

Subclassing the List Box

The methods, properties, and events for this control are the same as they were in Chapter 12. The main ones that we are going to deal with are SetConnection, Refresh, and SetCurrentDir. Rather than repeat all the information from the preceding chapter, I'm going to point out the enhancements in the control.

The first obvious enhancement is the capability of the control to display a directory icon next to each item. Support for displaying icons was needed because of the variety of Gopher file types available and the nature of the protocol. Therefore, in the PrecreateWindow event handler, we need to change the style of our list box to make it an owner-drawn list box, because the standard list-box control does not handle including pictures as part of the items.

The following code shows the class style settings for our list box:

```
BOOL CDirectoryCtrl::PreCreateWindow(CREATESTRUCT& cs)
{
        cs.lpszClass = _T("listbox");
        cs.style |= LBS_OWNERDRAWFIXED | LBS_STANDARD | LBS_HASSTRINGS;
        return COleControl::PreCreateWindow(cs);
}
```

I chose the `LBS_OWNERDRAWFIXED` style instead of `LBS_OWNERDRAWVARIABLE` for simplicity and because every icon in the list box will be the same size. If you want to allow the programmer to set the icons through properties, you need to set this style to `LBS_OWNERDRAWVARI-ABLE`. Also, I decided to let the control store all the items itself, rather than maintain a list in code, and that is why the `LBS_HASSTRINGS` style is there.

Handling *OCM_DRAWITEM*

Now that we are talking about the subclassing aspects of the control, let's write the code for displaying our list box. Because our control is owner-drawn, Windows sends us a message each time the control needs to be redrawn. Therefore, we need to add a handler for this message to our message map, as shown in the following code:

```
BEGIN_MESSAGE_MAP(CDirectoryCtrl, COleControl)
        //{{AFX_MSG_MAP(CDirectoryCtrl)
        //}}AFX_MSG_MAP
        ON_MESSAGE(OCM_COMMAND, OnOcmCommand)
        ON_OLEVERB(AFX_IDS_VERB_PROPERTIES, OnProperties)
        ON_MESSAGE(OCM_DRAWITEM, OnOcmDrawItem)
END_MESSAGE_MAP()
```

Your message map should resemble this code. Now write the routine for handling the `OCM_DRAWITEM` message and for drawing both the icon and the text. A great deal of code is involved, but don't get intimidated; it is not very difficult to decipher. First, we take care of the message by calling our `DrawItem` function, as follows:

```
LRESULT CDirectoryCtrl::OnOcmDrawItem(WPARAM, LPARAM lParam)
{
        DrawItem((LPDRAWITEMSTRUCT)lParam);
        return 1;
}
```

The DrawItem function basically obtains a pointer to the control's drawing surface and gets the dimensions for the item we are drawing. After that, it calls the DrawItemPicture function, followed by the DrawItemText function. The following code shows the DrawItemText function:

```
void CDirectoryCtrl::DrawItem(LPDRAWITEMSTRUCT lpDrawItemStruct)
{
        CDC *pdc;
        CPen* pOldPen;

        // Construct CDC object for drawing
        pdc = CDC::FromHandle(lpDrawItemStruct->hDC);

        switch (lpDrawItemStruct->itemAction)
        {
                case ODA_DRAWENTIRE:

                        //Draw item's picture
                        DrawItemPicture(&lpDrawItemStruct->rcItem, pdc);

                        // Draw item's text
                        DrawItemText((int)lpDrawItemStruct->itemID, &lpDrawItemStruct-
>rcItem, pdc);

                        // Break if item is not selected
                        if (lpDrawItemStruct->itemState != ODS_SELECTED)
                                break;

                case ODA_SELECT:

                        // If invert flag is set, invert item when selected
                        pdc->InvertRect(&lpDrawItemStruct->rcItem);
                        break;

                case ODA_FOCUS:
```

```
            // Draw focus rect when item gets the focus
            pOldPen = (CPen*)pdc->SelectStockObject(BLACK_PEN);
            pdc->DrawFocusRect(&lpDrawItemStruct->rcItem);
            pdc->SelectObject(pOldPen);
            break;
    }
}
```

Notice that there is code for inverting the selected item in the ODA_SELECT section and for drawing a focus rectangle around the selected item in the ODA_FOCUS section.

The *DrawItemPicture* Function

The DrawItemPicture function uses the same method that we used for rendering a bitmap on our invisible control that is visible at design time. Following is the code for DrawItemPicture:

```
void CDirectoryCtrl::DrawItemPicture(LPRECT lpRect, CDC *pdc)
{
        CBitmap bitmap;
        BITMAP bmp;
        CPictureHolder picHolder;

        // Load clock bitmap
        bitmap.LoadBitmap(IDB_DIRECTORY);
        bitmap.GetObject(sizeof(BITMAP), &bmp);

        // Set up draw rect
        int iSaveRight = lpRect->right;
        int iSaveBottom = lpRect->bottom;

        lpRect->right = lpRect->left + bmp.bmWidth;
        lpRect->bottom = lpRect->top + bmp.bmHeight;

        // Create picture and render
        picHolder.CreateFromBitmap((HBITMAP)bitmap.m_hObject, NULL, FALSE);
```

```
        picHolder.Render(pdc, *lpRect, *lpRect);


        lpRect->left += bmp.bmWidth;

        lpRect->right = iSaveRight + bmp.bmWidth;

        lpRect->bottom = iSaveBottom;


        bitmap.DeleteObject();

}
```

The *DrawItemText* Function

Finally, the DrawItemText function simply retrieves the item text from the internal storage of the list box. To do this, we send the LB_GETTEXT message to our control; then we output the string by using the API function ExTextOut. The following code shows the DrawItemText function:

```
void CDirectoryCtrl::DrawItemText(int nIndex, LPRECT lpRect, CDC *pdc)

{

        char sSelection[255];


        SendMessage(LB_GETTEXT,nIndex,(long)sSelection);

        if (strlen(sSelection) != 0)

        {

                // Draw text

                pdc->ExtTextOut(lpRect->left, lpRect->top, ETO_CLIPPED, lpRect,
➥sSelection, strlen(sSelection), NULL);

        }


}
```

Navigating Backward

Because the Gopher classes do not support navigating backward, we are going to have to remember each place we have been. In fact, there is no straightforward way to navigate at all. In FTP, the information we displayed in the list box was also used to navigate through the control. In Gopher, however, there is a description that has nothing to do with the actual location of the file. Therefore, our list box will handle storing our descriptions, but storing the locations of each file is up to us. For this reason, I created two classes that will serve for storage. I called my classes CGopherDirInfo and CGopherHistory. Following are the definitions of these classes:

```
class CGopherDirInfo : public CObject
{
public:
        CGopherDirInfo(CString sInfo);
        ~CGopherDirInfo();
        CString GetDirInfo();

private:
        CString m_sInfo;
};

class CGopherHistory : public CObject
{
public:
        CGopherHistory(CString sHistory);
        ~CGopherHistory();
        CString GetHistory();

private:
        CString m_sHistory;
};
```

Our control is going to maintain a dynamic array of each of these classes. When the control retrieves a level in the server structure, the locator string for each item is stored in an array of type CGopherDirInfo. This means that each time we clear the contents of the list box to display a new level, we need to destroy and recreate the array.

The CGopherHistory array works a little bit differently; it functions like a stack. When the user first connects, it is empty. When the user requests to go a different directory, the preceding directory is added to the stack. We allow the user to navigate backward by adding the (..) item as the first item in each subsequent directory. This item is stored in the CGopherDirInfo array with the text HISTORY. Therefore, when the user double-clicks the (..) entry, we retrieve the directory information and find the word HISTORY for the locator. Whenever the word HISTORY is found, we get the locator from the CGopherHistory array; it will be the last item in the stack. Finally, we remove it from the stack.

The code for implementing the array is available in the sample code on the CD-ROM that comes with this book. For our discussion, it is necessary only to point out the functions that I created to manipulate the array, as follows:

```
CString GetGopherDirInfo(int nIndex);
void AddGopherDirInfo(CString sDirInfo);
CString GetGopherHistory();
void RemoveGopherHistory();
void AddGopherHistory(CString sHistory);
```

Following are the member variables to hold the arrays:

```
CObArray *m_pGopherDirInfo;
CObArray *m_pGopherHistory;
```

As always, we ensure that all the variables are initialized in the constructor, as follows:

```
m_pFtpConnection = NULL;
m_pFtpFileFind=NULL;

m_pGopherConnection = NULL;
m_pGopherFileFind=NULL;

m_sSelectedLocator="";

m_pGopherDirInfo=NULL
m_pGopherHistory = NULL;
```

What? You are right. There is an extra member variable that we have not discussed: m_sSelectedLocator. I can't get anything past you. I will discuss this variable in detail when I talk about the user selecting a directory to view.

Also, we need to be very careful with freeing all the memory allocated for the arrays. Remember that each time the user double-clicks a directory, a new array is created. If we do not free the memory from the preceding array, your program is going to leak like a sieve.

Here is the code for the destructor:

```
CDirectoryCtrl::~CDirectoryCtrl()
{
        if (m_pFtpFileFind != NULL)
        {
                delete m_pFtpFileFind;
                m_pFtpFileFind;
        }

        if (m_pGopherFileFind != NULL)
        {
                delete m_pGopherFileFind;
                m_pGopherFileFind = NULL;
        }

        if (m_pGopherDirInfo != NULL)
                CleanGopherDirInfo();
        if (m_pGopherHistory != NULL)
                CleanGopherHistory();
}
```

The destructor checks to see whether there is any memory allocated for the arrays and invokes the appropriate clean function, if needed.

Here is the code for the clean functions:

```
void CDirectoryCtrl::CleanGopherDirInfo()
{
        if (m_pGopherDirInfo->GetSize() > 0)
        {
                // For each item
                for (int i = 0; i < m_pGopherDirInfo->GetSize(); i++)
```

```
            {
                    // Free item data
                    delete m_pGopherDirInfo->GetAt( i );
            }

            // Remove all items from item array
            m_pGopherDirInfo->RemoveAll();
            delete m_pGopherDirInfo;
            m_pGopherDirInfo=NULL;
        }
}

void CDirectoryCtrl::CleanGopherHistory()
{
        if (m_pGopherHistory->GetSize() > 0)
        {
            // For each item
            for (int i = 0; i < m_pGopherHistory->GetSize(); i++)
            {
                    // Free item data
                    delete m_pGopherHistory->GetAt( i );
            }

            // Remove all items from item array
            m_pGopherHistory->RemoveAll();
            delete m_pGopherHistory;
            m_pGopherHistory=NULL;
        }
}
```

Binding to the *Connection* Control

You have been patient long enough and you do not have to wait any longer. Here is the code that you have been waiting for (you are now entering the Gopher Zone):

```
void CDirectoryCtrl::SetConnectionHandle(OLE_HANDLE pHandle, short nHandleType)
{
    switch (nHandleType)
    {
    case CONNECT_GOPHER:
        m_pGopherConnection = (CGopherConnection *)pHandle;
        if (m_pGopherConnection != NULL)
        {
            if (m_pGopherFileFind != NULL)
            {
                delete m_pGopherFileFind;
                m_pGopherFileFind = NULL;
            }

            m_pGopherFileFind = new CGopherFileFind(m_pGopherConnection);
        }
        break;
    case CONNECT_FTP:
        ...
    if (m_pGopherConnection != NULL || m_pFtpConnection != NULL)
    {
        m_nConnectionType = nHandleType;
        if (m_pFtpConnection != NULL)
            SetCurrentDirectory("/");
        else
            SetCurrentDirectory("");
    }
    else
        Clear();
}
```

You may recall that in Chapter 12, we created a method called SetConnection. This method is used for binding the Directory control to the Connection control. The only differences are that an extra parameter—the handle type—is sent in to distinguish between an FTP connection and a Gopher connection, and that code is added to handle the Gopher connection. The code to handle a Gopher connection is very similar to the code for FTP. Basically, it stores the GopherConnection handle created in the Connection control and creates an instance to the CGopherFileFind class, used later to read a Gopher directory. The only other noticeable difference is the code that sets the current directory, which follows:

```
if (m_pGopherConnection != NULL || m_pFtpConnection != NULL)
{
        m_nConnectionType = nHandleType;
        if (m_pFtpConnection != NULL)
                SetCurrentDirectory("/");
        else
                SetCurrentDirectory("");
}
```

Notice that in the case of a Gopher connection, we set the starting directory to nothing. The truth is that we could have passed in the word *Pepe*, and the server would not care, because in the Gopher protocol, the top-level menu is always retrieved after a connection is established. In fact, any time that the Gopher server cannot resolve a locator string, it simply defaults to the top-level menu (also referred to as the default menu). Following is the code for the SetCurrentDirectory function:

```
void CDirectoryCtrl::SetCurrentDirectory(LPCTSTR sDirectory)
{
        switch (m_nConnectionType)
        {
        case CONNECT_GOPHER:
                m_sSelectedLocator= sDirectory;
                break;
        case CONNECT_FTP:
                m_pFtpConnection->SetCurrentDirectory(sDirectory);
                break;
        }

        Refresh();
}
```

The SetCurrentDirectory function mainly causes the Refresh to occur, which in turn causes the ReadDirectory function to get triggered. Remember the member variable that I sneaked into the constructor (m_sSelectedLocator)? Well, you still have to wait for the explanation.

You might be thinking that this code jumps around a lot. A triggers B, which causes C to occur, which alerts D. It is not quite as bad as that. There are good reasons for the jumping-around effect. The main reason is to avoid redundancy of code. When working with controls, you need to account for methods that are called externally as well as internally. For example, you do not want to read the server directory after making a connection to the server, because you would just end up duplicating the code for when the programmer issues the SetCurrentDirectory method. Also, you do not want to read the directory after the SetCurrentDirectory method, because that code would be duplicated when the programmer issues the Refresh method. Pretty soon, you would have a debugging nightmare at hand.

Try to minimize the number of places where a function gets called. The ReadDirectory function, for example, is called only from the Refresh method. Here is the Refresh method:

```
void CDirectoryCtrl::Refresh()
{
        Clear();
        if (m_pFtpConnection != NULL || m_pGopherConnection != NULL)
                ReadDirectory();
}
```

Reading Directories

This section discusses the heart of the control: the function that reads the directories from the Gopher server. I omitted the code for handling FTP directories; that was covered in Chapter 12. Listing 13-2 shows the code to read a Gopher directory.

Listing 13-2   Reading a Gopher Directory

```
void CDirectoryCtrl::ReadDirectory()
{
      CWaitCursor cursor;        // this will automatically display a wait cursor

      CString strSearch = _T("*");

      switch (m_nConnectionType)
      {
      case CONNECT_FTP:
      ...
      case CONNECT_GOPHER:
            {
                  BOOL bContinue;

                  if (m_sSelectedLocator == "")
                        bContinue = m_pGopherFileFind->FindFile(strSearch);
                  else
                        bContinue = m_pGopherFileFind-
➡>FindFile(CGopherConnection::CreateLocator(m_sSelectedLocator),"/*");

                  if (!bContinue)
                  {
                        // the directory is empty; just close up and return.
                        m_pGopherFileFind->Close();
                        return;
                  }
                  else
                  {
                        if (m_sSelectedLocator != "")
                        {
                              AddItem("..");
                              AddGopherDirInfo("HISTORY");
```

continues

Listing 13-2   Continued

```
                                        }
                                  }


                         while (bContinue)
                         {
                                  // FindNextFile must be called before info can be gleaned
➥from ftpFind
                                  bContinue = m_pGopherFileFind->FindNextFile();

                                  CGopherLocator gopherLocator = m_pGopherFileFind-
➥>GetLocator();
                                  DWORD dwType;
                                  gopherLocator.GetLocatorType(dwType);

                                  if (dwType == GOPHER_TYPE_DIRECTORY)
                                  {
                                          CString sDocumentName((LPCTSTR)gopherLocator);
                                          CString sDescription =
➥sDocumentName.Mid(1,sDocumentName.Find("\t")-1);
                                          AddItem(sDescription);
                                          AddGopherDirInfo(sDocumentName);
                                  }
                         }

                  m_pGopherFileFind->Close();
                  break;
                  }
          }


}
```

Reading the Top-Level Menu

After a connection is established with the server, we get the top-level menu or directory by using the CGopherFileFind class. We send an asterisk to denote that we want all the files. Then we loop through the files, using the following code, until all the files are read:

```
bContinue = m_pGopherFileFind->FindNextFile();
```

When this happens, the function returns False.

Once we move the file marker with the FindNextFile function, we can find the Locator information for that object. To do this, we use the following function:

```
CGopherLocator gopherLocator = m_pGopherFileFind->GetLocator();
```

If you remember the information on the Gopher protocol and the discussion pertaining to locator strings, you know that that is all we need to finish displaying the directories. From this locator string, we obtain the kind of object, and we use the identifier to filter out anything that is not a directory. The following code shows how to do the filtering:

```
gopherLocator.GetLocatorType(dwType);


if (dwType == GOPHER_TYPE_DIRECTORY)
```

All that is left to do is obtain the object description from the locator string and store the actual locator, so that the user can navigate the structure later, as demonstrated in the following code:

```
CString sDocumentName((LPCTSTR)gopherLocator);
CString sDescription = sDocumentName.Mid(1,sDocumentName.Find("\t")-1);
AddItem(sDescription);
AddGopherDirInfo(sDocumentName);
```

That's all there is to it (for the top-level directory, at least).

Reading Lower-Level Menus

Before issuing the FindFile command, we did a little check to see whether we were reading the top-level menu, as shown in the following code.

```
if (m_sSelectedLocator == "")
bContinue = m_pGopherFileFind->FindFile(strSearch);
else
bContinue = m_pGopherFileFind->FindFile(CGopherConnection::
➥CreateLocator(m_sSelectedLocator),"/*");
```

If we were not reading the top-level menu then we use the locator that we stored in the locator array to create a locator object. We then make the FindFile function use this locator object as its starting location; the new level will be read. That's why we needed that mysterious member variable to pass the locator that the user selected to the ReadDirectory function.

Navigating Between Directories

The function for navigating is the only thing left to show you. Here it is:

```
LRESULT CDirectoryCtrl::OnOcmCommand(WPARAM wParam, LPARAM lParam)
{
#ifdef _WIN32
        WORD wNotifyCode = HIWORD(wParam);
#else
        WORD wNotifyCode = HIWORD(lParam);
#endif

        switch (wNotifyCode)
        {
        case LBN_DBLCLK:

                switch (m_nConnectionType)
                {
                case CONNECT_FTP:
                ...
                case CONNECT_GOPHER:
                {
                        char sSelection[255];
```

```
                    int idListBox = SendMessage(LB_GETCURSEL,0,0L);
                    SendMessage(LB_GETTEXT,idListBox,(long)sSelection);
                    SetCurrentDirectory(GetGopherDirInfo(idListBox));
                    break;

                }
            }


        break;
        }


        return 0;
    }
```

All that this function does is retrieve the locator for the item selected in the list box from the CGopherDirInfo array and hand it over to the SetCurrentDirectory function, which triggers the Refresh function and then the ReadDirectory function.

This is a good time to get that blood circulation back and click that Compile button.

The List Control

I will not discuss the construction of the third control—the Document control— since it is so similar to the Directory control. The only modifications to be made to this control are to add pretty pictures for each of the possible file types and to reverse the filtering in the ReadDirectory function. Before, we wanted to display only directories; now we want to display everything but directories. Finally, we want to store the file-type identifier in the CGopherDirInfo array.

Nifty Things to Do with Gopher

Now that you have created these controls, what are you going to do next? Well, you can use your controls to make a Gopher client program that looks and feels like Windows 95. Also, it would be fairly simple at this point to make MiniBrowser into a more complete browser. All that is left to do is add support for HTTP (Hypertext Transfer Protocol), which is what Web browsers use to obtain Web-page information.

To add HTTP support to your controls, you need to modify the Connection control. Several classes were introduced in Visual C++ version 4.2 for handling connections to HTTP servers. Among these classes are CHttpInternetSession, CHttpConnection, and CHttpFile. The only thing that you would need to do after adding support for HTTP connections is create an HTML viewer control.

Chapter Summary

Let's summarize what you have learned in this chapter:

- ◆ You learned about Gopher and its origins.
- ◆ You learned about the new Internet classes introduced in version 4.2 of C++.
- ◆ You learned how to enhance the connection control from Chapter 12 to support Gopher connections.
- ◆ You learned how to create a list-box control that allows you to have pictures in it.
- ◆ You learned all that there is to know about navigating Gopher servers.
- ◆ You learned some tips for completing your controls and making them commercially distributable.
- ◆ You learned that programmers like to make jokes when they write long chapters.

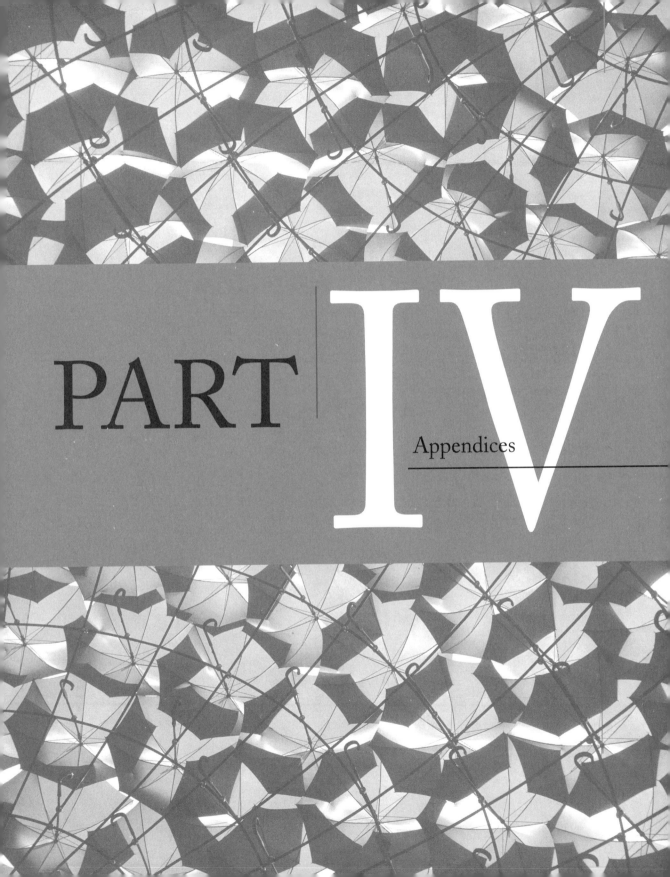

PART IV

Appendices

Appendix | A

Adding Licensing to Your Online Controls

by Markus Pope

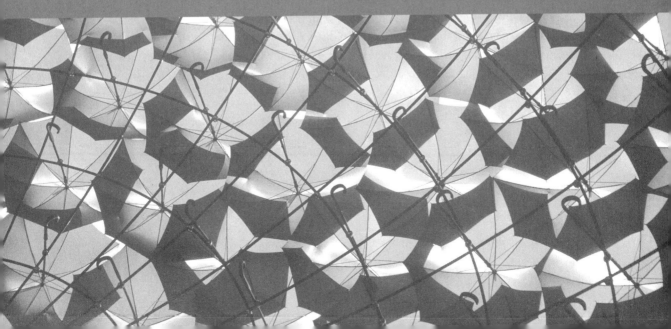

Component technologies, such as ActiveX controls, create markets for what Microsoft calls *ISVs* (independent software vendors). ISVs are third-party companies that create add-on components for other software vendors. For example, you and I could own a company that writes custom ActiveX controls and sells them to commercial software companies, such as Microsoft and Quarterdeck. Microsoft and Quarterdeck could then use our controls in software programs such as Excel and Procomm Plus.

Many third-party companies use the shareware concept to distribute their software. *Shareware* is the try-before-you-buy marketing strategy. Companies that market their programs through shareware allow users to download and use their programs for a specified period. After the grace period is over, users are expected to either pay for the software or discard it. This concept has worked very well for many companies.

Shareware programs are subject to theft, though, if they're not protected in some way. If there's no incentive for the user to register a shareware program, it's easy for the user to continue using the program and forget about paying for it. So most shareware programs use a licensing scheme that limits use of the product in some way. If the user doesn't have a license to use a product, he or she can't take full advantage of that product's potential.

Types of Licensing

Microsoft, in its infinite wisdom, saw the potential for an ISV market for ActiveX controls. During development of the ActiveX control specifications, Microsoft added a standard licensing API. Standard licensing allows control developers to develop components without worrying about how client applications deal with the license. At the same time, standard licensing allows software vendors to use ActiveX controls without worrying about how the controls handle licensing.

> **NOTE:** Don't worry—even though Microsoft has defined the licensing API, implementation of the license is still up to you. (The money that you spent on the encryption library won't go to waste!)

An ActiveX control is used by two types of users: developers and end users. Developers use the control when they integrate it into their software programs, and end users use the control when they install it as a component of a developer's software program. So the ISV must have some way to restrict the control, based on which type of user is using the control: developer or end user.

Development License

Development licenses regulate controls when the controls are used during development of software programs. If a developer inserts a control into a Visual Basic application, for example, Visual Basic uses the licensing API to determine whether the developer is licensed to use the control. If the developer is not licensed to use the control, Visual Basic prevents the developer from inserting the control into the application. (You write the code, though, so you can either reject the developer's request completely or just limit what the developer can do.)

Run-Time License

Run-time licenses regulate controls when the controls are used by end users. This allows the ISV to limit distribution of the control. A developer can insert a control into a Visual Basic application, using a development license, but that doesn't necessarily give the developer a license to distribute the control. ISVs may charge royalties, or additional fees, to allow distribution of components to end users. Microsoft's licensing API for ActiveX controls provides both development and run-time licensing.

Licensing Schemes

Licensing for ActiveX controls is very flexible. Microsoft just defines the interface and methods used to determine whether a control is licensed. Implementation of the interface and methods is left to you, the ActiveX control developer. Because the licensing API is so flexible, you can provide a wide variety of licensing, and you can regulate the use of your controls in many ways. Over the years, shareware vendors have developed many creative incentives to encourage users to pay for their software.

Most licensing schemes for shareware programs limit the programs in some way or just politely remind users that they can use the software only for a trial period. Even if you're not planning to distribute your components as shareware programs, you can use similar schemes to give your developers and users choices as to how they can license your components. Nag screens, crippling, and prevention are just a few schemes used by shareware vendors.

Nag Screens

Nag screens, which are the most basic licensing incentive for shareware programs, are windows displayed during program startup that remind the user that he or she is using an unlicensed or limited version. Nag screens are also used to advertise copyrights, trademarks, and patents used in a program. Using nag screens for ActiveX control licensing is very effective, because most development companies don't want your name showing up every time users run their programs.

Crippling

In addition to displaying nag screens, some vendors limit their software. Users are encouraged to upgrade to licensed versions of software to get bigger and better features. Some developers provide two versions of their software, based on whether users are registered. Other developers disable features, based on whether the user is licensed.

You find many levels of crippling in shareware applications. I've seen everything from disabling extended features to not allowing the user to save and reload data until the program is registered (that's a bit extreme). All are effective means of encouraging users to license software.

> **TIP:** Disabling features that are highly visible to users (such as pushbuttons in a dialog box) is effective but tends to frustrate users. Simply not providing a feature unless a user is licensed (hiding pushbuttons in a dialog box, for example) is less obtrusive and just as effective.

Because ActiveX controls are based on the component object model, ISVs can limit the properties and methods that a developer can use. If the developer or the end user doesn't have the correct license, the ActiveX control can return an error when a client application tries to use certain properties or methods.

Time Bombing

Time bombs probably are the most effective licensing scheme used by software vendors. When a program is started on a user's machine for the first time, it stamps itself with the date. Optionally, the program can stamp itself with the number of times it has been executed. The user can use the program a specific number of times or until a specific date. After the license runs out, the user must purchase a new license to use the software. (Ideally, your time bomb prevents the user from reinstalling the software to reset the timer!)

MFC-Provided Licensing

Licensing is handled by the IClassFactory2 interface, which is the interface that's responsible for instantiating your controls. IClassFactory2 implements licensing by using three methods: GetLicInfo, RequestLicKey, and CreateInstanceLic.

GetLicInfo is called when a development tool is inserting an ActiveX control into a container. GetLicInfo determines whether the developer has a license to use the control.

Development environments, such as Visual Basic, call RequestLicKey in building production versions of a control container. RequestLicKey returns a string that's passed to CreateInstanceLic during run time. CreateInstanceLic uses the string to determine whether the user is licensed to use the control. This determination can be as simple as comparing the string with another string stored in the control.

CreateInstanceLic is called at run time, when the end user is running the control container. CreateInstanceLic is responsible for ensuring that the end user is licensed and creating instances of the control. At this level, an ISV may decide to create or limit access to the control, based on the end user's license.

The COleObjectFactory class implements the IClassFactory2 interface, including the GetLicInfo, RequestLicKey, and CreateInstanceLic methods. COleObjectFactory provides three virtual functions that can be overridden to provide special licensing. When you create your control with the OLE ControlWizard, you can specify whether you want your controls licensed. If you choose to have licensing support, Visual C++ provides overloaded versions of VerifyUserLicense and GetLicenseKey.

VerifyUserLicense

COleObjectFactory::VerifyUserLicense is called when the development environment (also a container) calls the GetLicInfo method in IClassFactory2. The default implementation for VerifyUserLicense just returns a true value to indicate that the developer has licensed the control.

The version of VerifyUserLicense that's generated by the OLE ControlWizard calls AfxVerifyLicFile. OLE ControlWizard's COleObjectFactory::VerifyUserLicense looks like this:

```
BOOL COleObjectFactory::VerifyUserLicense()
{
        return( AfxVerifyLicFile( AfxGetInstanceHandle(),
                szLicFileName, szLicString ) );
}
```

AfxVerifyLicFile looks in the control's directory for a file called License.lic. If the file is found, AfxVerifyLicFile opens the file and reads in the first line, comparing it with a copyright notice generated by the OLE ControlWizard. If the file is found and the copyright notices match, VerifyUserLicense returns true; otherwise, it returns false. _szLicFileName and _szLicString are static variables created by OLE ControlWizard.

> **NOTE:** A custom implementation of VerifyUserLicense can check the registry or do something similar. It's not necessary for VerifyUserLicense to search for a file on the disk drive.

GetLicenseKey

COleObjectFactory::GetLicenseKey is called when the development environment calls the RequestLicKey method in IClassFactory2. MFC's default implementation for GetLicenseKey returns false.

The OLE ControlWizard generates a version of GetLicenseKey that looks similar to this:

```
BOOL COleObjectFactory::GetLicenseKey( DWORD dwReserved,
        BSTR FAR* pbstrKey )
{

      if( pbstrKey == NULL )
            return FALSE;


      *pbstrKey = SysAllocString( _szLicString );
      return( *pbstrKey != NULL );

}
```

dwReserved is not used. pbstrKey points to a buffer that receives the licensing key—the string that's passed to IClassFactory2::CreateInstanceLic when the control is instantiated. GetLicenseKey calls SysAllocString, which creates a character buffer and copies a Unicode string into it. pbstrKey is set to the buffer that contains the non-Unicode version of _szLicString. GetLicenseKey returns false if _szLicString is empty.

VerifyLicenseKey

COleObjectFactory::VerifyLicenseKey gets called when the container calls IClassFactory2::CreateInstanceLic to create an instance of a control. The OLE ControlWizard doesn't override VerifyLicenseKey. Instead, the ActiveX control framework relies on MFC's implementation. MFC's implementation of VerifyLicenseKey compares the string passed into CreateInstanceLic with the string returned by GetLicenseKey. If the strings match, VerifyLicenseKey returns true, and CreateInstanceLic creates an instance of the control. An instance of the control is not created, of course, if VerifyLicenseKey returns false.

Here is MFC's VerifyLicenseKey:

```
BOOL COleObjectFactory::VerifyLicenseKey( BSTR bstrKey )
{

      BOOL bLicensed = FALSE;
      BSTR bstr = NULL;

      if( (bstrKey != NULL) &&
      GetLicenseKey(0, &bstr))
```

```
        {
                ASSERT(bstr != NULL);

                UINT cch = SysStringLen( bstr );
                if ( (cch == SysStringLen(bstrKey)) &&
                     (memcmp(bstr, bstrKey, cch) == 0) )
                {
                        bLicensed = TRUE;
                }

                SysFreeString(bstr);
        }

        return bLicensed;
}
```

VerifyLicenseKey is also a virtual function, like VerifyUserLicense and GetLicenseKey. You can overload it to provide extended functionality. You may want to compare the string stored in the container with a string in the registry, for example, or you may want to use some sort of encryption scheme to verify that the string passed into VerifyLicenseKey represents a valid license.

To Sum Things Up

You can add custom licensing to your controls by overloading three virtual member functions in the COleObjectFactory class. Overloading VerifyUserLicense allows you to specify whether the developer has a design-time license to use the control with development tools such as Visual Basic and Visual C++. Overloading GetLicenseKey allows you to provide the string that's imbedded in controls when the design phase is complete. And by overloading VerifyLicenseKey, you can verify that the string returned by GetLicenseKey and imbedded in the control indicates a licensed end user.

Appendix | B

Diagnosing Problems with Your Online Applications

by Markus Pope

Finding bugs in a communication system isn't quite as straightforward as one might assume. Several layers in communication systems can fail. Failure can occur at the protocol level, at the client level, or even at the host level. Figure B-1 shows the levels of a communications system.

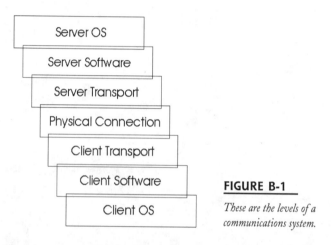

FIGURE B-1

These are the levels of a communications system.

As you've probably guessed, you must use a variety of troubleshooting techniques to isolate problems that you find in such a system. (The terminal control that you wrote in Chapter 5 is an example. Think about what it would take to troubleshoot problems with your terminal.) Although *Programming Internet Controls* can't give you everything that you need to find and fix your bugs, we can at least give you some of the basic ideas.

In this appendix, you'll learn how to determine the level at which a problem is happening. Additionally, you'll learn how to find the true nature of a problem—some problems are actually multiple problems combined. Figuring out how to fix those problems, once you find them, is up to you. Also, we'll talk a little bit about how you can add a monitor window to your Internet application. (The same basic principle applies to terminal programs as well.)

Finding the Problem

Working in the technical-support profession for many years gives you the opportunity to see a great many troubleshooting techniques; some are successful, and others are not. Technicians who are successful at finding and solving problems have a very clear understanding of the troubleshooting process.

The troubleshooting process involves varying the environments that problems live in and also testing to find the effects of those variations on the problems that you're troubleshooting (very similar to the scientific process). A good technician, just like a good doctor, realizes that highly visible problems are merely side effects of less visible problems.

Suppose that you've written a mail client. For some reason, your mail client is failing to send a mail message to markus@socketis.net. How can you tell whether you have a bug in your code, a bug in the mail server, or just a bad e-mail address? You start by determining which part of the mail system—the client or the server—actually has the problem.

Determining the Level

Finding the level on which the problem actually occurs is very important. Not knowing what part of the system a problem happens in can lead to days wasted on worthless debugging. Days wasted on worthless debugging cost you time and money. Start by thinking about how the system is supposed to work.

A mail client goes through a few steps to send a mail message. First, the mail client resolves the mail server's address and makes a connection to it. After that, the client sends the header for the mail message to the server. The client follows the header with the body of the mail message. Then the client saves the mail message and disconnects from the server. In Figure B-2, you can see the flow of a client/server communication.

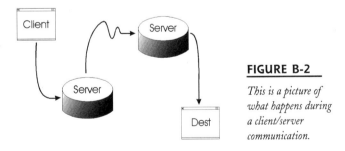

FIGURE B-2

This is a picture of what happens during a client/server communication.

After receiving the mail message, the mail server resolves the domain name that's included in the e-mail address of the person the mail message is going to. The mail server then makes a connection to the mail server that owns the domain name. After that, the originating mail server sends the mail message, using the same protocol that the client used to send it.

You can narrow down the problem described earlier (can't send a mail message to markus@socketis.net) by varying the environment. Start with the basics. Can you send a mail message to any other Internet address? If you can't send a mail message to anyone, you've narrowed the problem to either your client or the mail server. If you can send a mail message to someone else, the problem is either with the mail server or the destination. Let's pretend that you can't send a mail message to anyone.

Now that you've determined that the problem is with your client or the mail server, you can do more testing and narrow the problem even further. Open a different mail application. Try to send mail to the same addresses you tried with your mail client—preferably a commercial mail app. If you can send mail using another application, but not yours, you've narrowed the problem to your mail client. If you can't send mail with another mail client, the problem is with the server. (It's time to call your Internet Service Provider and make sure that the mail server is up!)

Simplifying

After you've figured out the level at which the problem occurs—in this case, the client—you can simplify the problem. You can use more traditional debugging techniques, such as stepping through the code or displaying messages to indicate program flow. In the case of the mail bug, you must determine whether the problem is happening when the mail message is sent or before. (Maybe the code to send the mail message is not even getting called.)

A little bit of gut feeling tells you that the problem is most likely happening when the mail message is sent. So you display message boxes at various places during the send, displaying responses returned by the server. You've struck it rich! Through careful execution of the troubleshooting process, you find that the server is returning a negative response on the e-mail address. Further investigation reveals a pointer problem. The mail client is sending garbage, including a few control characters, to the server. And the server issues a negative response when it receives the control characters.

That's how the troubleshooting process works. Over the years, I've learned that you can find a solution to any problem just by being faithful to the process. If you narrow a problem to its finest level and still don't have a clue what's causing the problem, you haven't narrowed the problem to its finest level.

Creating a Monitor Window

A useful debugging tool for communication applications is the monitor window. A *monitor window* (sometimes called a *status window*) is an area on the screen that displays messages about what programs are doing. Monitor windows are created and maintained by the programmer, unlike the debug window that's built into Visual C++. Some programs allow users to display their monitor windows; others display monitor windows only when they're compiled for debug.

There are two ways to create monitor windows in an MFC applications. Your first choice is to insert a CWnd object into your view class, create a window with a scroll bar, and use DrawText or TextOut to write messages to that window. The other method is to create a CDialog, attach it to a dialog-box template that contains a list box, and add messages to the list box. I prefer the second method, because it's a bit faster to code.

> **NOTE:** There's no need to get into details about how to add a new CDialog class to your project. That's covered in Chapter 4, "Plug-in Modem Dialer."

Writing Status Messages to a Monitor Window

Once you have a window in place that can act as a monitor window, at minimum, you need a function that allows you to write text to the window—similar to OutputDebugString for Visual C++. If you go the dialog-box route, you just need to create a public method in your CDialog class that gets a handle to the list-box control, attaches that handle to a CListBox object, and then calls the CListBox::AddString method to add the message to the list box.

Overloading the *CSocket* Object's Member Functions

You've learned throughout this book how to overload the members of the CSocket or CAsyncSocket objects and extend their functionality. In those overloaded functions, you can write as much debug information to the monitor window as you deem appropriate.

Be careful, though, because it takes quite a chunk of time to update and maintain the monitor window. Some communication protocols are time-critical. Writing too much information to your monitor window can cause more problems than it solves. Figure B-3 shows what a monitor window might look like.

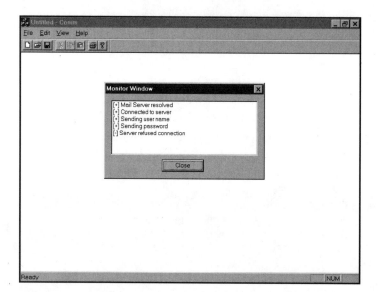

FIGURE B-3

This is a picture of what a typical monitor window looks like. Some applications include the monitor window as part of the interface, such as a status line.

For Internet applications, it's probably not necessary to write every character sent and received to the monitor window, even while debugging. Small status messages indicating what's happening and the server's response is good enough. Most Internet servers issue a negative response when a problem occurs. Figure B-3 also shows short (but descriptive) status and error messages. CSocket members that should write status information to a monitor window are OnSend, OnReceive, OnConnect, and OnClose.

Appendix | C

Installing the CD-ROM

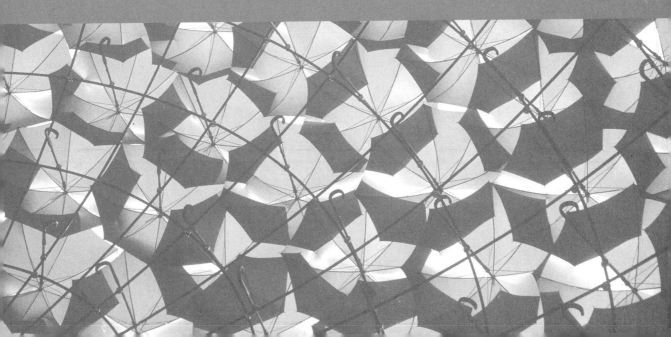

The CD-ROM that accompanies this book contains the controls built as examples in the book, as well as a collection of useful tools and utilities. The collection includes finger clients, FTP clients, and Telnet clients.

Running the CD

To make the CD more user-friendly and take up less of your disk space, we designed the CD-ROM so that no installation is required. This means that the only files transferred to your hard disk are the ones that you choose to copy.

> **CAUTION:** Significant differences among the various Windows operating systems (Windows 3.1, Windows 95, and Windows NT) sometimes render files that work in one Windows environment inoperable in another. For example, 32-bit programs that run under Windows 95 and Windows NT cannot run under Windows 3.1, which is a 16-bit operating system. In addition, the length and case of file names can make files invisible to one operating system or the other.
>
> Prima has made every effort to ensure that this problem is minimized; eliminating it, however, is impossible. Therefore, you may find that some files or directories appear to be missing from the CD. Those files are, in reality, on the CD but remain hidden from the operating system. To confirm this fact, view the CD in a different Windows operating system.

Windows 3.1

To run the CD-ROM in Windows 3.1, follow these steps:

1. Insert the CD into the CD-ROM drive.
2. In File Manager, choose **File**, **R**un to open the Run window.
3. In the **C**ommand Line text box, type **D:\primacd.exe** (where D:\ is the CD-ROM drive).
4. Choose OK.

Windows 95

Because there is no installation routine, running the CD in Windows 95 is a breeze, especially if you have autorun enabled. Simply insert the CD into the CD-ROM drive, close the tray, and wait for the CD to load.

If you have disabled autorun, place the CD in the drive and follow these steps:

1. From the Start menu, choose Run.
2. Type **D:\primacd.exe** (where D:\ is the CD-ROM drive).
3. Choose OK.

The Prima User Interface

Prima's user interface is designed to make viewing and using the CD's contents quick and easy. The interface contains four category buttons, four option buttons, and a display window. Click a category button to show a list of available titles in the display window. Select a title in the window and then click an option button to perform the desired action.

Category Buttons

- **Examples:** examples and source code from the book
- **HTML Tools:** a large collection of HTML editors, templates, and add-ons to help you create sophisticated Web pages
- **Internet:** finger clients, FTP clients, and other tools for getting the most from the Internet
- **Misc:** some Windows utilities to help you manage your files and improve your system's performance

Option Buttons

- **Install/Run.** If the highlighted title contains an install routine, selecting this option begins the installation process. If the title has no install procedure but contains an executable file, the executable is run. If neither an install nor an executable file is present (as in the case of a graphics library), the folder containing the information is shown. In the event that an application contains an executable file that will not run from the CD, the entire application is placed in a compressed ZIP file, which you can access by installing WinZip (included on the CD).

> **NOTE:** You can install some of the shareware programs that do not have installation routines by copying the program files from the CD to your hard drive and running the executable (.exe) file.

♦ **Information.** Data about the selection is shown, if available. This information is usually in the form of a read-me or help file.

♦ **Explore.** This option allows you to view the folder containing the program files.

♦ **Exit.** When you're finished and ready to move on, choose Exit.

The Software

This section briefly describes some of the software that you'll find on the CD. This list is just a sample; as you browse the CD, you will find much more.

♦ **Cute FTP:** simple and straightforward FTP software for beginners and pros alike

♦ **Finger clients:** C-Finger, WinWhois, Xfinger, and more

♦ **HotDog:** a stand-alone HTML editor that supports extensions from Microsoft and Netscape, as well as proposed HTML 3 elements

♦ **HTML Assistant:** a simple Web publishing tool for creating HTML Web pages

♦ **Kenn Nesbitt's Webedit:** the popular HTML editor for both novices and pros

♦ **Live Markup:** as close as you can get to a WYSIWYG HTML editor

- **Mapedit:** a WYSIWYG (What You See Is What You Get) editor for imagemap files
- **Telnet clients:** Anzio Lite, CommNet, and others
- **Vram:** a 32-bit virtual RAM file system driver for Windows 95 to speed your system's performance
- **WinZip:** one of the leading file compression utilities for Windows 95, Windows NT, and Windows 3.1

INDEX

Notes

Notes

Notes

Notes

To Order Books

Please send me the following items:

Quantity	Title	Unit Price	Total
_____	_____	$ _____	$ _____
_____	_____	$ _____	$ _____
_____	_____	$ _____	$ _____
_____	_____	$ _____	$ _____
_____	_____	$ _____	$ _____

Subtotal $ _____

Deduct 10% when ordering 3-5 books $ _____

7.25% Sales Tax (CA only) $ _____

8.25% Sales Tax (TN only) $ _____

5.0% Sales Tax (MD and IN only) $ _____

Shipping and Handling* $ _____

Total Order $ _____

Shipping and Handling depend on Subtotal.

Subtotal	Shipping/Handling
$0.00–$14.99	$3.00
$15.00–$29.99	$4.00
$30.00–$49.99	$6.00
$50.00–$99.99	$10.00
$100.00–$199.99	$13.50
$200.00+	Call for Quote

Foreign and all Priority Request orders:
Call Order Entry department
for price quote at 916/632-4400

This chart represents the total retail price of books only
(before applicable discounts are taken).

By Telephone: With MC or Visa, call 800-632-8676, 916-632-4400. Mon-Fri, 8:30-4:30.
WWW {http://www.primapublishing.com}

Orders Placed Via Internet E-mail {sales@primapub.com}

By Mail: Just fill out the information below and send with your remittance to:

Prima Publishing
P.O. Box 1260BK
Rocklin, CA 95677

My name is _____

I live at _____

City_____ State_____ Zip _____

MC/Visa#_____ Exp._____

Check/Money Order enclosed for $_____ Payable to Prima Publishing

Daytime Telephone _____

Signature _____

Other Books from Prima Publishing, Computer Products Division

ISBN	Title	Price	Release Date
0-7615-0801-5	ActiveX	$35.00	Available Now
0-7615-0680-2	America Online Complete Handbook and Membership Kit	$24.99	Available Now
0-7615-0915-1	Building Intranets with Internet Information Server and FrontPage	$40.00	Available Now
0-7615-0417-6	CompuServe Complete Handbook and Membership Kit	$24.95	Available Now
0-7615-0849-X	Corporate Intranet Development	$40.00	Fall '96
0-7615-0692-6	Create Your First Web Page in a Weekend	$24.99	Available Now
0-7615-0503-2	Discover What's Online!	$24.95	Available Now
0-7615-0693-4	Internet Information Server	$40.00	Available Now
0-7615-0815-5	Introduction to ABAP/4 Programming for SAP	$45.00	Available Now
0-7615-0678-0	Java Applet Powerpack	$30.00	Available Now
0-7615-0685-3	JavaScript	$35.00	Available Now
0-7615-0901-1	Leveraging Visual Basic with ActiveX Controls	$45.00	Available Now
0-7615-0682-9	LiveWire Pro Master's Handbook	$40.00	Fall '96
0-7615-0755-8	Moving Worlds	$35.00	Available Now
0-7615-0690-X	Netscape Enterprise Server	$40.00	Available Now
0-7615-0691-8	Netscape FastTrack Server	$40.00	Available Now
0-7615-0852-X	Netscape Navigator 3 Complete Handbook	$24.99	Available Now
0-7615-0751-5	Windows NT Server Administrator's Guide	$50.00	Available Now
0-7615-0759-0	Professional Web Design	$40.00	Available Now
0-7615-0780-9	Programming Web Server Applications	$40.00	Available Now
0-7615-0063-4	Researching on the Internet	$29.95	Available Now
0-7615-0686-1	Researching on the World Wide Web	$24.99	Available Now
0-7615-0695-0	The Essential Photoshop Book	$35.00	Available Now
0-7615-0752-3	The Essential Windows NT Book	$27.99	Available Now
0-7615-0689-6	The Microsoft Exchange Productivity Guide	$24.99	Available Now
0-7615-0769-8	VBscript Master's Handbook	$40.00	Available Now
0-7615-0684-5	VBscript Web Page Interactivity	$35.00	Available Now
0-7615-0903-8	Visual FoxPro 5 Enterprise Development	$45.00	Available Now
0-7615-0814-7	Visual J++	$35.00	Available Now
0-7615-0383-8	Web Advertising and Marketing	$34.95	Available Now
0-7615-0726-4	Webmaster's Handbook	$40.00	Available Now

License Agreement/Notice of Limited Warranty

By opening the sealed disk container in this book, you agree to the following terms and conditions. If, upon reading the following license agreement and notice of limited warranty, you cannot agree to the terms and conditions set forth, return the unused book with unopened disk to the place where you purchased it for a refund.

License:

The enclosed software is copyrighted by the copyright holder(s) indicated on the software disk. You are licensed to copy the software onto a single computer for use by a single concurrent user and to a backup disk. You may not reproduce, make copies, or distribute copies or rent or lease the software in whole or in part, except with written permission of the copyright holder(s). You may transfer the enclosed disk only together with this license, and only if you destroy all other copies of the software and the transferee agrees to the terms of the license. You may not decompile, reverse assemble, or reverse engineer the software.

Notice of Limited Warranty:

The enclosed disk is warranted by Prima Publishing to be free of physical defects in materials and workmanship for a period of sixty (60) days from end user's purchase of the book/disk combination. During the sixty-day term of the limited warranty, Prima will provide a replacement disk upon the return of a defective disk.

Limited Liability:

THE SOLE REMEDY FOR BREACH OF THIS LIMITED WARRANTY SHALL CONSIST ENTIRELY OF REPLACEMENT OF THE DEFECTIVE DISK. IN NO EVENT SHALL PRIMA OR THE AUTHORS BE LIABLE FOR ANY OTHER DAMAGES, INCLUDING LOSS OR CORRUPTION OF DATA, CHANGES IN THE FUNCTIONAL CHARACTERISTICS OF THE HARDWARE OR OPERATING SYSTEM, DELETERIOUS INTERACTION WITH OTHER SOFTWARE, OR ANY OTHER SPECIAL, INCIDENTAL, OR CONSEQUENTIAL DAMAGES THAT MAY ARISE, EVEN IF PRIMA AND/OR THE AUTHORS HAVE PREVIOUSLY BEEN NOTIFIED THAT THE POSSIBILITY OF SUCH DAMAGES EXISTS.

Disclaimer of Warranties:

PRIMA AND THE AUTHORS SPECIFICALLY DISCLAIM ANY AND ALL OTHER WARRANTIES, EITHER EXPRESS OR IMPLIED, INCLUDING WARRANTIES OF MERCHANTABILITY, SUITABILITY TO A PARTICULAR TASK OR PURPOSE, OR FREEDOM FROM ERRORS. SOME STATES DO NOT ALLOW FOR EXCLUSION OF IMPLIED WARRANTIES OR LIMITATION OF INCIDENTAL OR CONSEQUENTIAL DAMAGES, SO THESE LIMITATIONS MAY NOT APPLY TO YOU.

Other:

This Agreement is governed by the laws of the State of California without regard to choice of law principles. The United Convention of Contracts for the International Sale of Goods is specifically disclaimed. This Agreement constitutes the entire agreement between you and Prima Publishing regarding use of the software.